From CSCW to Web 2.0:
European Developments in Collaborative Design

David Randall · Pascal Salembier
Editors

From CSCW to Web 2.0: European Developments in Collaborative Design

Selected Papers from COOP08

 Springer

Editors
David Randall
Department of Sociology
Manchester Metropolitan University
Manchester, UK
d.randall@mmu.ac.uk

Pascal Salembier
Université de Technologie de Troyes
France
pascal.salembier@utt.fr

ISBN 978-1-84882-964-0   e-ISBN 978-1-84882-965-7
DOI 10.1007/978-1-84882-965-7
Springer London Dordrecht Heidelberg New York

Library of Congress Control Number: 2010924749

Springer is part of Springer Science+Business Media (www.springer.com)

Contents

Part III   Web 2.0 Problems and Solutions

Contributors

Aurélien Bénel
Université de Technologie de Troyes, France

Marco Bertoni
Lulea Technical University, Sweden

Susanne Bodker
Aarhus University, Denmark

Simone Braun
FZI Research Center for Information Technologies, Germany

Jean-Pierre Cahier
Université de Technologie de Troyes, France

Tommaso Colombino
Xerox Research Centre Europe (XRCE), Grenoble, France

Åsa Ericson
Lulea Technical University, Sweden

Thomas Herrmann
Ruhr-University of Bochum, Germany

Elke Hinrichs
Fraunhofer FIT, Germany

Ola Isaksson
Lulea Technical University, Sweden

Irina Kireyev
RWTH Aachen University, Germany

Peter Gall Krogh
Alexandra Institute, Århus, Denmark

Christine Kunzmann
FZI Research Center for Information Technologies, Germany

Andreas Larsson
Lulea Technical University, Sweden

Tobias Larsson
Lulea Technical University, Sweden

David Martin
Xerox Research Centre Europe (XRCE), Grenoble, France

Benjamin Moos
University of Siegen, Institute for Information Systems, Siegen, Germany

Jacki O'Neill
Xerox Research Centre Europe (XRCE), Grenoble, France

Anja Bechmann Petersen
Aarhus University, Denmark

Marianne Graves Petersen
Aarhus University

Michael Prilla
Ruhr University of Bochum, Information and Technology Management, Germany

Wolfgang Prinz
Fraunhofer FIT, Germany

Tim Reichling
University of Siegen, Germany

Carsten Ritterskamp
Ruhr University of Bochum, Information and Technology Management, Germany

Markus Rohde
University of Siegen, Institute for Information Systems, Siegen, Germany

Frederic Roulland
Xerox Research Centre Europe (XRCE), Grenoble, France

Andreas Schmidt
FZI Research Center for Information Technologies, Germany

Jutta Willamowski
Xerox Research Centre Europe (XRCE), Grenoble, France

Volker Wulf
University of Siegen, Institute for Information SystemsSiegen, Germany

Chao Zhou
Université de Technologie de Troyes, France

Introduction

David Randall and Pascal Salembier

The chapters in this book are extended and revised versions of selected papers from the Coop conference, which took place in Carry-Le-Rouet, near Marseille, in 2008. They reflect developments in CSCW, HCI, and related disciplines. This broad field has, for 30 years, been associated with support for complex work practices within organisations and a related concern with the relationship between traditional co-located work practices and newer, computer-mediated practices. It was founded on a critique – suggesting that new interactive or collaborative computer technologies could not be understood in the same way as prior generations of computer; that overly simplistic models of both the human actor and of the organisation would have to yield to a more complex understanding; and – perhaps most importantly – that new methods and analytic approaches would be required in order to furnish this understanding. Without question, and we say this in full knowledge that the marriage has not always been a happy one (Hartman 1995) the field has been a progressive one, characterised by an inclusivity in respect of the disciplines contributing to the work and the methods that might turn out to be appropriate and relevant. The result has been an interdisciplinary approach that had been enormously influential wherever one looks. Where 'design' had previously been largely understood in terms of the need for a more scientific, or at least engineered, view it became increasingly regarded as an activity that had to reflect the situated and occasioned nature of working life. Moreover, it is a sign of the healthy state of CSCW that these changes continue to be debated, for the world changes fast and gets no simpler. The papers in this collection reflect this. They deal with some of the ways in which the sands have shifted. New 'social' technologies, with concomitant affordances, have arrived with unprecedented speed (who had heard of 'tagging', 'tag clouds', 'social bookmarking' or 'Facebook' 5 years ago?). We still struggle to understand what application they might have in the near future. Our analytic interests, and the domains we focus our attention on, continue to evolve. There have been some significant moves, such that the notion of 'awareness of work' has come to mean more than the co-located orchestration of activities to be found in, for instance, command and control centres or indeed in any single organisation. A new emphasis, perhaps also prompted by a burgeoning interest in knowledge and expertise sharing, has been evident, whereby 'awareness of work' comes to encompass the problems of expertise and knowledge in complex environments (see for instance, Ackermann et al. 2003) and also entails a very heterogeneous view of 'what we need to know'. Sources of complexity might include the division of labour; socially and organizationally distributed skills and expertises, and the practical problems of information seeking. Section 1 of this book deals with those issues, covering such matters as the way in which knowledge has to be both 'past' facing and 'forward' facing; how the complexities of expertise and its social distribution impinge on a workflow system for colour printing, and how required knowledge can extend well beyond the shop floor into management-related activities.

A second theme is emerging, relating to CSCW's concerns with design methodologies. It has been well-attested that traditional approaches to design have been largely based on the engineering metaphor – and substantially remain so despite the intervention of ethnographic and other strategies. More recently, however, there has been something of a sea change in respect of a recognition of creativity in design. This is a fundamental shift, for it implicates the idea that the design process, whatever it might be, is not to be understood reductively. We do not necessarily improve design by managing the steps in the process ever more tightly. This may well have to do with the move of interactive computer systems into domestic and public spaces as well as their more traditional industrial and commercial locations and what would seem to follow from that, to whit that decompositional models do not easily describe environments where 'task' is largely irrelevant (or at least, extremely difficult to define). At the same time, and not entirely surprisingly, this change in mood or sentiment has not gone unchallenged, for it implicates some radical views about the relationship between description and prescription. The concern for creativity has sometimes been understood as reflecting a postmodern sensibility, and one in which the play of possibilities, or contingencies, is best understood by a critical engagement with actors. There is no little irony in the fact that an original CSCW complaint which had to do with the fact that we knew too little about actors, or underrepresented their interests is being challenged by a variety of contested stances concerning the degree to which actors' common sense understandings of their world constitute an appropriate starting point for design-related activities (see Crabtree et al. 2009 for a range of contested positions). It is not our place to engage in this debate here, and we will limit ourselves to the observation that it has arisen at precisely the time when new technology is increasingly being developed and marketed for purposes which are not tightly coupled with work-based tasks. Regardless, it is arguably the case that we still have neither a conceptual framework for understanding creativity in design, nor methodologies which might fully reflect this transition. The papers in Section 2 represent a move forward in attempts to deal with creativity through examination of failure in the design of systems which support creative activity; through attempts to provide a more rigorous approach to conceptualisation and thirdly through a case study which examines the way in which designers and participants can reconfigure their relationship.

A third significant tendency is the joint development of the participative web (Web 2.0) and the semantic web (a natural candidate for the Web 3.0 label according to many). The idea of Web 2.0 carries a number of different, and nuanced, assumptions with it, including not least a developing interest in the way in which the Web can be used to support collaborations of one kind or another and the emergence of virtual communities. Of course, this burgeoning area has moved well beyond the work environments that CSCW has been historically associated with and now encompasses blogs, wikis, social networking sites, and so on which can, in principal, be used for any number of different purposes. At the same time, there are other, somewhat more radical, assumptions embedded in the so-called semantic web, not least Tim Berners-Lee's original ambition that symbolic information can be embedded into computer systems in such a way that semantic information can become 'machine readable'. Already processes which range from the 'tagging' associated with folksonomic applications through to fully fledged ontologies with formal and specified knowledge hierarchies embedded in them have become common. This too has a consequence for new thinking about how users might be involved in the development and population of applications. The development and use of folksonomies, ontologies and related taxonomic or tagging techniques, we suggest, has opened up in a dramatic way a new scope for the consideration of design issues as heterogeneous and creative processes. Nevertheless, this is not without challenges of its own. New relationships between designer and user are again entailed, along with new problems of conceptualising exactly who our users might be and how they might be mobilised. In Section 3, chapters deal with the various ways in which this new challenge can be met. They range through a consideration of the relationship between our historical approach to collaborative work and the challenges of the semantic and socio-semantic web through the provision of new tools: how a maturity model might help us reconfigure the design process for ontology development; how user interface issues need to be taken seriously even in the new world of social tagging; and how lightweight forms of these new applications might be taken up in the business world (Cook 2008).

The papers here, we hope, reflect the inclusivity that we earlier suggested in respect of the different disciplines which can be enlisted for design, methodologies used, and the interest in the potential of radical new technologies. The book is divided into three parts. The first part we have titled, 'Awareness of Work' and the papers within it are in their different ways attempts to deal with 'awareness' as something distinct from the glances and gazes which have informed much of our understanding of interactional awareness hitherto. Following Schmidt (2002), we take the view that 'awareness' is a deeply confused concept, one which would repay a Wittgensteinian analysis (see Martin et al. Chapter 2). That is, the various ways in which the term might be used bear a 'family resemblance' to each other but do not describe a consistent phenomenon. To put it another way, the section is titled, 'Awareness of Work' because awareness might consist in many different activities and knowledges. We need to constantly reaffirm the eclectic possibilities entailed in the term. Prinz et al. discuss the idea of 'anticipative' awareness. They suggest that groupware has, for the most part, been associated with support for 'past-oriented' activity. They argue that groupware systems can, in principle, either store and display a history of events that took place in the past or can allow users to plan in advance by seeking future notifications. As they put it, "The future event can ideally be defined to encompass any combination of specific artifacts, specific activities and specific members of a workspace. None of the groupware tools we analyzed, however, allows specifying actions to be carried out by workspace members until a date in the future and then automatically verifies and notifies whether they were performed within the deadline or whether they were performed late or not at all." They go on to demonstrate how this future awareness can be built into a well-known and well-used tool, BSCW, which was developed at Fraunhofer FIT.

Martin et al. examine the work done to control colour production in graphic design and printing, focusing on the reasons why practitioners do not implement 'colour managed' workflows. The technical requirements of these systems, it turns out, are beyond the capacity of most people working in the industry – both in terms of equipment set-up and knowledge. The paper then provides a critical appraisal of infrastructure and workflow as a means of supporting cooperative work in design and printing, based on an extensive ethnography conducted by the authors. Here, rather than design for awareness, the issue is 'design with awareness'. Using Star and Ruhleder's well-known notion of 'infrastructure', they identify processes of embedding, transparency, conventionality and visibility which inform the degree to which any individual will be aware of the contingencies involved in the work of another. They suggest that their study is one of the first where infrastructural issues have been analysed in an area other than scientific practice and, moreover, shows that the different parties involved are not equal partners and had little or no input into the infrastructure's design or development and therefore had no ownership. Although the authors consider the design of alternatives to be problematic, they show quite clearly that one of the major limitations of generic design is lack of awareness of work.

In the third paper in this section, Reichling et al. discuss the notion of 'regional clusters' to discuss support for an entirely different form of awareness, and that is cross-organisational. As they say, "technical approaches aiming at fostering mutual awareness and collaboration among companies in regional networks are scarce". This chapter builds on previous research which examines tools and activities to support business 'networking', based on substantial long term enquiry into joint activities in and between a number of regional companies, the paper discusses a tool called, 'Business Finder' designed to improve mutual awareness among small and medium sized businesses. Their approach is founded on arguments concerning business 'clusters' (Porter 2000) which emphasise the interconnectedness of competition and cooperation. Using an action-research perspective based on informal discussions and semi-structured interviews, they suggest a new way of both fostering collaborative ventures and designing 'shared expertise' systems for dealing with the issue of developing organisational networks.

In Section 2, as suggested above, creativity is the theme which links three papers. More specifically, *collaborative* creativity is an emergent theme in CSCW literature, predicated on a longstanding interest in the functioning of teams and reflecting the move away from a step-by-step, functional view of team effectiveness. Nevertheless, arguing that functional specifications of team activity ignore the essentially creative nature of team outcomes is one thing. Spelling out what creativity might be and how it might vary from one context to another (or indeed whether it can be said to have 'universal' features is quite another. Creativity, it seems to us, is another 'black box' which needs to be opened if we are to avoid essentially heroic, and not terribly useful formulations of the creative act (although occasional examples of attempts to relate creativity to other concrete factors do pop up in the sociology and history of art (see for instance, Baxandall 1974; Becker 1982). Thomas Herrman draws on an existing literature to derive some central features of collaborative creative activity as an initial step in this direction. As he points out, creative activity is a complex challenge because actors often have different back-grounds, thought processes and methods of self-expression and, moreover, activi-ties are often only weakly structured and are highly flexible. Based on a series of interviews conducted with CSCW researchers, Hermann draws out a set of 'design heuristics' which include: supporting the large picture – the visualization of rich material; the malleability of shared material and stimulation of variations; support of convergence within evolutionary documentation; smooth transitions between different modes of creative collaboration; integration of communication with work on shared material, and support of role dynamics and varying modes of collabora-tion, thus creating what Hermann terms a, 'conceptual architecture' which might aid in disentangling the similarities and differences to be found in various sited of collaborative creative activity.

Krogh and Petersen, from the Alexandria Institute and Aarhus University in Denmark, take a different view of the creative process, and aim to show how 'users' can be a part of it in ways that are sometimes unanticipated. Of course, there is a long tradition in Participatory Design and elsewhere of user involvement but here the involvement of the user takes a new and creative form. The authors present an approach to design for collaborative *co-located* experiences among people sharing collective resources for controlling interfaces in places like libraries and the home. They claim, following Hindmarsh et al. (2005) that it is still the case that few sys-tems are designed to support interaction in these locations and a shift in emphasis towards, "what desirable place or situation are we forming together?" is necessary.

In this vision, people *become* designers in and through their playful interactions with each other and through prototypical systems placed in real-world contexts. This ludic vision, which has something in common with Bill Gaver's work (Gaver 2001, 2002), entails users creatively making technology at home in their world. To illustrate these themes, the authors present two design case studies , one in the context of a public library and one in a home context, where technologies are put in place with the explicit intention of engaging users collaboratively.

Bodker and Bechman Petersen, also from Aarhus in Denmark, emphasise the empirical issues surrounding support for creative activities by analysing the way in which a new collaborative technology, 'Napkin', was introduced to support cre-ative, integrative, cross-media production. This evaluative study shows how a com-plex technology designed to support news reporters, failed. They provide a detailed examination of the reasons for that failure, and in particular look at the different worldviews and commitments on the part of, for instance, journalists and editors. In a similar way to Martin et al. in Chapter 2, they point to the different and incom-mensurate practices of various parties to a creative activity- the production of multi-media news reports for several outlets including, 'radio, TV, web, a daily newspaper and several additional products'. In this way, the paper is a valuable reminder of what we have suggested above- that even when we are dealing with new and more creative endeavours, the same careful, empirically based evaluations will be necessary. As Bodker and Bechman Petersen point out, regardless of the kind of activity involved, there will necessarily be some kind of articulation work entailed (Strauss; Schmidt & Bannon, 1992) and that there is a considerable overhead to this when different groups have different narrative visions, as in this case.

Section 3 deals with various features of the move to "new forms of Web" (participative and semantic). We have argued above that the move to machine readable semantic information is hugely ambitious (and arguably foolhardy) but to turn our backs on semantic web would be foolish and to neglect further prospects in ontologies, intelligent agents and the like will not make them vanish into air. It seems to us that CSCW has an enormous amount to contribute to this evolving technology. Not least, and CSCW practitioners are well aware of this tendency, many of the hard-won lessons for design concerning the importance of solid, careful and detailed empirical work as a tool in the design toolkit are often ignored in the rush to do 'cutting edge' design. Nevertheless, in the context of Web 2.0 and semantic Web it does seem to us to be important that we reiterate that the empirical studies associated with design work which first came to prominence in CSCW existed to rectify a perceived deficiency – a lack of information about the ordinary, practical ways in which people go about their business. To our knowledge, no serious ethnographer has ever suggested that the results of such enquiries constitute *a solution* to design problems- rather that such studies are *a good place to start* in considering what kinds of problem design work may encounter. That there may be different analytic policies involved in the apparently simple business of doing empirical work- and how empirical results relate (or not) to theoretical issues – is beyond question, and these policies may not all serve the same purpose. Nevertheless, there is a danger that in inhabiting the brave new worlds of Web 2.0 and semantic Web, practitioners neglect the importance of the user, howsoever s/he is construed and, as a function of this, neglect the business of evaluating what we have achieved. By way of example, there is at least a 10 year history of 'ontology-based design' now. This is perhaps the most fully-fledged and ambitious example of a semantic application in Web technology. Ontologies in their most mature and widely-used forms are in the main associated with the bio-informational sciences, and the Gene Ontology (GO) would probably be the best known. It is surprising, then, to discover that approaches to ontology-building largely duplicate the top-down engineering assumptions of software engineering from 20 years ago (Gomez-Perez et al. 2004), and that there are few if any prolonged and systematic empirical studies of use (but see Lin et al. 2008). This, we suggest, is a critical omission since the successful application of various kinds of semantic engine will depend in large part on the domains in which they are applied and what we know about them. Not least, even in the most 'scientific' of domains, it turns out that there are more disputes about terms and their logical relations that one might expect. It follows that, in more heterogeneous contexts, those problems are likely to be magnified. Braun, Kunzmann and Schmidt, working at the FZI Research Center for Information

Technologies in Karlsruhe, Germany propose ways to deal with the design and implementation of an ontology for organisational purposes, including effective resource allocation, knowledge management and human resource development. We know already from a number of studies in both CSCW and elsewhere that knowledge management projects of this kind often fail, in part because competence is not well described and has a dynamic quality. A range of organisational barriers sometimes lead to incomplete and outdated information, and because the maintenance of knowledge bases is extremely difficult (for the reasons that Grudin originally pointed out) eliciting information for ontology-construction is a non-trivial task in this context. Braun et al. argue that, *'a lack of participation of all employees has been one of the key problems. To overcome this, we propose a collaborative approach based on Web 2.0-style people tagging and complement it with community-driven ontology engineering methods.'* they go on to suggest a combination of Web 2.0 'bottom-up' approaches using folksonomic processes and 'expert' led top-down approaches to produce an Ontology Maturation Model.

Larsson et al. working at Lulea University in Sweden, continue with the general theme of how Web 2.0 applications are likely to impact on organisational matters through a consideration of what they call, 'Engineering 2.0'. In a virtual enterprise setting, they argue, it becomes increasingly important to make sure that knowledge and expertise created in one discipline, domain or company is correctly understood and quickly utilised by other actors in the value chain. Virtual enterprises are those which exist for specific purposes, and are not defined in terms of buildings and personnel. They often consist of, for instance, groups which may, in other circumstances, be competitors. It follows, therefore, that if these groups are temporary and dynamic then the overhead of setting up technology support has to be taken very seriously, as do the problems of information security. The authors suggest that 'hard' engineering data is already well-supported by, for instance, CAD packages and so on, but that, *'... knowledge work also has a social dimension, e.g., learning and experiencing. The assessment of the result from a number of distinct computer analyses, i.e., 'putting two and two together', and what engineers know by experience influence many decisions in product development, but this kind of design reasoning is usually not made visible in the same way as technical product information.'*

They then explore the use of 'lightweight' technologies for supporting the creative use and re-use of information by design teams in this context.

In their paper Benel et al. introduce the notion of the "socio-semantic Web" as "the confluence of knowledge engineering and CSCW", and as an alternative to the formal approach of semantics promoted by the semantic Web. According to the authors, if the new web aims at supporting cooperation inside and between communities it has to be built upon a social-oriented view of ontologies rather than on a computational one. This view has direct effects on the delimitation of relevant theoretical objects (intersubjectivity, collaborative construction of meaning, trust between the actors, and so on) and on the nature of the technological commitment (semi-formal ontologies, micro-social tagging, visualisation of individual viewpoints, etc). This approach gave birth to a set of dedicated tools including Agorae, a web platform which supports the collaborative building of topic maps.

In the paper, the authors suggest methods for developing social tagging by incorporating multi-viewpoints, multi-tags selection and tag relations to produce interfaces which have a more directed purpose than just maximising utility for 'crowds' of user. An illustration drawn from a study performed in the domain of scientific archive is presented in more detail.

Prilla and Ritterskamp question whether the CSCW conception of collaboration support remains viable in the age of Web 2.0. As they point out, the success of low-overhead web-based technologies like Wikis seems to support the argument that web-based architectures provide specific benefits, such as simplicity of usage, immediate feedback on UI and structural level and feedback on user contributions (e.g. Grudin 2006). As they say, *"Web 2.0 orchestrates available technology in a way that encourages users to participate actively as its architecture of participation helps to balance effort and benefit even in work-related settings."* Nevertheless, they are optimistic for the future of collaboration support tools because they see no automatic translation between one set of functions, designed for mass collaboration – and another, designed for enterprise collaborations. The similarities and differences to be found in the distinction between collaboration support systems and Web 2.0 applications reside, in their view, in three main dimensions: goal and work orientation, communication and coordination among peers in groups and playfulness and user experience. and argue forcefully that new Web 2.0 tools complement and enhance the prospects for CSCW applications. They demonstrate through an examination of prototypes how successful strategies for combining the two can be found.

Overall, then, it is clear that the themes and perspectives that emerged in CSCW some 30 years ago have not gone away. At the same time, they are being progressively transformed as new technologies appear and as we adopt new methods for working out what to do with them. We argued at the start that CSCW has been enormously influential in a variety of fields, not all of them technology-related. The ethnographic 'turn' largely inspired by CSCW concerns has been appropriated and used in any number of interdisciplinary areas and shows no sign of exhausting its uses. Even so, new and creative versions of investigative technique are common and the papers in this collection demonstrate that fact. Equally, the advent of radical new technology provides a new lease of life and prompts lively discussion about the new relationships to be discovered therein. All in all, we hope these papers demonstrate the health of CSCW and its continued growth and maturity.

References

Ackermann, M., Pipek, V. and Wulf, V. (eds.) (2003) *Sharing Expertise: Beyond Knowledge Management*, Cambridge, MA: MIT Press

Baxandall, M. (1974) *Painting and Experience in Fifteenth-Century Italy: A Primer in the Social History of Pictorial Style*. Oxford Paperbacks: Oxford

Becker, H. (1982) Art Worlds. Berkeley: University of California Press

Cook, N. (2008). Enterprise 2.0 – *How social software will change the future of work*: London: Gower

Crabtree, A., Button, G., Rodden, T. and Tolmie, P. 2009, Proceedings of CHI 2009, Boston, Mass: ACM Press

Dourish, P. (2006) Implications for design? *Proceedings of the SIGCHI conference on Human Factors in computing systems*, Montreal, Canada

Gaver, W. (2001) Designing for ludic aspects of everyday life. *Ercim News*. No.47. www. ercim. org/publication/Ercim_News/enw47/gaver.html

Gaver, W. (2002) Provocative Awareness, *Computer Supported Co-Operative Work: The Journal Of Collaborative Computing, Amsterdam. 11. 47*. 5–93.

Gomez-Perez, A., Fernandez-Lopez, M. (2004) *Ontological Engineering: With Examples from the Areas of Knowledge Management, E-Commerce and the Semantic Web*, Springer

Grudin, J. (1988) Why CSCW Applications fail: Problems in the Design and Evaluation of organizational Interfaces. Proceedings of CSCW, 88. Portland, Oregon: ACM Press. 85–93

Grudin, J. (2006) Enterprise Knowledge Management and Emerging Technologies. *Proceedings of the 39th Annual Hawaii International Conference on System Sciences*. HICSS'06

Hartman, H. (1995) The Unhappy Marriage of Marxism and Feminism: Towards a more progressive union, in V. Lippit. *Radical Political Economy*. M.E.Sharpe

Hindmarsh J., Heath C., Vom Lehn D., Cleverly J. (2005) Creating Assemblies in Public Environments: Social Interaction, Interactive Exhibits and CSCW, Computer Supported Cooperative Work (CSCW). Vol 14 No 1

Lin, Y-W., M. Poschen, R. Procter, J. Kola, D. Job, J. Harris, D. Randall, W. Sharrock, J. Ure, S. Lawrie, A. Rector and C. Goble, C. (2008) Ontology building as a social-technical process: a case study. Oxford e-Research Conference, Oxford, UK. September.

Porter, M. E. (2000) Locations, Clusters, and Company Strategy. In: Clark, G. L.; Feldman, M. P.; Gertler, M. S. (Eds.); *Oxford Handbook of Economic Geography*. Oxford University Press: New York, S. 253–274.

Schmidt, K. (2002) The Problem with Awareness: Introductory remarks on awareness in CSCW, *Computer Supported Co-Operative Work: The Journal Of Collaborative Computing, Amsterdam Vol 11* (3–4) Springer. 285–298

Star S. L., and Ruhleder, K. (1996) Steps toward an ecology of infrastructure: Design and access for large information spaces, *Information Systems Research 7*(1). 111–134

Strauss, A. (1988) The Articulation of project Work. The Sociological Quarterly, Vol. 29 No.2. 163–178

Part I
Awareness of Work

Chapter 1
Anticipative Awareness in a Groupware System

Wolfgang Prinz, Elke Hinrichs, and Irina Kireyev

1.1 Introduction

Current asynchronous collaborative tools support awareness of changes in an electronic workspace in two ways. Either they store and display a history of events that took place in the past (awareness of past events) or they allow users to register an interest in an event in the future they want to be notified about (awareness of future events). The future event can ideally be defined to encompass any combination of specific artifacts, specific activities, and specific members of a workspace. None of the groupware tools we analyzed, however, allows specifying actions to be carried out by workspace members until a date in the future and then automatically verifies and notifies whether they were performed within the deadline, late, or not at all.

It is, however, the latter aspect of awareness – being notified of what has not happened rather than of what did happen – that is a frequent requirement in collaborative work as shown by the following typical situations. One team member writes a document and expects the other team members to read it, to review it, or to suggest improvements. A teacher asks her students to write an essay and wishes to "remind" the students later of the delivery when the deadline approaches. A call for papers is issued and abstracts have been accepted, but the conference committee needs to know who failed to deliver the full paper rather than who did actually deliver.

We propose to fill the obvious gap by complementing awareness of what happened in the past by awareness of events which will or will not happen in the future – we call this concept anticipative awareness or in short: expectations. Expectations allow users to be flexible in defining in detail what action by which participants and on which artifact they are interested to observe and until when.

W. Prinz (✉) and E. Hinrichs
Fraunhofer FIT, Germany
e-mail: wolfgang.prinz@fit.fraunhofer.de

I. Kireyev
RWTH Aachen University, Germany

D. Randall and P. Salembier (eds.), *From CSCW to Web 2.0: European Developments in Collaborative Design*, Computer Supported Cooperative Work,
DOI 10.1007/978-1-84882-965-7_1, © Springer-Verlag London Limited 2010

We decided to implement the concept of anticipative awareness within BSCW (Appelt 1999; Bentley et al. 1997), a shared workspace system developed by Fraunhofer and OrbiTeam (2007), www.fit.fraunhofer.de, and OrbiTeam, www. orbiteam.de, starting in 1995 and in operation ever since. BSCW has a large user community of an estimated million users worldwide. We chose BSCW as the baseline system for our implementation for three reasons. Firstly, we wanted to improve the tool we are using in our daily work. Though BSCW features a broad range of awareness functions, it can still be difficult to keep track of the state of work in large, shared workspaces with active team members. When deadlines are approaching, it can be quite cumbersome to find out who did not deliver – actually this has to be done manually. Automated notifications of these anticipated (non)events well ahead of time would be most welcome to many BSCW users. Secondly, the existing awareness features of BSCW made the implementation of our concept of anticipative awareness relatively easy. Thirdly, the large number of "real users who are doing real work" using BSCW offer excellent opportunities for a thorough evaluation and verification of our concept.

After reporting on related work in the area of awareness, we give a detailed account of our concept of anticipative awareness and of how we implemented this concept by integrating it into our shared workspace system BSCW. We then describe how we evaluated our work and "what the users said." This leads us to a critical analysis of what the users liked and what should be improved.

1.2 Related Work

Bernheim-Brush et al. (Prinz 2002) divide existing asynchronous awareness mechanisms in one or more of the following categories: informational, subscription-based, and peripheral.

With informational awareness mechanisms, details of the document activity are shown or can be queried from the workspace. The majority of systems concentrate on this type of awareness. ReadWear and EditWear technique (Hill et al. 1992), Version graph in COOP/Orm (Magnusson and Asklund 1996), and ActivityViewer in Palantir (Ripley et al. 2006) are just some examples of existing practices to provide information on changes in a workspace itself. BSCW already supports this type of awareness with event icons, event history, and AwarenessMaps (Appelt 1999; Bentley et al. 1997; Gräther and Prinz 2003).

In subscription-based awareness mechanisms, a user can register an interest to receive notifications on certain events in a workspace. Systems such as CVS-watch (Berliner 1990), Coven (Chu-Carroll and Sprenkle 2000), or Bugzilla (The Mozilla 2007) originate in the software engineering community, while the CSCW community contributed Khronika (Lövstrand 1991), Elvin (Fitzpatrick et al. 1999), and Nessie (Prinz 1999) to implement user-controllable notification mechanisms.

In peripheral-based awareness mechanisms, often widgets are applied to provide awareness at a glance outside the workspace, for example, like a sidebar in

Bernheim-Brush et al. (2002) or Cadiz et al. (2002). Peripheral awareness is mostly used in synchronous collaboration. But since the widget will also show changes that have occurred when the user was off-line, as soon as the user connects again, it can be valuable also for asynchronous awareness.

Existing collaborative tools use informational, subscription-based, or peripheral awareness mechanisms to represent events or activities that took place in the past or that take place in the present. The informational awareness mechanisms show all the events that occur in a workspace. In heavily used workspaces the number of events that occur can become very large and hence the mass of events tends to become overwhelming and it will be almost impossible for the user to view all the events. Subscription-based awareness mechanisms filter the events of interest for a user with respect to his awareness profile, but the number of notifications they generate can be also quite large, overwhelming, and annoying. Therefore, several approaches exist to combine events in an overview presentation (Pankoke-Babatz et al. 2004).

Nevertheless, none of the tools we have analyzed allows a specification of events or actions that should take place in a workspace in the future to automatically verify and notify a user whether they were performed or not.

For the development of our concept we used the framework by Tam and Greenberg (2006). It defines workspace change awareness as the ability of individuals to track the asynchronous changes made to a collaborative document or graphical workspace by other participants over time. In their theoretical framework they list the required information elements for change awareness. The set of questions that the workspace should answer is the following:

1. Where have changes been made? – the location of each change
2. Who has made the changes? – The author of each change
3. What changes were made? – The content of each change
4. How were things changed? – The actions that lead of each change
5. When did the changes take place? – The time of each change
6. Why were the changes made? – The reason for each change

We based the expectation user-interface forms and notification messages in our application on this list of requirements.

1.3 Anticipative Awareness

Our concept of expectation awareness enables a user to specify his anticipation of future activities on a certain artifact or a group of artifacts in a shared workspace. The users will be informed at a chosen point in time if the expected activities have happened or not. Our approach is based on the observation that after performing an activity on an artifact in a workspace, a user usually has a picture in mind of what activities on this artifact should be performed next by his fellow workers (or rather:

he anticipates next activities on the artifact). For example, after uploading a document, the user would probably anticipate that it will be read or modified; after making a poll, he probably waits for others to vote on it. Usually this anticipation also has a certain time limit, within which the activity should take place. We call this anticipation an *expectation*. Figure 1.1 illustrates the process of an expectation.

After an expectation is being created, the creator can either decide to notify the team members involved in the workspace about the expectation or to keep the expectation to himself. In addition, a periodic alarm mechanism is set to test

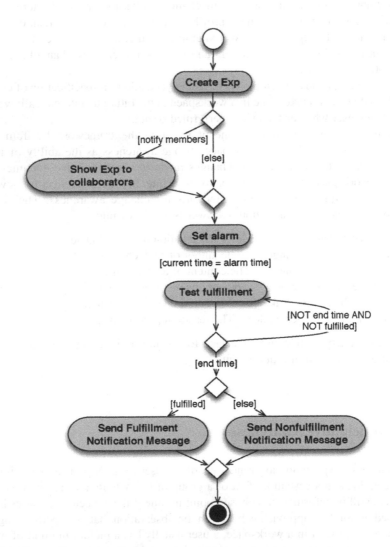

Fig. 1.1 Expectation process diagram

the expectation fulfillment at certain time intervals. As long as the expectation is not fulfilled, the periodic fulfillment tests are performed until the expectation end time. At the end time the last fulfillment test is performed and when the expectation is not fulfilled, a nonfulfillment message is sent. If the expectation gets fulfilled, the periodic test mechanism stops and waits for the expectation end time to send the fulfillment notification.

In practice, we model an expectation as an object with six basic attributes: creator, artifact, activity, participants, start date, and end date. Additional attributes can be defined to extend the usability and flexibility of an expectation. For example, a selection of a preferred notification mechanism or an option to inform the involved collaborators of an expectation is thinkable. The values of these attributes will be specified by the user when a new expectation is created.

An expectation changes its state after the deadline. The three basic possible states are *initial* (before the deadline), *fulfilled*, or *nonfulfilled* (after the deadline). An expectation itself, as any other object in the system, has operations to manipulate it. We consider as essential operations *create*, *edit*, *delete*, *check fulfillment*, and *view fulfillment status* (Fig. 1.2).

In the following we describe the major attributes of an expectation in more detail: artifact, activity, and participants.

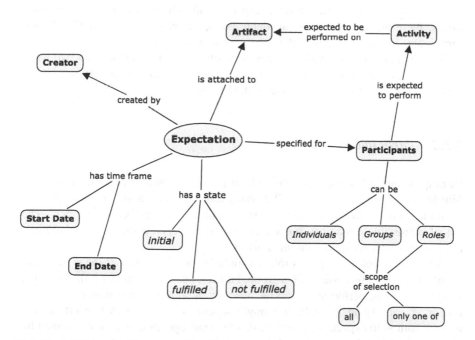

Fig. 1.2 Concept map of the expectation concept

1.3.1 Artifact

The artifact attribute refers to a shared object in a workspace, upon which the chosen activity should operate. We distinguish between a single artifact and a container of artifacts. A single artifact is an object that can be uploaded to or created in a workspace, such as a document or a note. A container of artifacts is a collection of artifacts, such as a folder, a blog, or a discussion.

For a set of artifacts, users should be able to decide whether the expectation is fulfilled when the expected activity takes place in all artifacts or in at least one of the artifacts. This selection will often depend on the expected activity itself. It is obvious to expect, for example, that the read operation will take place in all documents in a folder while the modify operation only on at least one of them.

An exceptional activity for this matter is the create activity. The create operation can be expected only in a container, such as a folder. Another consideration of interest is the case of a hierarchical structure of objects. Then it must be decided whether the activity should take place only in the uppermost level or in the whole hierarchy.

1.3.2 Activity

Activity is an action or operation expected to be executed on the chosen artifact or on a chosen container of artifacts. The list of possible actions is the operational semantics of a chosen artifact with respect to the chosen participants. In other words, these are the operations available on the chosen artifacts for the chosen participants in accordance with the access rights of the latter.

In case of an artifact containing other artifacts (e.g., a folder) there are two ways to define a possible list of actions: either an action common to all artifacts or an action that is executable only on one of the artifacts.

1.3.3 Participants

Participants are other members with whom the creator shares the selected object. Similar to an object, a single collaborator can be either a single member or a "complex" collaborator, such as a group or a role with a number of members. The list of admissible operations for a certain artifact depends on the collaborator's rights to perform operations on this artifact.

For members of a group or a role it should be decided, whether the expectation should be fulfilled by a role or by a group. Further, one must consider if the expected activity should be performed by all members or by at least one member inside of a role or a group. Again, this definition might depend also on the activity itself, since it is quite natural to expect, for example, that the read operation will be performed by all members of a role or a group while the modify operation by at least one of them.

Finally the fulfillment condition for the selected set of collaborators (counting a role or a group as one collaborator) can be specified, i.e., whether all collaborators must fulfill or at least one of them (Fig. 1.3).

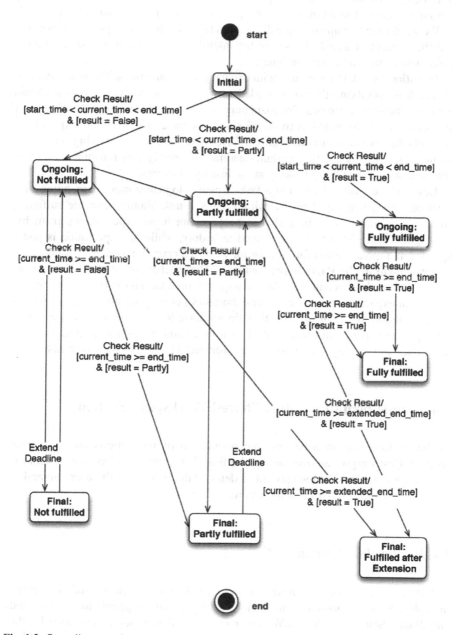

Fig. 1.3 State diagram of an expectation evaluation process

A user can decide whether he wants to make an expectation be visible to the other participants or not. By making an expectation visible, the user implicitly announces to other members what kind of activities he expects them to perform in a workspace. The intention is to establish a better understanding of the expected activities among the members of a project. This use of an expectation makes it very similar to another formal method of project management: task assignment.

We would like to emphasize the differences between the concept of an *expectation* and the concept of a *task*. These are the intention, the level of necessity, and the agreement of the participant assigned.

Intention A task is a work unit with a sequence of instructions. The main intention of a task is specifying the work needed to be done and assigning it to a certain person or number of persons. The main purpose of an expectation is providing better awareness on anticipated activities in a workspace. Creating an expectation supports the automatic summarization of events that the user is looking forward to occur in a workspace until a certain deadline. Currently this information can be obtained only manually by looking at the history of events.

Level of Necessity Assigning a task is psychologically more demanding than creating an expectation. The one who assigns a task should have the sufficient authority, while anyone in a shared project can have expectations from his colleagues. Tasks have to be performed as a duty, while an expectation is just a lightweight representation for looking forward to a certain action.

Agreement of the Participant Assigned The mechanism of a task assignment usually entails the agreement of the participant whom the task is being assigned to. During an expectation creation the collaborators not only do not have to agree to the expectation, but in most cases they do not have to know about an expectation. An expectation is just an expression of what its creator believes should happen in a workspace and an easy means for being informed whether it happens or not.

1.4 Implementation into a Shared Workspace System

In this section, we describe our implementation of the anticipative awareness concept. First we give an overview of the BSCW system – the baseline system for our implementation. Then we provide a detailed description of the user interaction and user-interface of expectations feature.

1.4.1 Baseline System BSCW

BSCW is a web-based groupware system implementing the shared workspace metaphor. Shared workspaces are established by groups of people to organize and coordinate their work. A BSCW server (a standard web server extended by the BSCW functionality through the Common Gateway Interface) manages any number of shared workspaces – repositories for shared information, accessible to the members of a group via any normal web browser using a user name/password authentication scheme. In general, a BSCW server manages workspaces for different groups, and users may be members of several workspaces (e.g., one workspace corresponding to each project in which a user is involved).

A workspace may contain different kinds of information, represented as information objects arranged in a hierarchical order. The objects may be of various types such as folders, URL links to Web pages, documents such as graphics, spreadsheets, and text documents, discussion forums, opinion polls, tasks, or user-specific address books and calendars. The system allows numerous operations – usually depending on the object type – that can be applied to objects, e.g., objects may be renamed, deleted, and undeleted, for URL objects the URL reference may be modified, documents may be put under version control, or users may add a comment to a discussion forum. Operations that have been carried out result in events, which are reported to the users by means of event icons so that they are aware of each other's activities in a workspace.

Some features of BSCW are given below (for more details see Appelt 1999 and Bentley et al. 1997):

Authentication People authenticate by name and password, before they have access to BSCW workspaces. Authentication algorithms include basic authentication, cookie authentication, and X.509 client certificates.

Version Management Documents within a workspace can be put under version control which is particularly useful for joint document production. Documents may be locked to refrain from others replacing them.

Access Rights The system contains a sophisticated access rights model using the notion of roles. Roles define access profiles and can be attached to any object in BSCW. This way, for example, some users may have complete control over an object in a workspace whereas others have only read access or no access at all.

Discussion Forums Users may start a discussion on any topic they like and the system presents the threads in a user-friendly manner.

Community Support BSCW supports so-called communities of interest which provide a new mode to bring people of common interests together for exchanging information. Communities can be open to self-subscription or semi-open where interested users have to apply for membership with the community managers.

Opinion Polls Users may create and manage polls. Polls provide means to collect and evaluate the opinion of other users on certain topics. BSCW provides an interface for editing, executing, and evaluating polls. Polls may be accessible to the general public or to the members of a workspace only.

Event Notification The event service of the BSCW system provides users with information on the activities of other users, with respect to the objects within a shared workspace. The system records the events, and presents the recent events to each user; this notification is integrated into BSCW's user-interface (by placing event icons next to artifacts). Events can be confirmed on a per-user basis at different levels, from individual objects to complete workspace folder hierarchies. Likewise event notification can be filtered on a per-object basis; this is to reduce both the noise induced by too many events and to make sure really important events are not missed. The entire history of artifacts cannot be removed from the system (except by a system administrator) and may be inspected at any time.

Daily Activity Report and Direct Email Notifications Users may additionally subscribe to a daily activity report which is sent to the user via email and which lists all events in any of the user's workspaces within the report period (in general 1 day). Upon user request direct email notifications are issued as soon as an event occurs.

Synchronous Event Notification An (optional) applet supports real-time synchronous awareness about who is logged on and what events are produced.

RSS News Feed BSCW offers an RSS news feed to external news readers enabling external access to BSCW events.

From a system developer's point of view, our main consideration for choosing the BSCW shared workspace system as a baseline system was its modularity and extendibility – new features can be added relatively easily to BSCW by using the BSCW packages mechanism; it allows switching a certain set of features on and off during runtime.

Consequently, the expectation feature was implemented as a BSCW package consisting of various class definition modules, utility routines and user-interface modules, XHTML templates, and cascading style sheets. The kernel software of BSCW was left unchanged.

1.4.2   User Interaction and User-Interface

Our user-interface design for expectations in BSCW was guided by the following principles:

1.4.2.1   Seamless Integration into the Existing BSCW User-Interface

User-interface elements (e.g., icons, forms, buttons) used by the expectation package are based on existing BSCW user-interface elements.

1.4.2.2   Multipurpose Self-Explaining Icons

An "expectation" icon appears after creation of a first expectation on an artifact. The icon is a link to the object's expectation list and its color indicates the state of the expectation. The same icon will indicate the state of further expectations created on an object. To promote an intuitive understanding of icons meaning, we have chosen to represent the meaning with colors matching standard signals of fulfillment (green –), nonfulfillment (red –), and not yet decided (yellow –).

1.4.2.3 Provision of Default Values, Keeping Forms Simple

User-interface forms provide default values. This allows quick creation and editing of expectations. Basically, an expectation can be created just by choosing the *Add New Expectation* option in object's menu and then clicking on the *OK* button.

1.4.2.4 Responsiveness

The state of the expectation is directly reflected by a change of icon (with a potential delay caused by the periodic alarm interval set by the system administrator). The email notification, however, will only be sent at the chosen end time.

1.4.2.5 Sparse System Messages

Our application sends only one email notification per expectation at the expectation end time, if the user chose to be notified at all (Fig. 1.4).

1.4.3 Creating an Expectation

A new expectation is created by invoking a menu command upon which a form opens (see Fig. 1.5).

The form consists of two parts: part one consists of mandatory parameters and part two provides advanced specification of collaborators to be observed (which is not described here).

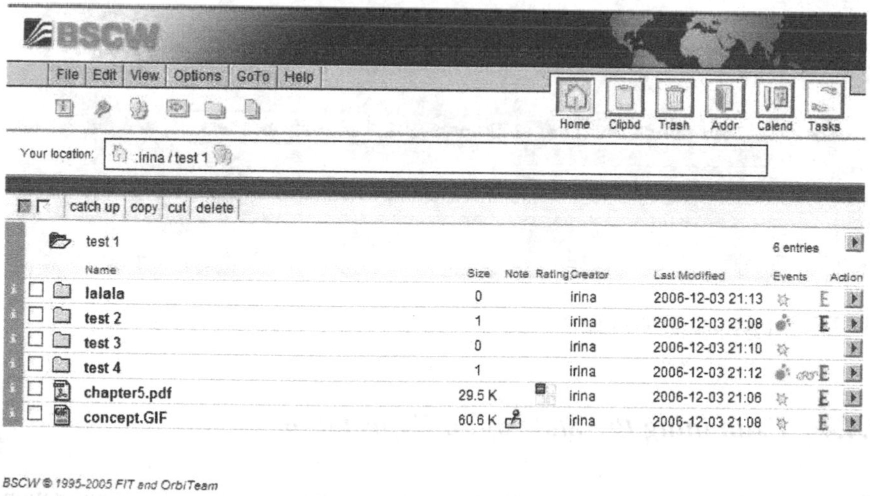

Fig. 1.4 Expectation indication in a BSCW workspace

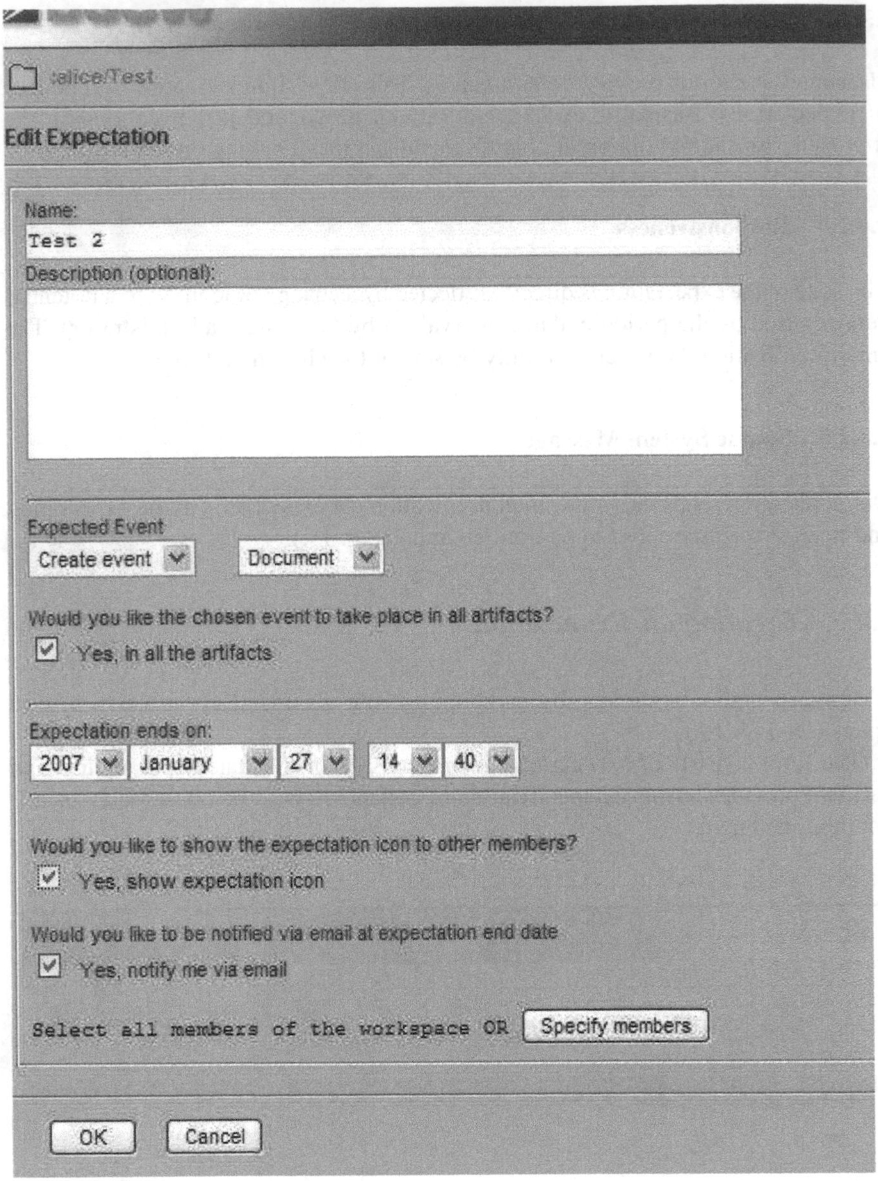

Fig. 1.5 Expectation creation form

1.4.4   Examining the State of an Expectation

The creator of an expectation can obtain information about the state of his expectation in several ways: by change of color in the expectation icon, by the expectation state page, and by email notification at the end of the expectation period (Fig. 1.6).

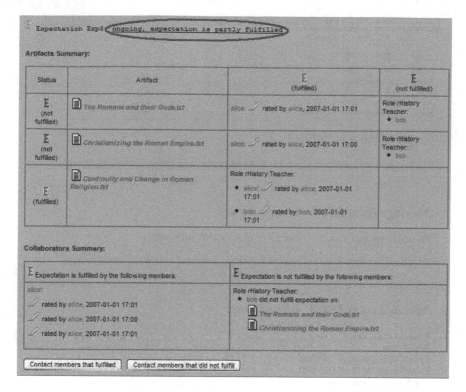

Fig. 1.6 Expectation state page

Figure demonstrates the state check of an expectation of a rate event. The expectation is on a folder with three documents and two users: Alice and Bob. Alice and Bob hold the role *History Teacher*. The user expects that all users must rate all documents. The state page shows that the user Alice fulfilled the expectation and the user Bob did not fulfill on two out of three documents. Alice appears in the column of collaborators that fulfilled for each one of the documents and in the summary. Bob rated only one of the documents and thus he appears in the column of the collaborators that fulfilled for this document, but he appears also in the column of collaborators that did not fulfill for other two documents and in the summary. The fulfillment state of the role "History Teacher" is not fulfilled because of its nonfulfilling member Bob. The overall expectation state is not *final*, because the end time is not over yet.

1.4.5   Email Notification

When the expectation period ends, an automated email is generated, if the expecting user wishes so. Figure 1.7 shows an example of such a notification message. The message is kept short on purpose, but includes a reference to the state page of the expectation for further details.

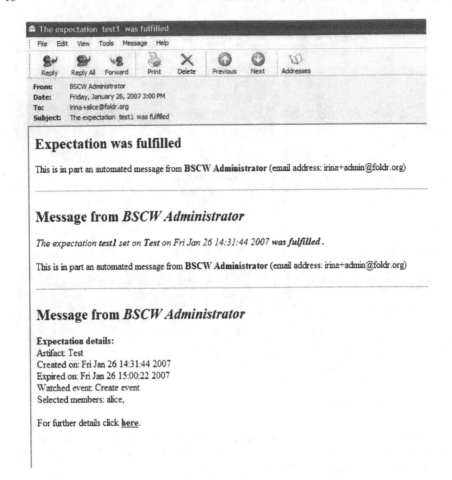

Fig. 1.7 Automated email notification at end date

1.5 Evaluation

In this section, we present the evaluation of the new expectations features in BSCW. The evaluation consisted of tests carried out by ten representative participants from our target group: experienced BSCW users who are responsible for the management of large international projects using BSCW workspaces with many (>30) members. Each test was held by one person at a time and it took 30–45 min.

The evaluation began with a short briefing and a hands-on experiment to get used to the system functionality and use. Afterwards the test persons were asked to perform several tasks on their own. The tasks became more and more elaborated and they covered the whole set of expectations functionality, including the advanced features for creating an expectation on roles and groups. Each participant created or fulfilled five expectations during the test. Out of these, four were to be created by the test participant in accordance to a given task-scenario. One expectation was prepared in advance by the facilitator. It had to be understood and fulfilled by the participant.

After an expectation was created by the test participant, it was fully fulfilled, partly fulfilled, or not fulfilled at all by the test facilitator. Then the test participant was asked to look at the result and to describe it to the facilitator. Each expectation had to be created on a different artifact in a workspace.

The users were asked to provide comments (thinking aloud) or to ask questions while executing the tasks. These questions and comments, together with usability issues identified during the user tests, were collected in a log book.

After each test we conducted a semi-structured interview including questions about the overall impression of the system; whether the expectation concept was clear and easy to learn, estimation of the usefulness of such a feature, possible use cases, and improvements to the user-interface.

Next, we summarize the difficulties encountered during the tests, the suggestions made by the users, and the overall opinion and impressions that the users expressed in the semi-structured interviews.

Difficulties were mainly identified with the expectation creation form and navigation to the expectation actions. No difficulties were encountered in reading the expectation result or in changing an existing expectation. All the test participants could successfully solve the task.

The struggle with the expectation creation form was due to understanding the meaning of the advanced participant selection for an expectation. The options to select all members or at least one member for a role or a group, often required further explanation. The majority of the participants preferred to select members, one by one, instead of selecting a role or a predefined group. However, in another task, where a specific group had to be selected for an expectation, all participants configured the expectation correctly.

Difficulties with the navigation to expectation actions were mainly due to multiple clicks that were needed to get to the expectation result page. Users expected to see the fulfillment state directly after clicking on an expectation icon.

In addition to these usability issues, a number of suggestions were collected that relate to the icon design (improvements for color-blind users), the selection of a deadline (a date is sufficient, a precise time is not needed), and the format of the notification email (more details were required).

All test participants found the expectation concept easy to understand and the expectation result simple to read. All the test participants considered the expectation feature as a very useful extension to the awareness features of the shared workspace system. Some users argued that they would use the feature mostly in large workspaces for awareness, especially to establish anticipative awareness. The majority said that they prefer expectations over tasks since they are less demanding than a task assignment.

Based on this positive and encouraging feedback we have improved the expectation functionality. It is currently being provided at a workspace server for three large European research projects with over 200 users. After the announcement of the feature to the user group a number of expectations have already been created by the users. Until today we have received very positive feedback about the easiness to monitor the status of an activity and in particular to supervise outstanding activities

1.6 Lessons Learned and Future Work

The user tests have shown that the expectation concept is easy to learn, the implementation is responsive and stable, and the expectation result is easy to read. Nevertheless, further consideration is needed to improve the expectation icon, the expectation creation form, and the navigation to expectation operations. In the following we describe the realized improvements.

The expectation icon now leads directly to the expectation status page instead of the configuration page. This is due to the observation that users are more frequently monitoring the expectation status than updating it. Furthermore, it is planned to include a tooltip for the expectation icon that displays further expectation details such as name, event type, creation date, and end date.

The selection of single users, roles, and groups as participants of an expectation has been simplified by moving the role and group selection into an advanced options window, while the selection of single members remains on the main page of expectation creation. This enables the creation of standard expectations in one step. The selection of "at least one" or "for all" conditions, on members inside roles and groups and on members including roles and groups, requires further consideration. Since it is also a cognitive challenge to understand these specific set operations, the creation of an easy-to-use user-interface for this task remains a challenge. To ease the navigation, additional expectation operations have been added to the context menu of an artifact in a shared workspace.

Currently, the expectation fulfillment evaluation is triggered by a periodic alarm. Thus it may happen that an expectation has already been fulfilled, although the state has not yet been updated, due to the triggering interval. To increase the responsiveness of the system, it should be triggered by each operation that takes place in a workspace. However, this requires changes to the kernel of BSCW which was avoided for the first version of the application.

With respect to the expectation concept, the following extensions are planned. In our concept an expectation can be set either on a single artifact or on all artifacts in a container. Furthermore, it is desirable to enable the selection of several artifacts (not necessarily from the same container) for a single expectation. However, we expect that this may cause user-interface challenges. Thus the usefulness of this extension remains to be evaluated.

Vice versa, our expectation concept is currently limited to the creation of an expectation on an entire artifact. But, often expectations refer to specific artifacts elements or parts. Developing a more sophisticated concept of expectations enabling users to describe how they expect the future contents being cooperatively developed will be the next step.

Finally, we suggest the evaluation of the usefulness of expectations in other domains such as software development, architectural design, web content and knowledge management, e-learning, and collaborative problem solving. In this context it will be necessary to extend the presented concept from a single CSCW application (i.e., shared workspace system) to several applications in a cooperative working environment including workflows, instant messaging, and application sharing.

1.7 Conclusion

This work presents a new approach in the area of awareness in groupware. We have made a first step toward supporting both conventional, past-oriented and anticipative, future-oriented awareness by suggesting a conceptual model for defining expectations of actions in a shared workspace and for an automatic check and notification of fulfillment or nonfulfillment of these expectations. Our approach is people-centric and is based on a real-life mental state: the state of anticipating certain events in a workspace. After having studied previous theoretical and practical research on awareness and having analyzed several current collaborative systems, we developed a conceptual model of expectations in shared workspaces. We then implemented our approach as an add-on package to the shared workspace system BSCW. Having evaluated our system with a group of BSCW users we analyzed their feedback and came to the conclusion that all test users declared the concept of anticipative awareness useful and the implementation on the whole usable. Based on the comments of the test users we propose several improvements of the implementation.

References

Appelt, W. (1999) WWW Based Collaboration with the BSCW System. SOFSEM '99 Conference (Milovy, Czech Republic). *Springer Lecture Notes in Computer Science 1725.*

Bentley, R., Appelt, W., Busbach. U., Hinrichs, E., Kerr, D., Sikkel, S., Trevor, J. and Woetzel, G. (1997) Basic Support for Cooperative Work on the World Wide Web. *International Journal of Human-Computer Studies 46*, 6. pp 827–846; Special issue on Innovative Applications of the World Wide Web.

Berliner, B. (1990) CVS II: Parallelizing software development. *Proceedings of the USENIX Winter 1990 Technical Conference.*

Bernheim-Brush, A. J., Bargeron, D., et al. (2002) Notification for Shared Annotation of Digital Documents. *Proceedings of the SIGCHI conference on Human factors in computing systems: Changing our world, changing ourselves.* ACM Press.

Cadiz, J., Venolia, G., et al. (2002) Designing and Deploying an Information Awareness Interface. *Proceedings of the Conference on Computer Supported Cooperative Work, (CSCW 2002).* New Orleans, USA: ACM Press.

Chu-Carroll, M. C., Sprenkle, S. Cove (2000) Brewing better collaboration through software configuration management. *ACM SIGSOFT Software Engineering Notes, 25.* pp 88–97.

Fitzpatrick, G., Mansfield, T., et al. Augmenting the Workaday World with Elvin (1999) *Proceedings of the Sixth Conference on Computer Supported Cooperative Work. (ECSCW '99)*. Copenhagen: Kluwer Academic Publishers.

Fraunhofer FIT and OrbiTeam. BSCW – Basic Support for Cooperative Work. http://bscw.fit.fraunhofer.de/, 2007.

Gräther, W., Prinz, W. (2003) Visualizing Activity in Shared Information Spaces. In *Human-computer interaction*. J. Julie: pp 1096–1100.

Hill, W. C., Hollan, J. D. et al. (1992) Edit Wear and Read Wear. *Proceedings of the SIGCHI conference on Human factors in computing systems*.

Lövstrand, L. (1991) Being selectively aware with the Khronika System. In *Proceedings of the 2nd European Conference on Computer Supported Cooperative Work*. Amsterdam: Kluwer Academic Publishers.

Magnusson, B., Asklund, U. (1996) Fine Grained Version Control of Configurations. In COOP/Orm. Lecture Notes In Computer Science; *Proceedings of theSCM-6 Workshop on System Configuration Management*. Springer.

Pankoke-Babatz, U., Prinz, W., et al. (2004) Stories about Asynchronous Awareness. In F. Darses, R. Dieng, C. Simone and M. Zacklad, *Cooperative Systems Design – Scenario-Based Design of Collaborative Systems*. IOS Press: pp 23–38.

Prinz, W. (2002) NESSIE: An Awareness Environment for Cooperative Settings. *Proceedings of the Sixth Conference on Computer Supported Cooperative Work*, (ECSCW'99). Copenhagen: Kluwer Academic Publishers.

Ripley, R. M., Sarma, A., et al. (2006) Using Visualizations to Analyze Workspace Activity and Discern Software Project Evolution, in UCI ISR Technical Report. http://www.isr.uci.edu/tech-reports.html.

Tam, J., Greenberg, S. (2006) A framework for asynchronous change awareness in collaborative documents and workspaces. International Journal of Human-Computer Studies (64). 583–598.

The Mozilla Organization (2007) Bugzilla Bug Tracking System, http://www.bugzilla.org/.

Chapter 2
'Colour, It's Just a Constant Problem': An Examination of Practice, Infrastructure and Workflow in Colour Printing

David Martin, Jacki O'Neill, Tommaso Colombino, Frederic Roulland, and Jutta Willamowski

2.1 Introduction

Two interrelated topics that have been of enduring interest to researchers in studying cooperative work practices and the design and use of technologies to support those practices are workflow and, to a slightly lesser extent, infrastructure. Workflow systems are a classic form of technology employed to coordinate cooperative work along a process of production where different workers (potentially in different companies and locations) complete different tasks along a 'line' of production. The workflow and the technologies that embody or enforce it are designed to maintain adherence to procedure and coordination across time and place. The central issues surrounding the treatment of workflow in Computer Supported Cooperative Work (CSCW) and related disciplines have been the problem of getting workflow systems to mesh with the particularities of local flows of work among people. Since Suchman (1983, 1987), at least, there has been a presiding concern with the ways in which workflow models fail to take into account the local, embodied, non-prescriptive and emergent manner (responding to dynamic local circumstances) in which people organise their work. Workflow systems have been criticised for being designed from 'elsewhere' – with an inadequate, overly idealistic or abstracted understanding of the work they are meant to assist. People end up having to organise or translate (potentially after-the-fact) their work, so it fits with the workflow system or workaround or ignore the technology completely (see Bowers et al. 1995) for an example from the print industry).

Consequent to such studies, there has been considerable work in looking at the possibility of adaptive workflow systems that could be altered to fit disrupted and evolving work patterns during a period of 'domestication' (see for example the Klein et al. (2000) special issue on such systems) and are informed by an awareness of the contingencies of work practice.

D. Martin (✉), J. O'Neill, T. Colombino, F. Roulland, and J. Willamowski
Xerox Research Centre Europe (XRCE), Grenoble, France
e-mail: david.martin@xrce.xerox.com

D. Randall and P. Salembier (eds.), *From CSCW to Web 2.0: European Developments in Collaborative Design*, Computer Supported Cooperative Work, DOI 10.1007/978-1-84882-965-7_2, © Springer-Verlag London Limited 2010

However, it is now being more clearly acknowledged that while it may be easy to take the stance of 'bad fit' of system with existing practice, this ignores the fact that new systems are often specifically bought and deployed to transform work in some way – sometimes purely with the intention of making things more efficient, other times with notions like improving quality or conditions. A more sophisticated analysis of the situation, which also acknowledges the perspective of the software product developer, has developed. It is a complex task to provide generic products that can still be useful over a wide series of circumstances (Martin et al. 2005; Pollock et al. 2007), and part of the process for success in this area is to make apparent to customers the benefits of changing their organisation's ways of working to fit the product, rather than vice versa. This may seem counter-intuitive, but when we witness the success of products such as enterprise resource planning (ERP) systems from companies such as SAP (see Section 5), we can understand that while some customers 'lose', and for some employees of customers the process of deployment and change is painful, many buyers of these systems are – in the long run at least – satisfied customers.

While the process of design or choice of system is clearly very important, more recent research has also focused on examining the process of system tailoring and the social process of 'change management'. Deciding what practices need to be preserved, which may be transformed and how this is handled 'politically' may be crucial to the success of systems involving workflows. And, going further, new technology possibilities such as service-oriented architectures (SOAs), gradual, sensitive (to users and other impacts) roll-out and more tractable domains (like banking) may allow workflow systems to be a success (Brahe and Schmidt 2007). In some ways, the literature on infrastructure (Star and Ruhleder 1996; Star 1999; Lee et al. 2006; Olsen et al. 2006) presented in venues such as CSCW has a similar flavour to the literature on workflow. Although it deals with, for example, the technical structures that 'sit behind' the interface level and thus may be less visible to the user, these still impact on how their work is achieved. This literature has been concerned with infrastructure as a 'relational concept' – specifically with the relations between certain identified people, their work and the infrastructural technologies that serve as a 'substrate' for that work. In following this agenda the research has looked at the impacts and mismatches between people, their work and infrastructures and the work to produce and manage infrastructures. Interestingly it has predominantly also focused on infrastructures for global scientific communities to carry out *e-scientific* research and has been interested in the problems of community building, particularly concerning trust and the sharing of data as well as technical issues. More recent research has focused on the crucial role of people ('the human infrastructure of cyberinfrastructure' cf. Lee et al. (2006) in promoting, supporting and maintaining infrastructures.

In this study we are clearly moving into a domain quite different from these other studies. However, Star and Ruhleder (1996) identified several features of infrastructures that are useful for this study. Infrastructures tend to be *embedded* (sunk into other structures, technologies and social arrangements), *transparent* (not noticed), *linked with conventions of practice*, and they *become visible upon breakdown*. They are seen as relational in that what constitutes one person's infrastructure is not the same for another depending on such things as their relative jobs. In this paper we examine the relation between the work of graphic designers and print workers, the workflows and technologies they employ, and the technical infrastructure embedded in their software and devices. This infrastructure is placed there for the purpose of managing colour (communicating and translating it from device to device and application to application).[1]

We believe that this study is interesting and important in both a specific and general way: specifically because managing colour across a distributed workflow is a complex cooperative problem and generally because this work builds upon classic topics concerning practice, workflow and infrastructure. We believe it builds on these topics in a manner that illuminates them in a different way, mainly because: (1) other studies of infrastructure have not looked at infrastructure in relation to a *product production workflow*, instead in relation to *data sharing when conducting scientific research*. *Thus* this research is novel in that it specifically looks at an interrelation between infrastructure, workflow and practice; (2) the different parties involved are not equal partners but service providers and clients; (3) the different parties had little or no input in the infrastructure's design or development and have no ownership; (4) while this infrastructure is problematic it is difficult to imagine any reasonable alternative; and (5) the ways in which it impinges on work and is misunderstood by practitioners are, of themselves, interesting.

2.2   The Problem of Colour Print Production

Producing colour prints is complex and when problems occur, understanding their root causes, where they are located (in the workflow, in the file, or at the printing device and just where exactly within any of these) and how to solve them is very difficult even for domain experts. Putting aside problems with print devices – how they are calibrated and maintained, and issues to do with humidity, temperature, and how inks and toners react – one of the main problems of producing colour is achieving the 'correct' or at least a 'good' mapping between what is created and observed on screen and what is produced in print.

The technologies involved in colour work – input (e.g. scanners and cameras), display (e.g. monitors) and output (e.g. printers) devices – have device-centric ways of producing and encoding colour (i.e. different colour spaces). Colour is produced differently on screen, by combining red, green and blue (RGB) light sources, than in print, made of cyan, magenta, yellow and black (CMYK) ink or toner pigments which are applied to some substrate (e.g. paper). On top of this, different devices (even different devices of the same order, e.g. two printers) have

---

[1] As an example of the relational (rather than absolute) features of infrastructure one can see how the CM infrastructure for graphic designers' work is the topic of research and development for colour scientists rather than being an infrastructure that supports their work.

different gamuts[2] (ranges of colours) they can produce. Furthermore, design choices, technical constraints and manufacturer preferences also create differential colour production. This clearly sets up an issue for how files or documents, passed between devices, are represented. There needs to be some method of translating between these different colour spaces, particularly for deciding how colour definitions within one gamut should map on to those in a different gamut.

Colour management (CM) was developed by The International Colour Consortium (ICC).[3] CM is an industry-standard technical system designed to enable translation between different colour spaces and colour devices (monitors, printers, etc.). Essentially this means that when a file is transferred from one device to the other, it should come with a profile that indicates how to interpret its colour information. This profile is then translated into a device independent colour space defined by the ICC before it can be re-interpreted correctly in terms of the new device. CM is a technically correct solution, in that the system, when used properly, can translate colours between say a screen and a print device such that colours seen on screen should correlate as highly as possible with those printed out.

Over the last 2 years we have been studying the work involved in creating and producing graphic designs, with a focus on colour printing. Our studies show that the successful implementation of properly colour managed workflows is rare in the print industry, and that achieving printed results that satisfy the customer is often a complicated business involving a number of print-proof-adjust-reprint cycles. Practitioners mostly do not have any kind of systematic understanding of what it is, in particular, about a certain document that when printed on a certain machine will cause a particular type of problem. It is not that they do not have any knowledge of problems, their causes, and potential solutions; it is just that this knowledge maps in complicated (not always accurate) ways to what is actually going on.

2.3   The Prospect of New Markets

It might seem strange to talk about the prospect of new markets after discussing the problems of current colour printing practices. However, some points are worth making that explain why this is relevant. Firstly, colour printing is a multi-billion dollar industry and is likely to remain so for some time. Secondly, the problems of colour do not curtail the industry; they just make achieving the desired output more costly, or compromises must be made on quality. That is, it takes more print-proof-and-adjust cycles in order to get the desired product or the accepted product

---

[2] The range of colours – gamut – a device can produced are defined mathematically in a multi-dimensional space. Colour spaces both overlap and diverge. Translating colours from one space to another involves mapping colours in one space to the other according to various algorithms. Various compromises are made for mapping colours that occur in one space but are outside the gamut of the other.

[3] http://www.color.org/index.xalter

is of lesser quality than it might be. Thirdly, there is an ongoing competition between offset printing where a printing plate has to be produced for each individual page, versus digital printing, which requires no plate, meaning every different page is produced at the same cost. Because of the need to produce plates, offset printing is more expensive for short runs (i.e. numbers of copies), but is generally understood (by designers and printers) to produce more aesthetically pleasing prints. This is generally seen as a feature of having a higher resolution and wider colour range of richer inks, but is also probably a product of technology maturity and greater practitioner experience. So, offset is widely understood as having the edge on quality. Due to this many printing decisions are made on quality-amount-cost calculations with a number of copies threshold[4] below which offset is not economically viable unless there are specific quality requirements the client is prepared to pay for.

However, intriguingly, digital opens up a variety of different business propositions whereby printing multiple variations of the same document on-the-fly, or single documents for mass populations, or tailored products becomes possible for the same *printing* price per page as printing a longer run. This offers possibilities for capturing a mass consumer 'long tail' market (Anderson 2006) previously untapped in high-quality printing, for example, where many consumers construct various semi-bespoke products (e.g. calendars) out of their own photographs. It also opens up a market for software products and applications that make the production of variable tailored printing products easier and dependable, and crucially, cheap enough. These printing products are very attractive to businesses who wish to employ personalised 1–1 marketing (specific products and services are targeted to individuals, rather than in a blanket fashion to all customers). This type of marketing is thought to be much more effective in getting customers to 'bite'.

In both of these markets web 2.0 is important, as is the notion of 'mass customisation' (Piller and Stotko 2002) Mass customisation is the idea of providing tailored or personalised products to customers for around the same cost as mass produced. Being tailored, these products or services should necessarily have higher value to the customer. The Internet can help to achieve this in a number of ways – through digitisation, quicker, more efficient customer interactions, and the ability to collect and analyse customer data. If the product is entirely digital (e.g. music) the entire process of selection, tailoring and delivery, and the ongoing customer relationship can be managed on-line. If the product is material, e.g. clothes (or as in this case printing), while it still needs to be delivered, many aspects of the customisation (giving exact measurements, choosing colours, emblems, etc.) and the relationship can be achieved through the Internet. Other products like specialised advice can be done completely on-line. Mass customisation has become an important topic for printing; firstly, for allowing print shops to offer web submission and web-based products that can be personalised and tailored, and for reaching mass market customers. Secondly, this opens up the market

---

[4]This number can vary considerably depending on the specific technology in question and the nature of the print job, but is generally considered to be around 2,500 copies.

for new technologies that make it easy to implement and manage workflows for producing 1–1 marketing, that manage and assess digital printing assets (images, photographs), that provide templates for tailorable documents and so forth. In this way, high-quality production printing is moving into web 2.0 and related technologies territory. But the question of assuring quality – particularly in colour – remains.

2.4 Method and Settings

The paper describes the findings of a series of ethnographic studies undertaken at a number of print shops and graphic design agencies in the UK and Europe over a 2-year period (cf. Randall et al. (2007) for a guide and exposition of this work in CSCW and Bowers ct al. (1995) for a pertinent study in the print industry). We carried out this work in conjunction with colleagues working at another research laboratory within our organisation in North America. During this time we also consulted market research carried out internally and externally to our company. Having compared our results with the North American work and the market research, and having found that they were repeated, this allows us to make reasonable claims about the generalisability of our findings.

Observation is our primary method, supplemented by in situ interviewing, with site visits varying between 2 days and 3 weeks. Our fieldwork data were audio and video recordings, photographs, notes and artefacts from the sites. Our materials were gathered and analysed with an ethnomethodological orientation (Garfinkel 1967; Sharrock and Anderson 1986) which emphasises how work is organised as a recognisable social accomplishment. To achieve this we observed and analysed the real-time details of work, interaction between participants, and interactions with technologies and artefacts. From this analysis we were able to uncover how practitioners understood, oriented to, reasoned about and managed colour, and this is presented below.

It is also worth explaining how our materials are presented here, and for what reasons, as some readers may be looking for transcripts of audio or video, or detailed notes on unfolding action, none of which they will find here. The purpose of our project was to find out how colour was being managed and why CM technology was not being properly exploited. As we discovered how design work unfolds by studying our materials we also found the ad hoc methods used to manage colour and that the way in which practitioners reasoned about colour was radically different to that which would be required to use CM workflows. It is these methods, that reasoning and the schism between these and what would be required to use CM workflows that we present here.

2.5 Infrastructures and Workflows

CM is a technical 'infrastructure' upon which CM workflows can be built to achieve consistent colour reproduction (most faithful to the original source, most consonant with what is seen on screen, etc.). Every screen-to-print workflow uses some CM technology components whether, and this as we shall see, is crucial, this is the knowing intention of designers and print workers or not. Although CM is not in itself a workflow system, to use it successfully, necessarily implies a workflow where a specific instantiation is *rigorously followed* and *understood* (at least in a functional sense, by following a strict set of procedures, making the correct selections, etc.) *by all* of those involved in the process.

Unfortunately developing a correctly operating workflow and adhering to it is not simple. Different devices offer different settings for handling (e.g. recording, producing) colour. Different design applications offer various settings for working with documents and encoding colour data in files, including differing default settings. Successfully managing colour across a screen-to-print workflow requires that the users ensure that 'appropriate' profiles are always attached to files and that these are translated in the 'correct' places. Users must be able to understand the separation between how an image is displayed and how it is encoded, as well as potentially taking into account the capabilities of the print device. Defining the appropriate workflow requires a degree of technical knowledge not normally found among design and print professionals. Ordinarily, or at least as an aspiration, in the realms of computing, the complexity 'going on behind the scenes' is hidden from the user, often with a 'graspable' workflow sitting on top of a complex infrastructure. Here, implementing a good workflow requires a sophisticated understanding of just how the CM infrastructure works.

In our studies of print shops (firstly) and graphic designers (secondly) the most obvious finding was that properly colour-managed workflows were not implemented anywhere, even in a fine art museum. In our studies of print shops (O'Neill et al. 2007) we became aware that most files reaching the print shops contained no colour profiles (attachments indicating the CM information), and that those that did, had the profiles discarded by the print workers as untrustworthy. We also became aware that tools on print devices, designed to be used with colour-managed files were being used 'inappropriately' or 'creatively' to try and effect aesthetic changes. Our initial belief was that the problem might lie with the graphic designers and it certainly seemed to originate in their work. This led us to look upstream in the process, to graphic designers, to try and understand why CM was not being used by them. Our research indicates that because CM is very complex – both in itself and in the way it is presented in tools and technologies – practitioners all along the process have varying knowledge and understanding of it but do not have the understanding, desire or resources to implement a properly colour-managed workflow. In many cases this applies to print-shop workers just as much as graphic designers. When it comes to the customers who commission graphic designers, they are often initially even more in the dark, about the problems associated with colour translation and production.

The situation is made even more difficult due to the fact that different people in different organisations using different technologies work to produce and print designs with elements from different sources (e.g. graphics, photos, text). Indeed, such a finding is reinforced by the fact that it is photographers who are the people who are most likely to colour manage. They can exercise more direct control over their workflow as it involves fewer people and they are often interested in *preserving* the colour data from camera to print. In our interviews with them we have realised that they orient to trying to keep what they capture with the camera, whereas graphic design is much more about *creation* and *production* that involves the assembly and transformation of material from several sources.

2.6 Non-CM Workflows in Graphic Design and Printing

Our studies of graphic designers added strength to the idea that CM was proving too technically complex to understand and implement across the print workflow. Graphic designers showed variable levels of understanding of CM and it was seen as too complex to implement properly. There was, also, a degree of confusion about elements of CM; few had anything approaching an in-depth knowledge.

In the absence of CM workflows, designers and print shops strive to control colour in more local and practical ways. Practitioners were found to have developed several related techniques and practices for achieving the colour results they required, or at least reducing the inconsistencies and uncertainties between screen and print. And most obviously graphic designers develop relationships with print shops that they trust; who help them achieve good prints, without necessarily inquiring into what it is about the print shop (their set-up, staff, equipment) that enables this.

Indeed, this is a very interesting question, since the industry-scientific and best-practice view on producing quality prints resides with the notion of being able to design and implement a CM workflow. Whereas, configurations of people and technologies that can still produce quality in the absence of a properly colour-managed workflow – and what that quality consists in – are poorly understood. In the following section we detail various ad hoc practices used to control colour and note that the interesting thing that unifies them is their *tangibility* and *comprehensibility*; they deal with samples and more straightforward, everyday ways of viewing and encoding colours such that the reproduction is close to something they have previously seen. This stands opposed to the mathematical models of colour encoding embodied in CM.

2.7 Examples of Ad Hoc CM

In our previous paper (O'Neill et al. 2007) we noted that CM did not seem to be used at all in print shops and discussed the ways in which print workers tried to correct problematic colour in prints by adjusting several controls. We also described how print shops worked with customers to set up colour libraries for important colours like brand colours and that they tried to educate customers both about the potential problems with files and colours and about how they might be improved. Looking at graphic designers has reinforced our understanding of the importance of relationships in printing; graphic designers often have favoured print shops that help them to produce a quality product. Although print shops often do more of the correctional work, graphic designers orient towards problems with colour and try and control colour in ways in which they are able. They may also spend considerable time managing customer expectations, e.g., making them aware of colour differences between screen and print. Designers' basic advice on colour is that offset is better than digital, if one has strict colour requirements; spending time (and more money) proofing with the print shop is crucial; and Pantone inks (proprietary ink formulas used in offset printing) are the most dependable ways of getting colour right. It should be noted that the advice of both printers and graphic designers for customers is experientially based rather than grounded in a scientific perspective and understanding.

2.7.1 Pantone Swatch Books

The Pantone Inc. Corporation produces a range of inks, swatch books and charts (see Fig. 2.1) of their proprietary colour space, that show the colours that can be reproduced, given the substrate (coated or uncoated paper), print technology (e.g. between offset printing and different types of digital press), and ink formulas (proprietary Pantone inks, or four colour combinations) that are used. The colours themselves, their 'intensity' and general look and feel vary across the range. When used properly – i.e. the correct book for the correct print device technology and for the correct substrate – Pantone technology can be used to specify and print individual colours with good accuracy. The designer can select the desired colour from the guide book or chart and then can encode the colour as a Pantone in the image file and it will be interpreted as such by the print device (Fig. 2.2 shows a leaflet

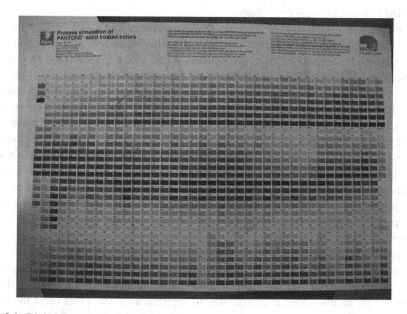

Fig. 2.1 Digital Pantone swatch chart

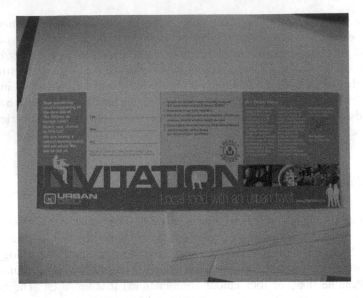

Fig. 2.2 Deli flyer (produced from the swatch chart)

produced by using the chart in Fig. 2.1). We observed a widespread use of Pantone swatch books and charts for selecting and controlling colour in all the design houses we visited. In the best cases, the designers were using print device and substrate (e.g. coated/uncoated) appropriate Pantone swatch books bought by them or provided to them by their print shop.

For example, one of the UK agencies had just invested in a full set of Pantone swatch books and the designers showed us that they now had an offset process colour swatch book that had been giving them particularly good results. However, some design houses used Pantone swatch books that were not 'correct' for the printing press or substrate they were going to print on. Instead, they had one Pantone book and believed that this was relevant to all presses and substrates. In these cases, the relationship between the chosen Pantones or CMYK process colours and what the print device could produce was more variable. A key problem from the perspective of designers is that the Pantone system is confusing. Pantones are stipulated as a set of equidistant numbered colours within the range (gamut) that can be produced by a machine. This means that a specific Pantone number may well be a different colour when produced on different machines. Unfortunately this is not widely known and many people labour under the misapprehension that choosing a specific Pantone (e.g. for a brand) will ensure consistent reproduction across print devices and substrates.

Furthermore, the differentiation between Pantones and their CMYK process versions was, again, understood differently in different locations. A number of designers that we have observed choose a palette with reference to a Pantone guide in their design, simply as this seems a sensible way to stipulate a palette. Later on in the process it may well turn out that either the customer does not want to pay for specifically mixed Pantone inks, or the design will be printed on digital (which in most cases means that special inks cannot be provided). At this point the designer will either get their software package to convert the Pantones into CMYK versions or will leave this to the printer. Either way, the CMYK versions may vary in the extent to which they match the original Pantones often leading to confusing results. It was during the course of our studies that we found out that even different releases of the same software package can have different conversions!

This problem in often exacerbated in situations where a design with the same palette is printed on both offset and digital, as differing results would be likely. For many designers and – it would surely seem the default expectation – the belief is that Pantones are a system of absolute value, but that reality is that, although in the 'same ball-park' they are actually relative to one another across formats.

A great advantage of using Pantone swatches is that it allows the matching of colours by eye, which unsurprisingly, given its simplicity and tangibility, is one of the designers' preferred methods. Although, they are aware that matching colours individually between screen and swatch book is somewhat imperfect due to the different media of instantiation. Importantly, Pantones can only be used for specifying spot colours in vector graphics objects (graphic blocks of colour) and not for bitmap regions within the page (such as photographs or elements of a photograph).

2.7.2 Work in Default CMYK Colour Space to Help with Gamut Issues

Two design houses we observed work by default in a CMYK 'emulation' space (see Fig. 2.3) on screen when they are producing a printed product. By working in CMYK they believe the discrepancy between what they see on screen and what will eventually be printed is minimised (i.e. in comparison with working in RGB). Working in CMYK means that designers are showing some orientation to printing in their work. In general the effect of this is that they are less likely to choose colours for their designs that are out of gamut; there will be generally a greater consonance between what is seen on screen and what will be printed. However, understanding just how what appears on screen will relate to a print is still complicated, especially if using an un-calibrated[5] monitor, as different colours will be closer or differ more from their on-screen equivalents.

This is exacerbated when the user does not know which settings they have and their impacts, e.g. in one of the settings CM tools were turned off, while in the other they were set at a North American default setting (it was in the UK). In both cases

---

[5]Calibration is a process where the colorimetric response of a device (the way the device reproduces specific colours) is measured using a spectrophotometer. The resulting measurements are used to adjust the device and maintain consistency in colour reproduction over time. Calibration needs to be performed regularly on all devices (monitors and printers) in a CM workflow.

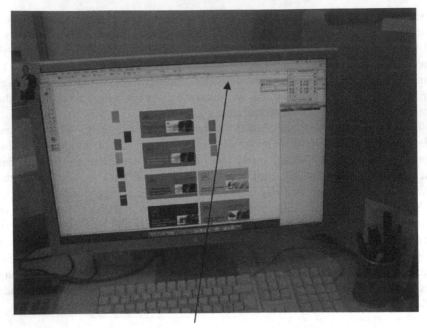

Fig. 2.3 Designing in CMYK emulation space

(even when apparently turned off) CM is setting and altering the colour values in the files for printing. This can lead to some unexpected effects on printing.

2.7.3   Preferred Palettes and Known About and 'Simple' Colours

Graphic designers we observed had 'preferred' palettes and 'known about' colours. These are colours and sets of colours that, by experience, designers had found seemed to print well. This was not simply a matter of perceived consonance between screen and print but was also to do with having seen the colours printed a number of times and having been pleased with the results. When colour choices were left open they tended towards guiding customers to one of those colours if they felt it was appropriate for the product. On the other hand, certain colours were known to be problematic. For example, vibrant orange is difficult to reproduce using process colour (CMYK) combinations. This was one of the UK Universities' corporate colours for which they had found a specific, preferred, print shop that could produce the colour well.

Another method that designers used to manage colour is to use 'simple' colours in their designs. What this amounts to varies, with some renditions clearly more easy to produce and others may amount to practitioner misunderstanding.

For example, simple colours might be considered to be colours made up of 100% C, M, Y, or K; or a mixture of just two of CMYK. Single colours or simpler combinations of just two colours were intuitively understood to be more dependable in output. However, some designers prefer regular breakdown percentages like 25% C 50% Y, etc. as opposed to 17%C 39%Y, etc. The extent to which a colour made up of varying percentages of four colours is 'complex' is open for discussion. Some designers reported that the reason they consider colours composed of irregular percentages more complex is not to do with mixing colours but rather that it is more difficult for them to know how a colour composed in a more complex way will look 'in real life' when it is printed out. For example, in one situation observed, a brown with a high magenta content looked like a rich brown on screen or printed on offset, but printed on a digital print device it was burgundy in colour. Another technique designers used was to use shades (lightening/ darkening) of the same colours. As we were told, an issue between screen and print is that of harmony between colours – combinations that look harmonious on screen can be dissonant in print. Tricks of the trade like using shades ensure a harmony between the colours.

We have two examples of designers using 100% cyan (Fig. 2.4). In the first, the brief was to provide some 'straightforward/clean' designs for a plumbing parts company. The catalogues were black and white with one extra colour. Looking through various samples of previous work the designer noticed that out of four colours used, one appeared to be 100% cyan. As one of the four colours in colour printing (CMYK), it is easy to 'hit' this colour consistently, as it does not involve mixing any colours (Fig. 2.5).

Fig. 2.4 Mission rubber 100% cyan

Fig. 2.5 CMYK key for block colours

At another design agency, the designer was showing us a university newsletter and noted how he had picked 100% cyan as the key colour along with black, white and grey because it looked good and was easy to produce.

2.7.4   Work with the Print Shop to Set the Colour Values

In situations where customers have very strict colour requirements, they or the designers must put in extra work with the print shop (and pay more) to ensure that the colour requirements can be met. This is done through printer (machine and person) selection, through encouraging customers to pay for Pantone inks and through process colour proofing, and proofing in general (Fig. 2.6). In this way tolerable/desired colours are achieved. We have seen these colours encoded as keys on files and print samples (Figs. 2.7). Certain print shops also get the reputation of being able to do certain things. For example (as pointed out above), the University designers went to a certain print shop when needed "because they could produce a really strong orange". We observed the design of boxes for curry spice recipes (Fig. 2.7) where the design house sent the customer to the print shop because the customer had 'very particular' colour requirements. They were particular in that she wanted very specific colours (like the 'jade' green above) with very little tolerance but did not want to pay for specific Pantones. The designers told her that she needed to go to the print shop and work out the precise CMYK mixes that fitted her requirements. In Fig. 2.7 the CMYK process mixes have been added to the image as a key. The same process occurred for this design house when producing a set of boxes for some 'puddings' (see Fig. 2.3 for early designs and for colour proofs). By getting the customer to

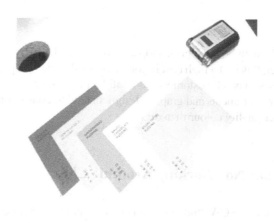

Fig. 2.6 Colour proof test prints

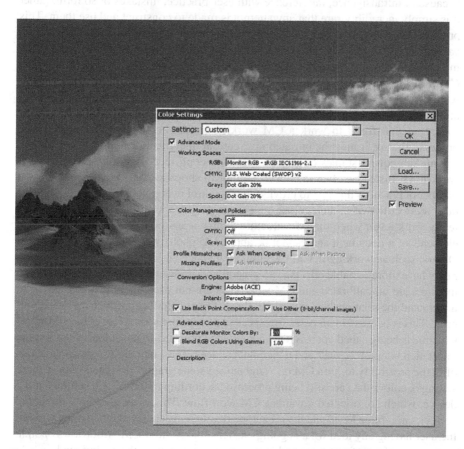

Fig. 2.7 Photoshop CM settings dialogue – working spaces, CM policies (turned off), conversion options, advanced controls

collaborate directly with both the print shop and the design house, good colour can be achieved. However, this is at a high cost if, for example, the run is expected to be short. Some design houses may tell customers who will be printing on digital that they must relax their colour requirements and graphic designers tend to consider that offset printing produces better quality colour than digital.

2.8   Discussion: No 'Working Around' CM

A common feature of CSCW studies of workflow systems is that people often *work around* difficult elements of such systems. What is interesting here is that, being an infrastructure, it is not possible to truly work around CM. In our studies, supported by other work (Riordan 2005), we did not see any examples of properly implemented CM workflows. It is not that CM workflows are tried and fail in implementation because of intransigence, interference with user practice, mistakes or so forth, rather it is simply incredibly rare that any attempt is made to construct and use them. This produces the consequent problem that the colour resulting from printing can be highly variable in relation to what was expected. Our studies of print shops showed that the majority of files that arrived at the shops did not have profiles attached containing CM information. Furthermore, even when files arrived with profiles attached these were discarded as not being trustworthy. When problems occurred, print operators attempted to solve them, but effecting a solution often proved difficult. CM is *non-robust*, in that for it to work a CM workflow must be followed throughout the process. That is, it must be initiated upstream at document design.

Our subsequent studies of graphic designers confirmed they were not using CM workflows. Instead – often in concert with print shops to some degree – they use a number of practices that aim to provide some control over colour. Some of these practices (correct use of swatch colour books, use of 100% cyan) are practices that can really work, even when the infrastructure is misunderstood, but they only work for elements of a document and cannot be applied to photographs or complex graphics. Others, such as working in CMYK emulation space and using 'simple' colour mix ratios have more variable effects. The general and persistent effect, however, is when monitors are un-calibrated and CM workflows are not used, there is no clear way to understand the relationship between all the different colours on screen and what will print. This is because in *all cases* (irrespective of conscious knowledge) the CM infrastructure is being called upon as it is *impossible* to produce digital colour without some translation between devices and their colour spaces. Thus, although some applications offer the possibility to 'turn CM off' (and indeed some graphic designers choose these settings), colour data are still being processed according to the default settings of the device, which are oriented towards a CM workflow. This work goes on without the correct 'encryption keys' and thus is automatically translated wrongly – often without the user having any idea what is going on. This makes 'non-CM' workflows *opaque* as a variety of transformations and encodings are going on in the background.

We suggest that colour production printing is an intriguing example of cooperative work that enabled us to examine some issues concerning infrastructure and workflow. These provide a different 'take' to the investigations of workflow systems previously presented in the CSCW literature. What marks this investigation out from previous work is the fact that we investigate the link between a particular infrastructure and the workflows that it implies. The nature of CM as an infrastructure means that even when using non-colour-managed workflows it still necessarily impacts on the way colour is processed and rendered and therefore affects the appearance of colour in documents. CM is an infrastructure which is 'scientifically' correct. It makes sense from a purely technical point of view, but it is very complex to put into place the workflows required to successfully make the infrastructure work to produce consistent and good colour. To make informed choices between the many possibilities offered by applications and devices, one needs to have a technical understanding of how CM actually works, i.e. some awareness of colour science. Currently such specialised knowledge and skills are largely absent in the design and print industries. Below we list three points which illustrate the complexity of CM and its presentation to the average user.

2.8.1 Confusing Presentation of CM Functions and Options

It is clear that the way in which CM options and controls are presented on the graphical user interface (GUI) of common editing and design applications means that the average user has problems understanding if they are operating, how they are operating, what would be the best option for 'this document' and so forth. For example, colour translation takes place, irrespective of whether CM is supposedly 'switched on or off', or whether the practitioners know what the settings are.

The CM options offered up are often opaque to practitioners and explanations are not ready-to-hand (rather they are hidden in the help systems) nor articulated in a way which is comprehensible to them – the potential sophistication of the system means the novice is presented with a dizzying set of options. In popular design applications when an image or photograph is imported the user will be given options that regard the preservation, conversion or removal of the file profile, and also whether they would like to preserve the profile but work in a different 'emulation' (or *working*) space (i.e. the appearance on screen). There are also various options for dealing with different types of image element differently (e.g. for CMYK versus RGB), as well as dictating how any conversion of profiles should work, as well as various advanced options. The implications of making certain choices are not self-evident unless one understands the underlying process of conversion between different colour spaces, and decisions not based on a clear understanding will often lead to unexpected results when the document is printed.

2.8.2 No Means of Recovery

There is a related issue around recovering information about the document creators' colour intent from documents at different stages of the workflow, in particular in situations where the colour as rendered by a specific device does not match the user's expectations. In the absence of a properly colour-managed workflow, neither the system nor the user will necessarily know just how the current set of encodings actually relates to what was intended or desired. Operations like colour space transforms may be applied without the user's knowledge and there is no meaningful audit trail or history. This may point to an issue with the 'intelligence' of the CM system and it is necessary to consider how useful information about the relationship between colour values and the way they are rendered on any given device can be communicated to the user. Currently there is no way to backtrack to an earlier state, beyond reverting to a previous version of the document or the assets contained within it – once a transform is applied to an element the values have changed (and therefore the colours have changed in some way). This issue and the lack of audit trail make the system particularly impenetrable to users. Once the design is some way 'down the road' to completion users often have no idea what the colour information is contained in their files, whether different elements have different profiles and so forth, and there may be quite a marked discrepancy between what colours they see on screen and how they will print out. This is clearly very problematic as it does not facilitate user learning by being able to analyse document (and document element) profile (and profile transformation) histories. We are not saying that this would be an easy solution to colour (re) production but it would allow users to compare and contrast good and bad results on, for example, photo quality or colour reproduction.

2.8.3 Difficult to Understand Impacts of Selections

That colour is an issue which those in the design workflow strive to control is evident in the many non-colour-managed workflows we observed. These methods tend to be far more *visible, tangible* and *collaborative*. However, because these methods do not specifically orient to the way in which infrastructure operates they produce varying results. Examining these methods raises a second issue; CM by its nature is somewhat abstract and the complexity of the possible workflows makes it very hard to make *concrete visual* mappings between the colour choices, encodings and their effects on a current document and a future print. To some extent colour must be understood abstractly. Furthermore, to take up a couple of points made in the previous section, managing colour according to CM protocols means: (1) making principled decisions on how to handle graphical elements at all stages (i.e., actively making a number of decisions and understanding their implications), (2) keeping some kind of memory or record of those decisions so users can keep track of where they are, and (3) having an understanding of how the colours they see on screen, relate to the colours recorded in the profile and ultimately to what they may print. The nature of the tasks and abilities required to colour manage are difficult and potentially unintuitive for practitioners, as they not only are complex and badly supported by the technology, but crucially they work against the normal everyday ways people apprehend, work with and understand colour.

2.9 Conclusion: New Technology and New Markets

While it might seem easy to make a critique of CM on the basis that it is not used, not understood and does not fit with the work of practitioners, this would not easily point us to a better solution of this difficult problem, with a long history and many complex features. Colour has intrigued many great scientists and philosophers – for example, from Newton to Goethe to Wittgenstein, and in many ways the work on colour leads us to a central, still unresolved problem which is the relationship between colour as a physical property and colour as perceived and reasoned about by people. To boil this argument down to a simple instantiation, there is no simple relation between colour as objectively measured and colour as perceived, talked about and understood by people. Colours are scientifically measured using standard, arbitrary values, such as hue (the colour, e.g., yellow), saturation (intensity) and value (lightness–darkness) under a given lighting condition. People – even though it is likely that our visual systems, if we are not colour blind 'perceive' colours in the same way – show great variability in responses to colour. Our perceptions are impacted by context – and not just visual context, but also what we are doing, who we are interacting with, what our knowledge is, how we *look* (our visual practices). We also can precisely discriminate colours side by side but if asked to recall (by picking out) a precise colour at a later date, we are shown to have poorer memory. We see familiar objects as always having the same colour, even when lighting conditions mean they do not. For example, our prior knowledge of the colour of an object 'instructs' us when seeing a New York taxi-cab to see yellow, or for an (old UK) telephone box, red. Even at night. Our response to colour in applied contexts (i.e. 'real world'), beyond what we know about the human visual system and colour perception from an experimental point of view, is not properly understood (Armour 1996; Goodwin 1997). However, for example, Wittgenstein (1978) in his usual slightly enigmatic way, points us to the importance of context in perceiving colour (in terms of *other colours*, in terms of *discernable objects and features*, and within a *coherent 'assembly' of 'things'*) by way of a thought experiment:

> Imagine a painting cut up into small, almost monochromatic bits which are then used as pieces in a jig-saw puzzle. Even when such a piece is not monochromatic it should not indicate any three-dimensional shape, but should appear as a flat colour-patch. Only together with the other pieces does it become a bit of blue sky, a shadow, a high-light, transparent or opaque, etc. Do the individual pieces show us the real colours of the parts of the picture? (Aphorism I-60) [20]

The important point to take from this is that even if CM worked in all cases, it would not necessarily mean everyone was happy with their 'prints'. A print is still different from an image on screen, and the (same) red in the print may not seem like the red I saw (some time ago) on screen. Also, choosing a colour from a small swatch surrounded by white is different to seeing it in a large block on a poster, or against other colours, or up close or faraway. And, furthermore, my perception of a colour as looking 'good' or 'correct' can be influenced by both other peoples' views of it and my faith in the people, actions and technologies that produced it.

However, the fact is that there must be some system in place to transfer colour information from application to application and device to device. CM is an infrastructure that provides for a standard means of translation enabling diverse manufacturers to produce products that can integrate successfully with others to communicate colour information across that workflow. We understand that unfortunately CM has to be complex but somehow this complexity needs to be further reduced in the way it is presented to users or the problem of non-use and misuse will not go away. One can think about the problem as a classic interoperability problem but with a twist; providing translation between devices that 'speak different languages' or do things different ways is a classic computing problem, however, one that is usually solved by engineers and kept hidden from the users. In the case of CM not only must the users understand – at least to some extent – the processing and translation of colour but there must be close coordination and strict adherence to specific procedure across the workflow. This raises questions about who in the process should be responsible for recruiting the required expertise to design, implement and manage such a workflow, and whether this would make economic sense in the light of possible benefits. In this paper we have not sought to provide answers to questions such as these, but rather to provide insight into a complex problem. Although many colour scientists may not understand why CM is not used, we feel these issues will be familiar to those in the CSCW community.

2.9.1 A Mediating and Correcting Technology

One solution to these problems could be an additional software layer to bridge the gap between the current CM infrastructure and the actors of the workflow, such that there could be some translation of CM, or the requirements for CM, to make them more tangible and understandable for users. Our research also shows how far the current practices, knowledge and perspectives of those involved in graphic design and printing are from those required for the CM infrastructure to work correctly. We can infer from this that any attempt to design and implement a mediating technology that nevertheless still required a strict adherence to CM (albeit with translation) would lead to a failure in adoption or to the introduction of new attempted workarounds. Using ethnographic work studies as a resource for developing technology innovation, we have been exploring technological possibilities based on these findings. They have led us towards the design of technology supporting the workflow that is based on two principles: (1) that achievable, 'good enough' colour is what is strived for in most situations rather than technically correct colour reproduction and (2) that it should be possible to assess non-CM documents for detectable and correctable colour problems prior to printing. To this end we are in the process of developing a tool that can provide an assessment of non-CM documents prior to printing. It is based on integrating some technologies that can detect a number of colour problems – mainly when certain colours are likely to be printed out in a manner rather differently to how they appear on screen – and highlight these graphically and textually and offer various potential 'corrections' to these problems. This seems to tally well with our findings that certain colours are more important than others in documents, that large changes in colour are more problematic, while at the same time clients are mainly looking for a good enough result.

2.9.2 Preparing for Web 2.0 Markets

How does this work relate to the World Wide Web and mass customisations? Put simply, it seems clear that if the new business of printing is going to take off (web submission of documents by customers essentially 'unknown' to print shops, capturing the 'long tail' with a mass of customers printing single items, 1–1 marketing with variable pictures and text-tailored for individual clients) better, more predictable colour results are required in digital production printing. There may be a number of barriers to implementing these solutions, one such being the relative lack of expertise in programming, database management and automating workflows within the design and print industries. However, this expertise does exist in other communities so it may be imported into the industry. But, another key feature of these potential growth areas is that none of them afford the time for extensive print proof cycles. In fact, in the web submission long-tail markets the idea would be that the full transactions would be carried out over the Internet, with no iterations and no direct conversation between customer and print shop, save perhaps some textual exchanges.

In the case of the 1–1 variable market the configuration is slightly different, as in many cases it is likely that there will be some kind of direct relationship. Setting up a bespoke database and workflow with variable text and images for tailored products is a relatively complex affair. Often this will take some time and a certain amount of interaction between customer, print shop and graphic designer. A key issue here though is proofing – it simply is not practicable to proof each individual item. Ideally, proofing should be automatic or carried out by eye on a small 'representative' sample.

In both these cases, our concept for technology design would provide a means of capturing problems at an earlier stage. It could work as a part of a web submission portal to assess and correct problems, as well as to gather additional information from customers in the absence of direct contact. Furthermore, it could run as an automatic checker on variable 1–1 documents and flag up problematic cases. In this way it might well be useful in helping to open up these markets. We will report further on this technology as it develops.

Acknowledgements Many thanks to all of the staff of the graphic design agencies and print shops that allowed us to study their work for this project.

References

Anderson, C. (2006). *The Long Tail*. Hyperion, New York

Armour, L. (1996). *A Study of Colour: Wittgensteinian and Ethnomethodological Investigations*. PhD thesis, Department of Sociology, Lancaster University.

Bowers, J., Button, G., & Sharrock, W. (1995). Workflow from Within and Without: Technology and Cooperative Work on the Print Industry Shopfloor. *Proceedings of ECSCW'95.*

Brahe, S. and Schmidt, K. (2007). The Story of a Working Workflow Management System. *Proceedings of Group 2007*, November 4–7, Sanibel Island, Florida, US: ACM press.

Garfinkel, H., (1967). *Studies in Ethnomethodology*. Englewood Cliffs, N.J.: Prentice-Hall.

Goodwin, C. (1997). The Blackness of Black: Color Categories as Situated Practice. In Resnick, L., Säljö, R., Pontecorvo, C. & Burge, B. (Eds.) *Discourse, Tools and Reasoning: Essays on Situated Cognition*: Springer. pp 111–140.

Klein, M., Dellarocas, C., and Bernstein, A. (2000). Special Issue "Adaptive Workflow Systems". *Journal of CSCW. Volume 9*, Nos. 3–4. Springer.

Lee, C., Dourish, P. and Mark, G. (2006). The Human infrastructure of Cyberinfrastructure. *In Proceedings of CSCW 2006*. Banff, Canada: ACM Press.

Martin, D., Rouncefield, M., O'Neill, J., Hartswood, M. and Randall, D. (2005). Timing in the art of integration: 'That's How The Bastille Got Stormed'. Proceedings of Group '05, November 6–9th, Florida, USA, pp 313–322: ACM Press.

O'Neill, J., Martin, D., Colombino, T., Watts-Perotti, J., Sprague, M., Woolfe, G. (2007) Asymmetrical collaboration in print shop-customer relationships. *Proceedings of ECSCW 2007*: Springer.

Olsen, J., Olsen, G. and Zimmermann, A. (eds.) (2006). *The Collaboratories Handbook*, Cambridge MA, MIT Press.

Piller, F. and Stotko, C.M. (2002) Four approaches to deliver customized products and services with mass production efficiency, *Proceedings of the IEEE International Engineering Management Conference*, Cambridge University, UK, 18–20 August 2002. pp773–778.

Pollock, N., Williams, R., D'Adderio, L. (2007). Global Software and its Provenance: Generification Work in the Production of Organizational Software Packages. *Social Studies of Science 37*. 254–280

Randall, D., Harper, R., Rouncefield, M. (2007). *Fieldwork for Design. Theory and Practice* Series: Computer Supported Cooperative Work: Springer.

Riordan, M (2005) Variation in premedia color and the potential automation of imaging tasks. PICRM-2005-05 Printing Industry Research Center at RIT.

Sharrock, W. and Anderson, R. (1986). The Ethnomethodologists. Chichester: Ellis Horwood.

Star, S.L. (1999). The ethnography of infrastructure. *American Behavioural Scientist. Vol. 43*, No. 3. 377–391.

Star S. L., and Ruhleder, K. (1996). Steps toward an ecology of infrastructure: Design and access for large information spaces, *Information Systems Research 7(1)*. 111–134

Suchman, L. (1983). Office Procedures as Practical Action: Models of work and systems design. *ACM Transactions on Office Information Systems, 1*(4). 320–328.

Suchman, L. (1987). *Plans and Situated Action: The Problem of Human-Machine Communication*. Cambridge: Cambridge University Press.

Wittgenstein L (1978). *Remarks on Colour*. Berkeley & Los Angeles: University of California Press.

Chapter 3
Toward Regional Clusters: Networking Events, Collaborative Research, and the Business Finder

Tim Reichling, Benjamin Moos, Markus Rohde, and Volker Wulf

3.1 Introduction

Networks of regionally collocated organizations improve the competitiveness of their member companies. This is not only a result of lower transportation costs when delivering or purchasing physical goods but also other matters such as mutual trust or a higher diffusion of specialized knowledge among companies that have emerged as important aspects of regional networks. Even increased competition among collocated companies can lead to comparative advantages over externals as a result of an increased pressure for innovation. While the reasons *why* regional networks of companies offer comparative advantages has been widely investigated, the question arises as to *how* networks can be developed in terms of higher interconnectedness and deeper connections.

Until now, technical approaches aiming at fostering mutual awareness and collaboration among companies in regional networks are scarce. When searching for companies or services in general, we can use web search engines such as Google or Yahoo, which cover web sites of all kinds. Nevertheless, their results cannot be easily limited to companies in specific regions. We can also find directories of regional companies, hosted and maintained by regional business development agencies. However, they often suffer from outdated or incomplete profiles and require significant effort to keep them up-to-date. Recent approaches to knowledge management aim at networking among human actors within organizations (see, e.g., Ackerman et al. 2003; Reich ling et al. 2007). While they may offer potential for regional development, they have not yet been applied to networks of companies.

Research in the domain of regional networks of companies has been carried out by Porter (1998a, b, 2000). Porter's theories are strongly directed toward highly interconnected networks of geographically close companies along a value chain, so-called *clusters*. Popular examples of regional clusters are Silicon Valley,

T. Reichling (✉), B. Moos, M. Rohde and V. Wulf
Institute for Information Systems, University of Siegen, Siegen, Germany
e-mail: tim.reichling@uni-siegen.de

D. Randall and P. Salembier (eds.), *From CSCW to Web 2.0: European Developments in Collaborative Design*, Computer Supported Cooperative Work, DOI 10.1007/978-1-84882-965-7_3, © Springer-Verlag London Limited 2010

Hollywood, or, for the metal industry, the Ruhr Area in Germany. Porter holds that both cooperation and competition are important elements of regional clusters. Both coexist within a cluster, which means that they do not exclude each other and are even necessary for a successful development.

While Porter's argument primarily addresses clusters, we assume that less dense networks among regionally collocated companies may create similar benefits even though no distinctive cluster structures are present. Since networks are dynamic constructs, which grow and shrink vigorously, information technology (IT) support can contribute to their creation and development by improving interconnectedness. With regard to the domain of KM, expertise recommender systems have proved to be promising technologies for networking among human actors within organizations (cf. Hinds and Pfeffer 2003; Huysman and Wulf 2004; Reichling and Veith 2005; Reichling et al. 2007). We assume that these technologies can be applied to successfully support awareness and visibility in networks of regional companies too.

In this chapter, we present an integrated and holistic research approach we performed over 5 years in the region of Siegen-Wittgenstein (Germany). Our approach covers a series of social events and interventions carried out in collaboration with actors of regional companies. The entire set of these research activities was realized in two Action Research cycles. The first cycle features qualitative empirical methods, aiming at gathering a better understanding of the dynamics in our field of application – the media and IT sector of the Siegen-Wittgenstein region. In the second cycle we turned to a more technical approach. Following demands for technical support, we designed a search engine (Business Finder) that supports regional companies in finding potential customers, suppliers, or cooperation partners.

3.2   Related Work

A variety of studies indicate that regional proximity and interconnectedness are important factors for the success of companies. While globalization and new media appear to outperform these seemingly antiquated assets, they seem to maintain their significance nevertheless. Porter (1998a) labels this phenomenon *The Location Paradox*. Lower costs for transportation or resources cannot explain sufficiently why companies of a given sector appear to settle down in the same region.

Donhauser (2006) finds incentives for regional concentration in an increasing potential for innovation, productivity, and growth by better preconditions for cooperation. These are a result of different circumstances: First, regional proximity leads to vivid informal communication among human actors even across companies, resulting in a rapid diffusion of expertise and best practices. Second, the regional proximity often goes hand in hand with the creation of a highly specialized "Labour Pool" (Schiele 2003) from which regional companies can select their staff and thus save time and costs for training. Thirdly, another issue concerned with knowledge dissemination among actors of interconnected enterprises is trust (Porter 1998b). Since trust is a property of social ties, *social capital* (SC) affects processes of knowledge dissemination (Huysman and Wulf 2004). Social capital is not transferable among human actors. It encourages the actors' willingness to mutually support each other, initiate business cooperation, and share knowledge.

Besides the aspect of an improved information exchange, clusters are also characterized by stronger competition and improved transparency as a result of a large number of enterprises in the same sector. According to Porter (1998a) "[companies] can mitigate many input-cost disadvantages through global sourcing, rendering the old notion of comparative advantage less relevant. Instead, competitive advantage rests on making more productive use of inputs which requires continual innovation. [...] Without vigorous competition a cluster will fail." Porter realizes that cooperation and competition can coexist within a cluster and do not exclude each other. In fact, both are required for successful clusters.

We now turn to the question of how IT can contribute to the development of regional networks, which may lead to the formation of cluster structures. With respect to cluster support, Porter (1998a) suggests that IT systems could create awareness of other players within a cluster. Similarly, Leuninger and Held (2003) – without specifying certain technological approaches – argue for an IS-based address and communication platform. Krätke and Scheuplein (2001) propose IT support for cluster recognition and analysis. IT should support and influence political decisions and interventions to foster cluster development. Krätke and Scheuplein (2001) demand for IT tools to visualize internal interconnections and to compare regional and superregional clusters.

Until now, IT had little significance in dedicated cluster support and is neglected in the literature. Instead, existing technologies from other domains appear promising for network development. For instance, Resnick and Varian (1997) recommend IT systems that perform algorithmic matching on model based descriptions. These approaches gain importance in different domains of information and communication technology (cf. Resnick et al. 1994; Balabanovic and Shoham 1997), especially knowledge management (cf. Hinds and Pfeffer 2003; Huysman and Wulf 2004; Reichling and Veith, 2005; Reichling et al. 2007). In the context of KM, expert recommender systems can foster mutual awareness of skills and activities of human actors in organizations. They can also create visibility of corporate competencies of entire organizations or subunits or help to identify competence gaps. Different authors (cf. Ackerman et al. 2003; Huysman and de Wit 2004; Huysman and Wulf 2006) mention the important role of social capital in knowledge-intense processes among human actors. Recent KM approaches (a so-called second wave of KM) aim therefore at fostering as well as exploiting this resource within networks of human actors.

Organizational affiliation plays an important role when dealing with regional networking activities. Thus, it appears meaningful to apply the concept of social network building to regional networks of companies. In this way social capital may be fostered across different companies to improve awareness of others' competencies and needs, create mutual trust, and disseminate specialized knowledge.

The existence of clusters as highly developed regional networks of companies that exist over considerable periods of time, illustrates how important these structures are.

The scientific work presented here – first of all Porter's (1998a, b, 2000) theories about clusters – offers descriptive models that explain why clusters exist and which benefits they provide for their members. However, we are not aware of empirical studies on how these theories can be applied to create or strengthen structures of regional networks of companies that are not yet well enough developed in terms of their interconnectedness and sufficient coverage of the value chain. Economic approaches of cluster support have not yet proven to be successful, neither in creating clusters nor in supporting clusters (Alecke and Untiedt 2005).

In the subsequent paragraphs, we describe an integrated, holistic approach of "Regional Networking" which aims at developing interconnectedness and mutual awareness among players' competencies and activities in the Siegen-Wittgenstein (Germany) region. Our approach covers a variety of different methods, which we have applied over a couple of years. The different interventions were driven by the vision of a denser and stronger network of companies in the region, resulting in stronger cooperation ties between the companies and an increased competitiveness of the whole region.

3.3 Field of Application and Research Methods

In the following, we will describe the regional setting, particularly considering the software and media industry and the university. We also introduce the research approach and methods we applied to foster regional networking. The university's IS group plays a central part for the regional network support since it defines itself as a facilitator of regional networking. The authors are part of the IS group. The university had gained some regional reputation already before, as knowledge transfer and cooperation with industries has been a focus of the IS department's earlier activities.

3.3.1 The Regional Setting

Siegen-Wittgenstein is located in the state of North-Rhine-Westphalia. The region is almost the geographical center of the western part of Germany, about 100 km east of Cologne. Siegen, the region's center is a city of about 100,000 inhabitants. The university is located in one of its suburbs. The Siegen-Wittgenstein region has a long tradition of heavy industries, especially steel production. At the end of the nineteenth and the beginning of the twentieth century, the region was an important location for mining in iron ore. Since the mines were closed and most steel mills disappeared afterwards, mid-size companies in the business of specialized machinery and plant manufacturing and foundries play an important role in the regional economy. These companies are typically export-oriented toward the world market. The official unemployment figure is approximately 7%, which is below the federal and the state average.

During the last 30 years, software and media companies were founded in this region. Some of the companies were created by former students of the university's media science, computer science, or information systems programs. The regional business development department maintains a database in which about 380 small-to-mid-size companies from the software and media industry were registered in spring 2008. These companies employ about 4,500 workers and are generally considered to be of central regional importance.

The action research program presented in this paper was conducted by researchers at the University of Siegen's department of Information Systems. The research group works in the field of human-centered computing, specifically in the subfields of Computer Supported Cooperative Work, Participatory Design, End User Development, and Communities and Technologies. Supported by research funds from different government sources and industries, the IS group grew during the time of investigation from two to 15 staff members (faculty and research associates) and a similar number of students working as research assistants. Research is organized around specific, typically externally funded projects. Research practice develops within individual projects or bundles of related projects.

3.4 Research Methods

The research group started its regional network activities within the local software and media industries in 2002. At the beginning, there were mainly two motivations to become engaged in regional activities: (1) access to regional companies was seen as an important element in information systems' education (cf. Rohde et al. 2007) and (2) cooperation between university and local industries was necessary to receive research funding by the German national government and the European Union. These funding schemes usually require joint applications from industries and academia. While local partners are not essential, it can be argued they are preferable to large and dispersed networks of industrial partnerships.

We adopted an action research perspective, using three of Lewin's (1946) principles of action research:

- Researchers are not just external observers but intervene into the field of application. In our case, we tried to increase the level of social capital in the region and link different communities of practice (CoPs, cf. Lave and Wenger 1991; Wenger 1998) in the software and media industries.
- Research is a process of mutual learning of researchers and practitioners. It is based on an emergent process which takes shape as understanding increases.
- Researchers and practitioners join in tackling an issue of shared interest. When starting the process, we assumed that fostering regional networks of companies would be a desirable goal for the regional software companies, as well.

The research activities presented here can be understood as two cycles of an action research study that were performed over 5 years (2002–2007). In the first cycle we did not start with an overall phase model or plan for the different interventions. The interventions emerged due to a variety of opportunities and context factors. However, they followed the vision of increasing social capital and bridging among different regional CoPs (Lave and Wenger 1991; Wenger 1998). In the second cycle, we turned to a more directed set of actions, including technological components from the field of knowledge management that were applied and (briefly) evaluated.

In the first cycle we gained an initial understanding of the particularities of the regional industry by informal discussions with senior faculty at the university, the head of the regional authority's support unit, and some company owners. Supported by the regional authorities, we conducted an initial networking event which again led to new insights and contacts. From this starting point, a series of events were initiated which will be described subsequently. Especially, an innovative education program, called "Courses in Practice (CiP)" was an important aspect of the networking process in which students were supposed to learn by enculturating into regional companies' CoPs.

In the last 5 years, we conducted a series of semi-structured interviews and additional observational studies. As part of the first cycle, the CiPs were an important research focus; we conducted 25 explorative semi-structured in-depth interviews with students, supervisors from academia and industries, and officers of the regional administration. Fourteen students, six company practitioners, three academics, and two officers were interviewed in total. The interviews lasted between 60 and 180 min. We were specifically interested in their experience in establishing regional networks and their evaluation of our joint activities in fostering regional networks among local industry including the university. All interviews have been recorded with a DAT recorder and have been transcribed fully. In the evaluation, the answers were transformed into a table categorizing the role of students, academics, and industrial supervisors.

In the second cycle, a series of 16 semi-structured interviews were conducted with managers of regional media and IT companies. The interviews explored requirements for a search engine to support networking among regional companies. These interviews focused on internal and external cooperation, communication with partner companies and customers, and the use of IT infrastructures. Additionally, the interviewees were asked about their strategies to find new partners and to identify specific interests, expertises, and competences of internal colleagues, external partners, and potential customers. The search engine was supposed to be used by employees of regional companies in order to find suitable customers, suppliers, or cooperation partners within the region. Based on these requirements we designed and launched an experimental search engine called Business Finder. We combined two existing technologies: the database that was hosted by the regional business development department (see below) and an expertise-finding system that was developed for matching individual actors within organizations (Reichling et al. 2007).

3.5 Fostering Regional Networking

Our approach to regional networking includes a set of different interventions that we performed with a selection of companies located in the region of Siegen-Wittgenstein over 5 years (from 2002 to 2007). The interventions were carried out in two successive cycles (see above). The goals of our approach were (1) to gain a better understanding of how networking among companies can be supported by purposeful interventions and (2) create comparative advantages for the regional companies. Finally, in the second cycle, our approach applied the concept of recommender systems to improve visibility and create mutual awareness among the regional companies. For this purpose we introduced the Business Finder which supports finding suitable customers, suppliers, or cooperation partners for the companies in the region. Demands for IT support were gained during the social events that were accomplished in the first action research cycle. More explicit design requirements for IT support were gained in the second cycle which was directed toward IT support. The activities we carried out in both cycles are described subsequently.

3.5.1 First Action Research Cycle: Increasing Visibility and Connecting Actors by Means of Networking Events

As a result of the talks with the regional business development department, a concept for a series of networking events was developed, called "Lyz Media Breakfast" (because of the location in which the meetings took place). It tried to reach out to heads, or upper management, of regional software and media companies. Following an invited talk in the early morning (starting at 8:30 a.m.), there was a joint breakfast for the participants to network with each other. It was planned in a way that allowed the participants to leave at 10 a.m. to go on with their daily work.

At the first of these events, the head of the IS research group gave an introduction to the work of his group at the University of Siegen. The regional business development department had sent invitation letters to the heads of approximately 380 software and media companies stored in its database (see below). The first event had some 25 participants and led to discussions and talks among the participants. The first instance of the events was considered to be successful, which made the coordinating unit decide to organize more events. Although it was planned to have around four meetings a year, from 2002 to 2007 only four meetings took place.

Concerning the specific local situation in Siegen, the fostering of regional networks local companies and between local companies and the university revealed several critical factors:

(1) In the Siegen region, the density of software and media companies is not very high. Therefore, networks of practice focusing on specific aspects of software technology are difficult to establish. Thus, networking among different companies needed to be understood covering a broader range of practices, or a rather broad understanding of common practices.

(2) Because the regional market for IT services is limited, as well, there is strong competition among those software and media companies that target this market. This competition limits the chances to foster networking of regional companies for regional learning, at least on the CEO level.

(3) With regard to the size (especially of small companies) and the strong competition between the local companies, cooperation in regional networks is rather

weakly developed. The exchange of practical experiences seems to be more likely to be achieved within larger companies (e.g., local software company clusters in Silicon Valley). Within and between these larger companies' networks, a fluctuation of employees takes place, and people change from one local company to another one. Contrary to that, in the Siegen region, competition and the risk of "takeovers" of employees is considered one of the central problems.

3.5.1.1 Bridging Between University and Industry: Courses in Practice

Based on earlier experiences in entrepreneurial education, we have developed CiP as a didactic concept which bridges communities of practice of regional software companies and the IS group. Originally, the concept was developed to offer learning opportunities to students by integrating student teams into the CoPs of local IT companies (cf. Rohde et al. 2007). The CiP approach works as follows: IT companies define projects close to their core business. The student teams work on these projects inside the companies. When working in industries, the students are additionally coached by members of the IS group. Each group is supported by an academic supervisor. CiPs have the duration of typically one term (4 months). During this time about five meetings among the students and their academic supervisors take place. Coaching the CiP groups very closely is crucial for our concept. The student teams are connected to each other and to their supervisors in academia by means of a community system.

With regard to the setup of the CiP, the Siegen IS group could refer to the experiences of some of the group members with a similar CiP at the University of Aachen. Based on these former experiences, the initiative in Siegen aimed at establishing longer-lasting relationships between university and industry, to involve more stable companies (instead of very young start-ups), to build up "strong ties, 'to establish social capital, and therefore, to succeed in more than short-term effects and real' regional learning."

After nearly 1 year of building up relationships with regional companies, the first CiP at the IS faculty of the University of Siegen was announced for summer term 2003. At the end of the term, the students and their company advisors presented the results of their projects in public. The students gave a 20 min talk on their results on which the company advisors commented for about 10 min. Finally, the results were discussed publicly. This event was announced in the region. The participation of the faculty's dean and the engagement of the regional administration guaranteed a certain level of public interest. Thus, typically some 30 employees of other companies, faculty members, journalists, and students joined the presentations which ended with a small reception. These events became occasions for further networking among the regional actors as well as for acquiring new companies and students.

Since 2003, four instances of the CiP have been conducted. Eight student teams, two every year, consisting of overall 19 students got encultured in the CoPs of four different software companies. Two of the four companies participated more than once in the course: one of them four times, the other company two times.

With regard to the evaluation of the CiPs, the interviews brought evidence of some factors that influenced the success of the project groups, the networking between university and industry and the degree of mutual learning:

Long- Versus Short-Lasting Activities Some of the project tasks were embedded in longer-lasting activities within the companies' practice, whereas others just were defined for the project and its duration. Some interviewees stated that it was important that their project task was embedded in longer-lasting activities for the degree of involvement of company practitioners, for cooperation structures, and for the success of the project. Longer-lasting activities in the companies' practice do not mean that the university was engaged with these companies for a longer term, but that the projects' tasks and results took place within longer-lasting processes and projects of the company itself.

Collocation/Physical Presence Collocation of students and company practitioners had an influence on the establishment of cooperation structures between students and company practitioners. Students who were not collocated with the companies' practitioners but worked on the project tasks at home or at the university were less likely to build trustful relationships and social capital with the companies.

Relevance of the Project Task Some of the project tasks defined by the companies' executives had strategic relevance for the company and its product development, whereas other projects were defined more according to the company's peripheral interests. It showed that involvement, success, and enculturation are influenced by the strategic relevance the project task has had for the companies' practice.

Success of the Projects Regarding Task Fulfillment The success of projects can be measured by the fulfillment of the project task according to the assessment of the companies' supervisors. In terms of project success, one project has been evaluated as not successful. A second was eventually successful but could not be finished within the originally envisioned time frame. The other four projects have been assessed as successful by the companies according to task and goal definitions.

Enculturation in the Companies' Practice Successful enculturation into the companies' practice is one hint for gaining apprenticeship and therefore for socio-cultural learning. These enculturation experiences were made by students who collaborated in teams within the companies and felt integrated into the companies' practice. In the three CiPs, a successful enculturation of university students into the companies' practice even means that the students continue their relationship with the companies after the CiPs end. In three cases, CiP practitioners have been employed by the companies after the project.

3.5.1.2   Bridging Regional Industries: a Funded Networking Project

Another branch of activities was centered around externally funded cooperative research projects between industries and academia. In 2004, the European Structural Fund (ESF) provided grants for a regional networking and business development project in the IT and media sector. We were funded by this initiative to consult the participating companies individually and set up consortia meetings to foster expertise sharing among them. Managers from six companies met once a month to exchange experiences in the domain of marketing.

At the same time, we took part in the process of establishing a joint research center (Media Design and Experience Lab) in the field of interactive television (iTV). The center was supposed to focus on research and development of innovative technological features and suitable formats of iTV. We partnered with a local software company which had moved into the entertainment computing market. While the project was never realized due to changes in the anticipated funding scheme, it strengthened our cooperative ties with the company.

Finally, we have developed research proposals together with different member companies of the regional network. Many research programs of the German government and the European Union require participation of the industry. Some of them explicitly require SME participation. Thus, it made sense for the IS group to include regional companies into their research proposals if there were matching interests and converging practices. The participating companies were both involved in the CiP program (see above) and in the ESF-funded networking project. Thus, the research proposals were grounded in an already well-established cooperation between university and industry. While some of these applications failed, the opportunity to receive public funding via the university's activities stabilized the regional network to some extent.

3.5.2   Second Action Research Cycle: Support for Intra Organizational Knowledge Management

As a result of the action research activities carried out in the first cycle, it became clear that fostering expertise sharing and creating mutual awareness among companies could be beneficial. Therefore, we directed additional research activities toward technical tools to deal with those demands. An early approach of technical support was carried out by the regional business development department which had set up a company database Directory of Regional Companies (DRC[1]) containing about 380 different firms from the media and IT industry in the region of Siegen-Wittgenstein. This database contains the main address data and some keywords regarding the companies' core business. However, enquiries showed that the database was felt to be less informative than the companies' web sites. Log files of DRC confirmed that it was rarely used, and thus, had little impact of fostering regional cooperation.

In order to increase the perceived value of DRC, we approached ways of improving the DRCs performance by extending it with elements of an expert finding system. The ExpertFinding (EF) system (Reichling et al. 2007) had originally been developed

---

[1]DRC (Directory of Regional Companies), which is actually not the real name, denotes the database of the business support of Siegen-Wittgenstein, containing 381 media and IT companies (seen 2007/07/26): http://www.lyz-media.de/datenbanken/index.htm

to foster cooperation between human actors in large or distributed organizations. It has been designed based on requirements that were gathered in a major European industrial association (Reichling and Veith 2005). We took the approach of merging EF and DRC technologies in order to foster the development of regional networks of companies.

The EF system helps the development of an awareness of expertise by making individual knowledge and interests visible. The system's core feature is the so-called keyword profile, which is generated by a set of text documents the user selects from his recent workspace (local hard disk or server drives). These documents are expected to reflect the user's interests, skills, and recent activities, since users are requested to properly select folders and documents that are strongly associated with their actual working context or their abilities (Reichling et al. 2007). Those *keyword profiles* can be understood as large vectors of keywords which are ordered according to the frequency of the individuals' keyword usage in the users' documents. That keyword listing can be edited by the individual user and is then pushed toward the central server. Therefore, users always have insight and control of the contents of their profiles.

An extensive evaluation of the EF system with a set of pilot users in the industrial association showed that the concept was highly promising for the case of intra-organizational knowledge management (cf. Reichling et al. 2007). The participants considered the keyword profile-based search results to be accurate in most cases. At the same time the creation of the keyword profiles was felt to be easy and not time consuming, as only representative documents or folders had to be selected instead of entering keywords directly. Moreover, no privacy concerns were violated by the system since the users controlled the information the system provided about them.

3.6 Business Finder: Support for Regional Networks of Companies

The requirements analysis we performed in the second cycle shows that regional companies are mostly willing to cooperate with each other. Since trust is a major precondition for cooperation, networking mainly happens by personal recommendation. However, in Siegen-Wittgenstein, where few large-scale enterprises reside, regional cooperation is structurally hampered due to missing large-scale orders in the IT domain. Especially for suppliers of IT services (web designers, software developers) it is easy to transfer their "goods" over far distances, so no compelling reason for regional cooperation exists. Hence, unlike other industry sectors, geographical proximity is no necessary precondition for cooperation. Besides this obvious argument concerned with the IT sector, other (more subtle) reasons for super regional cooperation were discussed. The companies were "too small and insignificant" to carry out large-scale orders, as one participant stated. Similarly, another participant judged that regional companies were not likely to offer large-scale orders which were the only orders they could profitably accept.

With regard to the selecting cooperation partners, participants stated that mutual trust between representatives was the main precondition for successful cooperation. In order to maintain the level of customer satisfaction, the actors value the cooperation partners' high-quality demands that fit to their own demands. When former unknown partners shall be assessed, the actors rely heavily on oral recommendations given by trusted partners. As one interviewee states: "See, it works just about personal contacts or word-of-mouth recommendation, based on trust."

We further asked the interviewees for their attitude on existing databases, search engines and yellow page directories. We found that all the companies that were covered by our inquiry had registered to numerous Yellow Pages (YP) directories. However, from their experience participants were very skeptical about these this kind of systems: YP directories actually had little value measured against the effort of keeping the companies' profiles up-to-date. At the same time the effort increases with the number of systems that companies were subscribed in. Merely two of the interviewees reported successful business transactions as a result of the system subscriptions. Hence, companies limit their efforts to a small number of well-chosen systems.

Essential criteria of choosing YP directories that were given by participants are quality and up-to-dateness. Furthermore, the participants' impression of the operators in terms of maintenance and care is an important criterion. Again, trust toward the directories' operators appears to be a central factor. As one participant stated, he had lost trust in one directory after he discovered "massive spelling mistakes in name or address [...] such that you get the impression [...] they try to make you update your profile."

Controversy perspectives showed up concerned with the directories' focus. While some participants found highly specialized and sector specific directories useful, others demanded comprehensiveness. In both cases completeness in terms of the covered companies and a critical mass of registered companies is required. At the same time, the actors worry about potential masses of advertisement (spam) that might go along with a large number of subscribers.

According to their attitude toward existing databases (see above), the maintenance efforts and the disadvantages of such traditional business databases, all the interviewees expressed their interest and willingness to contribute to a new Business Finder system following another strategy.

3.6.1 Introduction of the Business Finder

The participants' statements illustrate that actuality and effort spent on maintaining are central concerns. Hence, in order to minimize this effort, the Business Finder is capable of creating and updating profiles from existing data sources automatically (see below). This data should consist of specific text documents related to the company. While companies' web sites may be updated rarely, newsletters provide up-to-date information about products, offers, or services. Privacy and data security concerns were also discussed with the interviewees. We learned that product specifications, flyers, advertising material, or newsletters do not collide with privacy concerns since these data are (semi-)public by definition.

The Business Finder system is designed to integrate directory approaches and web search engines with expertise recommender technology such as the EF. In order to semi-automatically create meaningful profiles of companies, we gathered data from three different sources (see Fig. 3.1): (1) Content of the DRC (see above) that is hosted by the business development department; (2) companies' web sites; and (3) arbitrary documents that happen to describe the companies' products, services, processes, methods, or special offers (newsletters, product descriptions, price lists, advertising material, flyers, etc.).

The implementation of Business Finder (BF) is based on the EF system (Reichling et al. 2007), an expertise recommender system for large or distributed enterprises. Its main purpose is creating awareness of activities, expertises, and experiences of actors within an organization in order to foster transparency and collaboration of the staff. While EF is essentially knowledge management technology, from its purpose it is very similar to BF. The EF client system provides a software tool which allows users to easily select documents or folders from the local file system, specifying path, age, author, and file format (typically doc, pdf, ppt, etc.). From these specifications EF creates keyword profiles which are an aggregate of the textual contents of all specified documents (cf. Reichling et al. 2007). For privacy concerns, all this takes place locally on the client machine. Users are given the opportunity to inspect and eventually correct their keyword profile before uploading it to the server.

As EF provides basic technology that can be used for BF as well, we decided to ground the BF on EF technology. Meanwhile, BF differs from EF in some elementary points: First, BF contains companies' profiles instead of user profiles (which is merely irrelevant from a technical point of view). Second, since arbitrary text documents, newsletters, and web sites are included, documents reach the server via manifold ways. (1) Via the web-based front-end (see Fig. 3.2a) users can select and upload single documents in order to create the keyword profile. As in EF, keyword profiles can be edited in order to remove single keywords. (2) In order to receive newsletters,

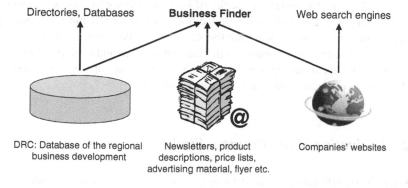

Directories, Databases   **Business Finder**   Web search engines

DRC: Database of the regional   Newsletters, product   Companies' websites
  business development   descriptions, price lists,
                    advertising material, flyer etc.

Fig. 3.1 Basic concept of Business Finder including three sources of data

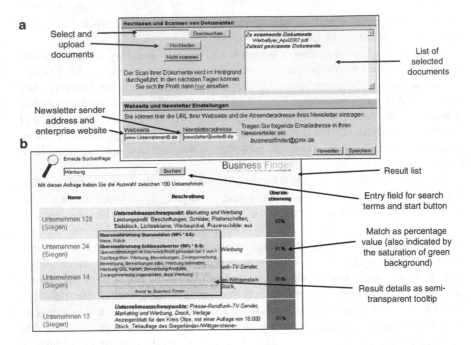

Fig. 3.2 (**a**) Uploading documents and specifying URL of the companies' websites and (**b**) result list of matching companies

we set up an email account which the letter can be sent to – so mailing lists need to be extended with that address in order to automatically include the newsletter into the keyword profile. (3) The web front-end further provides facilities to enter the companies' web site's URL (see Fig. 3.2a). A dedicated server side component of BF periodically scans all the registered web sites, just as web search engines do. The BF system was installed on a machine at the regional business development. It has direct access to the DRC database in order to access its elementary data.

Figure 3.2b shows the searching facility of BFs web front-end. The way it works is analogous to web search engines and needs no further explanation. Exemplary, Fig. 3.2b shows the search results for the search term Werbung (advertisement). Multiple keywords can be entered as well. The semi-transparent tooltip in Fig. 3.2b shows further details about the search results. Since rich data of the companies are stored, tooltips appeared to be a suitable way of visualizing.

3.6.2 Evaluation of the Business Finder

In March 2007, BF was presented to representatives of regional economy and launched shortly afterwards. We evaluated the design of BF on two levels. First, we presented the application to four different companies. Two of them were regional small-sized IT companies which offered software products and services. The other two companies, a large brewery and a producer of switching cabinets, both large-scale enterprises which demand IT services on the regional market. In a second phase, we did a comparative analysis of search results created by BF and those of Google, Google Maps, and two regional databases for IT companies. It should be mentioned that at the time of the evaluation elementary data from the former DRC and web sites were the only input to BF to create profiles from. No further documents like advertising materials or newsletters were used. Hence, the participating companies did not have any efforts to create their profiles (by means of selecting appropriate documents).

When presenting the system to the regional companies, the participants could try out the system and evaluate the search results. We also asked the participants for potential improvements. While all of the participants tested BF's search engine, the participants from the IT service providers also tested the profile creation facilities. The overall judgment of the participants with respect to usability and profile creation was positive. Concerns, however, were expressed with regard to the danger of manipulation by competing companies. The participants of the two IT companies feared that competitors could manipulate the keyword profiles by uploading large amounts of documents in order to appear in the result lists more frequently and in higher positions.

To evaluate BF in comparison with results from other search engines, i.e., Google and the local database of IT companies, we looked for six terms that we judged to be relevant within the IT industry: Internet, database, PHP, Server, programming, and Java. We chose Google as a representative search engine which is widely said to return satisfactory results. Since Google is not geographically restricted we added the region's name "Siegen" as an additional search term. We chose the local database of IT companies as another point of reference in order to assess potential advantages of BF. With regard to each term of the search queries, BF outperformed both the local database and Google. As expected, Google delivered many results which were not hosted by companies.

Participants expressed some skepticism with regard to the choice of search terms. They found them too unspecific. Therefore, they were asked to enter arbitrary keywords they found relevant to find a specific local IT company – the IT companies' participants aimed at finding their own companies via BF and entered related keywords. In each case, this company was among the top five BF results. Google and the local database of IT companies performed worse. Looking for his own company, one participant of an IT company expressed satisfaction with BF's results, especially when considering that they did not have to input or update their profile: "...because you see, I was found even though I did not maintain any profile" (see above).

In a second evaluation phase, we carried out a comparative search analysis with regard to the findings recall and precision. We compared the search findings of Google, Google Maps, and two local databases for IT companies using 10 IT relevant search terms. Again, we added the region's name as a search term in the cases of

Google and Google-Maps. We took the 20 topmost results as representative for the search engines' results. Recall denotes the ratio of relevant results to the overall number of (potential) relevant results. Precision is defined as the ratio between the relevant results and the number of results. A result was judged to be of "relevance" in case the company was located in the Siegen-Wittgenstein region and fits the search term(s). Figure 3.3 gives an impression of the BF performance compared to the other four search engines.

With regard to both dimensions – recall and precision – BF is doing well, even though in each dimension it was outperformed by one competitor. While Google Maps appears to have the best recall (Fig. 3.3a) it does not perform well with regard to precision (Fig. 3.3b). Only 47% of its results were actually regional companies. One of the regional databases (DRC) does best with regard to precision, which is not too surprising since all of its entries are by definition from the Siegen-Wittgenstein region. However, it does not perform well with regard to recall since there are quite some companies which are not registered in the database. Combining the results for recall and precision, BF performs best.

Furthermore, we tested the ranking of companies in different search engines with regard to characteristic keywords (cf. one example of the company L in Table 3.1). These keywords have been named by companies' managers, like they would expect customers searching for their products or services. This test showed that the search with BF resulted in the best (highest) rankings for these companies. Their services are found, although nobody had filled the database before or did any other related activity. One company owner remarked: "One can see, I shall be found even without having maintained my data."

The results of the evaluation further confirm the findings of the prestudy. The interviewees' already hinted to the fact that the existing databases of regional IT companies do not cover a sufficient amount of subscribed companies and hence do not offer a critical mass. Even if companies are registered, they may not be found due to the poor profiles kept in the database.

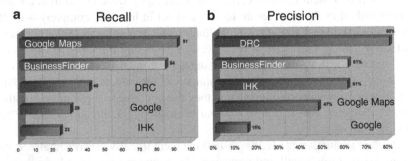

Fig. 3.3 (a) Recall and (b) precision of the search engine

Table 3.1 Ranking of company L, according to characteristic keywords with different search engines/databases

Keyword	BF	Google	DRC
Internet	24	–	69
Databases	3	179	4
PHP	1	–	3
Server	21	–	–
Programming	6	139	14
Java	1	364	2

3.7 Conclusion

Based on the theoretical approaches of Social Capital and Communities of Practice, we attempted to facilitate regional networks in the IT industry. The interventions aimed at fostering interconnectedness and strengthening existing network ties. Following an action research approach, empirical evaluations of these measures by means of qualitative interviews showed achievements and shortcomings of the attempt: The close cooperation with local authorities helped to trigger networking of IT companies. The CiP approach helped to build trustful relationships among the university's IS research group, IS students, and regional software companies. In an ESF-funded project, six software and media companies exchanged experiences with regard to their marketing and management practices.

However, we experienced some obstacles to networking: Certain regional actors were excluded by others when building up network structures. Due to historically evolved personal animosities and structures of competition, some networking attempts failed. Furthermore, egoistic strategic actions and opaque communication behavior of certain actors led to conflicts and set back the trust-building process. To be able to act as facilitators, the academic actors needed to invest a reasonable amount of time and dedication in order to just understand the social dynamics and to be accepted by the regional actors. Given differences in goal sets, practices, and culture between industry and academia made enculturation processes as part of the CiP program sometimes difficult. Limitation in European Union funds administrated by the region's department of business development led to competition among different industrial sectors. Negative decisions with regard to their project proposals created disappointment among the researchers.

The presented case within the IT and media industries describes a university-driven attempt to foster regional exchange of expertise. The study indicates that universities can develop different techniques of intervention and play a facilitating role in this process. However, processes of networking and enculturation require substantial efforts from regional companies as well as from academic actors. Mutual trust between regional companies and academia needs to be built over time through cooperation in various regional activities (cf. Fischer et al. 2007). From an academic point of view, such an action research program can help gaining insights into facilitating and hindering conditions for regional networking and foster the development of conceptualizations and theory.

A first evaluation of the Business Finder system showed promising results: The search results of Business Finder were judged to be more useful than those of the former DRC or common search engines like Google or Google Maps. However, further empirical research is necessary in order to gain deeper insights into the appropriation of the system in practice and its impact on the development of regional networks of companies.

References

Ackerman, M.; Pipek, V.; Wulf, V. (2003). *Preface to Sharing Expertise: Beyond Knowledge Management. Cambridge*, MA.: MIT-Press,

Alecke, B., Untiedt, G. (2005). Zur Förderung von Clustern – "Heilsbringer" oder "Wolf im Schafspelz"? Website of GEFRA – Gesellschaft für Finanz- und Regionalanalysen GbR Münster, http://doku.iab.de/veranstaltungen/2005/gfr_2005_alecke_untiedt.pdf (seen Jan 29 2008).

Balabanovic, M, Shoham, Y. (1997). Fab: Content-Based, Collaborative Recommendation. *Communications of the ACM, vol. 40*, no. 3. ACM Press. 66–72.

Donhauser, S. (2006). Aktivierung von Wachstumspotenzialen durch Netzwerke – Clusterbildung in Baden-Württember. *Statistisches Monatsheft Baden-Württemberg 4*, S. 18–23.

Fischer, G., Rohde, M., Wulf, V. (2007). Community-based Learning: The Core Competency of Residential, Research-based Universities. *International Journal on Computer-Supported Collaborative Learning (iJCSCL) 2007 (2):* Springer. 9–40

Hinds, P. J. and Pfeffer, J. (2003). Why Organizations Don't "Know What They Know", in *Sharing Expertise – Beyond Knowledge Management.* Cambridge: MIT Press. 3–26.

Huysman, M., de Wit, D. (2004). *Knowledge Sharing in Practice.* Dordrecht: Kluwer Academic

Huysman M. and Wulf, V. (2004). *Social Capital and Information Technology.* Cambridge, MA: MIT Press.

Huysman, M. and Wulf, V. (2006). IT to Support Knowledge Sharing in Communities: Towards a Social Capital Analysis, in: *Journal on Information Technology, No. 1,* Vol. 21. 40–51

Krätke, S.; Scheuplein, C. (2001). Produktionscluster in Ostdeutschland: Methoden der Identifizierung und Analyse –Kurzfassung. Eine Studie. Berlin: Auftrag der Otto Brenner Stiftung.

Lave, J.; Wenger E. (1991). *Situated Learning: Legitimate Peripheral Participation,* Cambridge, UK: Cambridge University Press.

Leuninger, S; Held, H (2003). Kommunale Wirtschaftsförderung im Umbruch – Kundenmanagement in Bestandsentwicklung und im Standortmarketing praxisorientiert umsetzen. *Standort – Zeitschrift für Angewandte Geographie 4, S.* 161–166.

Lewin, K. 1946: Action research and minority problems. *Journal of Social Issues,* 2. 34–46

Porter, M. E. (1998a). Clusters and the New Economics of Competition. In: Edward, Elgar (Eds.): Systems of Innovation: Growth, Competitiveness and Employment. Cornwall: MPG Books Ltd. 309-322.

Porter, M. E. (1998b). Clusters and Competition – New Agendas for Companies, Governments, and Institutions. In: *On Competition* (Harvard Business Review). Boston: McGraw-Hill Professional. 197–288.

Porter, M. E. (2000). Locations, Clusters, and Company Strategy. In: Clark, G. L.; Feldman, M. P.; Gertler, M. S. (Eds.): *Oxford Handbook of Economic Geography.* New York: Oxford University Press. 253–274.

Reichling, T. and Veith M. (2005). Expertise Sharing in a Heterogeneous Organizational Environment. Proceedings of ECSCW. Dordrecht: Springer. 325–345.

Reichling, T, Veith, M. and Wulf, V. (2007). Expert Recommender: Designing for a Network Organization, *Computer Supported Cooperative Work: The Journal of Collaborative Computing (JCSCW), Vol. 16*, No. 4–5

Resnick, P., Varian, H. R. (1997). Recommender systems. *Communications of the ACM, special issue, vol. 40.* 56–58

Resnick, P., Iacovou, N., Suchak, M., Bergstrom, P., Riedl, J. (1994). GroupLens: An Open Architecture for Collaborative Filtering of Netnews, in Proceedings of Computer Supported Cooperative Work, North Carolina: ACM Press. 175–186.

Rohde, M.; Klamma, R.; Jarke, M.; Wulf, V. (2007). The Reality is our Lab: Communities of Practice in Applied Computer Science. *Behavior and Information Technology (BIT), volume 26* issue 1.

Schiele, H. (Hrsg.) (2003). Der Standort-Faktor. Wie Unternehmen durch regionale Cluster ihre Produktivität und Innovationskraft steigern. 1. Aufl., Wiley-VCH Verlag GmbH & Co KGaA, Weinheim.

Wenger, E. (1998). Communities of Practice: Learning, Meaning, and Identity. Cambridge: Cambridge University Press.

Part II
Work and Creativity

Chapter 4
Support of Collaborative Creativity for Co-located Meetings

Thomas Herrmann

4.1 Introduction: Collaborative Creativity

The complexity and dynamics of ecological and economical challenges in the context of global labor division cannot be met by standard solutions. Design activities, which offer new, creative ways of looking upon the problems, are required, from different perspectives and with the goal of providing new choices for products, services, and processes. Therefore, creativity is needed.

As a first pass, creativity can be defined as the "ability to produce work that is novel … and appropriate" (Sternberg 1999, 3). It is not only the individual who decides whether an idea is new but also the experts of a field who have to recognize the novelty of the idea and accept the appropriateness so that they agree to include the new idea in their domain (Csikszentmihalyi 1996, 27).

Therefore, the novelty and appropriateness have to be related to the perspectives of the different stakeholders who are involved. Creative ideas are usually found at the beginning of innovations, which also include that the ideas are partially implemented and disseminated. The possibilities of achieving creative ideas probably increase if they are developed by different stakeholders who have differing backgrounds and expertise. This complies with Csikszentmihályi's (Csikszentmihalyi 1996, 23) observation that "*an idea or product that deserves the label 'creative' arises from the synergy of many sources and not only from the mind of a single person.*" We call this phenomenon "collaborative creativity" (Mamykina et al. 2002). We consider collaboration to be a process where people usually know each other and work together and at least have the possibility to give feedback to each other's ideas and work. Fischer et al. (2004) outline that collaborative creativity (in their words "social creativity"[1]) draws advantage from including different people

---

[1] We prefer this term to "social creativity" (Fischer et al. 2004) since every kind of individual thinking is of a social nature.

T. Herrmann (✉)
Ruhr-University of Bochum, Germany
e-mail: thomas.hermann@rub.de

D. Randall and P. Salembier (eds.), *From CSCW to Web 2.0: European Developments in Collaborative Design*, Computer Supported Cooperative Work, DOI 10.1007/978-1-84882-965-7_4, © Springer-Verlag London Limited 2010

with different backgrounds (spatial, temporal, cultural, etc.) and conceptual collisions can enrich the collaboration.

There is a wealth of literature on creativity and its psychological background as well as techniques to support creative thinking. Sternberg (1999) provides an overview, and we can draw upon several summaries in the field of creativity research such as Greene's (2001) detailed framework of 42 models. The relevant literature is also summarized in the field of HCI (Shneiderman 2000), requirements engineering (Maiden et al. 2004), and CSCW; a good overview is provided by Farooq et al. (2005). It is obvious that the endeavor of achieving creativity is just the opposite of the repetition of routinized, anticipatable activities or of a well-structured, effectively manageable project. Therefore, supporting collaborative creativity means dealing with a wicked problem (Rittel and Webber 1973).

If creativity is based on collaboration, the question of technical support has to be related to the research field of CSCW (Computer Supported Cooperative Work): What kinds of CSCW-features are useful for collaborative creativity, what needs to be improved, and how can we recognize whether a CSCW-application is feasible or not in this context? Obviously, a technical collaboration support is needed which goes beyond those kinds of software features that promote individual creativity, e.g., by improving the presentation and comprehensibility of complex collections of information or by means of simulation and exploration (Shneiderman 2000). Typical CSCW-Systems, which have to be taken into consideration, are GDSS (group decision support systems DeSanctis and Gallupe 1987) and EBS (electronic brainstorming systems) or electronic meeting support (Nunamaker et al. 1991). Furthermore, very common CSCW-features such as shared whiteboards, joint editing, awareness, and knowledge management support are highly relevant. Since collaborative creativity benefits from the heterogeneity of the group working together, the selecting of tools also has to reflect the heterogeneity of requirements with respect to socio-technical support. For instance, if a group of a software-engineer, a chief physician, an architect, and a business administration manager starts to develop ideas for a new type of hospital, it is not reasonable to offer them collaboration and documentation tools, which are specifically adapted to one of these professional domains. By contrast, some kind of documentation support is required that allows them to articulate their different perspectives and represent them in a shared artifact, which can be the basis for their ongoing process of developing, planning, and modifying of the new concept for hospitals.

To achieve a better understanding of the aspects and requirements that have to be taken into account for the design or selection of appropriate CSCW-tools in the context of collaborative creativity, we conducted a series of 12 interviews with various CSCW-researchers. The goal of this empirical work was to contribute to the elaboration of the design principle "support collaboration," which was one of 12 principles developed at an NSF-workshop (Resnick et al. 2005) with respect to creativity support. Analysis of the interviews provided the opportunity to derive design heuristics that can help to evaluate whether certain CSCW-configurations comply with the needs of creative collaboration. The interviewees emphasize playfulness, iteration, back-and-forth considerations, and aha-moments, which point to a kind of emergent phenomena as decisive characteristics of creativity. These aspects make clear that the design guidelines for supporting creativity in collaborations are different to those principles that are appropriate for cooperative work in general.

We derived six design heuristics, which we applied and evaluated in the context of co-located meeting support in a facilitation collaboratory at the University of Bochum, Germany. The centerpiece of the investigated type of meeting support in Bochum is a large, high-resolution interactive wall (480 × 120 m; 4,320 × 1,050 pixels), which seamlessly integrates three rear projection boards (see Fig. 4.1). Touches are recognized via six cameras, which view the reflection of infrared light that is caused by fingers or pens. The angles of view of the cameras overlap to support uninterrupted dragging actions over the entire wall. Data can be entered and manipulated directly on the screen or via laptops that are connected via Wlan. At the moment, certain types of software are available, mainly the Microsoft™ office suite, an editor for process diagrams (www.seeme-imtm.de), and the SMART™-software, which is used to control the interaction with the board and also provides means for making notes, handwriting recognition, annotations on PowerPoints, etc.

Furthermore, we identified some web applications (Google Docs, Mindmeister, bubbl.us) that support collaboration within and between the meetings. With this equipment, the ModLab in its current state has strengths and weaknesses, which can be related to the developed heuristics. They can be used to detect most of the

Fig. 4.1 The Modlab

weaknesses, and some of the problems which became apparent lead to a completion of the heuristics.

This paper presents design heuristics which help to develop or evaluate the tools which support co-located meetings or a series of workshops of heterogeneous design teams in their creative phases. In the next section we describe our methodological approach. Section 4.3 derives dimensions and characteristics of collaborative creativity from the empirical work, and characterizes the typical barriers which have to be overcome. Subsequently, we describe the design heuristics and present the comparison with related work (Section 4 5) and concluding remarks about how to use the heuristics.

4.2 Methodology

To understand the problems which can occur when using CSCW-features for collaborative creative work, we analyzed interviews with 13 people all of whom generally represent the following characteristics (Table 4.1):

CSCW-researchers who are involved in interdisciplinary creative collaborations from time to time, and are used to employing groupware functions.

Interdisciplinary orientation of every interviewee, varying focuses such as computer science, anthropology, business administration, information systems, psychology, philosophy, and usability engineering.

Few interviewees only are directly involved in research into creativity.

Table 4.1 Guiding questions for the semi-structured interviews

- What are – from a subjective point of view – relevant aspects of creativity – on an individual as well as on a collaborative level?
- Which kind of creativity and phases can therefore be differentiated between?
- What kind of groupware features and web-applications could be used, are really used, should be improved to support creativity [certain aspects were mentioned such as shared material, mobility, anonymity, experiments, awareness, community building to stimulate the discussion]?
- How can switches be supported (between creative work and routine tasks, between retreated thinking and communication, between synchronous and asynchronous communication)?
- In which kind of situation can groupware features be successfully employed for creativity and what are the characteristics of the appropriate situations?
- Which organizational issues have to be considered with respect to creativity support with groupware features?
- What triggers unconventional thinking?
- What are the important differences between academic and industrial settings with respect to creativity?
- What are the future trends to improve creativity with respect to groupware features and web-applications?

Different relations to CSCW: methods of software-engineering and design, developing and implementing concrete systems or features, studies on the usage of groupware, workplace studies where collaboration is especially relevant, evaluation of concrete systems.

Getting used to reflecting on their own practices and being willing to try out new technology in the field of CSCW.

The set of interviewees covers experience with different types of collaboration such as meetings, asynchronous work with dislocated colleagues, and synchronous communication.

The interviewees intensively take part in the CSCW-research community, e.g., 11 of them have served as PC-members or chairs of CSCW-conferences. With one exception, they all work in the USA (8 of them as faculty member at 4 different Universities, 3 of them at different research institutes).

The rationale behind the selection of interviewees is twofold: On the one hand, they are open-minded about using CSCW and they understand the principles of CSCW and its functionalities, and on the other they have advanced experience in describing troubles in this area. We suggest that those problems which prevent these people from using CSCW for the purpose of creative collaboration also keep other non-CSCW background users away. Therefore, the overcoming of the problems derived from the experience of CSCW researchers should become a priority and be used to inspire design heuristics. On the other hand, the selection of interviewees represents a wide range of different characteristics and therefore complies with the intention to conduct an explorative study. Although the interviewees do not represent the experience of the whole group of CSCW-researchers, they help to understand a broad variety of behavior and needs with respect to creative collaboration. We did not intend to analyze the interviews with statistical methods but to identify problems and requirements which stem from practical, reflected experience with CSCW-usage.

Conducting and analyzing the interviews took place in the following way: interviews took place at various locations in the USA in January and February 2007. Interviews always began with an explanation of the background and were semi-structured. The average interview length was 90 min and they were audio-recorded. Relevant categories were identified and derived and relevant data transcribed and assigned to the categories. Divergent descriptions were combined to understand the wide range of differing needs which have to be taken into account. We have supposed that every kind of differing need or problem can occur in heterogeneous teams and has therefore to be met by appropriate technical features.

The following description refers to the interviews by using "In" in parentheses followed by an indication of the interview's number (see Table 4.3).

After analysis of the interviews, the results were aligned to various dimensions. Design heuristics are one of these dimensions. They refer to the described problems with creativity and CSCW-features as well as to expectations or proposals for improvement. The heuristics were further elaborated by relating them to the

Table 4.2 Workshop experience as background of the heuristics

Supporting the larger picture – visualization of rich material

W1: Adding questions (prompts) as inspirationW2: Adding captions or enlargement of
  keywords within paragraphs

W2, W5: Adding pictures and other material as inspirations

W2,W5 Expressing various relations between elements, such as text paragraphs or collected
  ideas

W3: Adding textual comments (e.g., to a diagram)

W4 Anonymity and possibility of recognizing which items one has contributed (by using
  pseudonyms)

W4: Demonstrations of prototypes

W4: Making new contributions easily trackable

Malleability of shared material and stimulation of variations

W2: Highlighting and changing the size of words in text

W4: Sketching into prototype screen shots … need for multiple layers

W4: Sometimes the feeling occurred that not all important aspects are taken into consideration
  and dealt with

W5: Transformation from one medium into another (table into freely arrangable text items)

Support of convergence within evolutionary documentation

All workshops: continuous documentation but with varying degrees of displaying itW3: Adding
  comments and explanations

W4: Lack of time to consider the collected ideas

W4: Using an additional writer for collecting brainstorming items (+ checking whether it was
  appropriately noted down)

W5, W6: Need for prioritizing became obvious

Smooth transitions between different modes of creative collaboration

W1, W4: Parallel work in solitude and collaborative collection of ideas were combinedW1, W5:
  Seeing what others have just produced was possible during work in solitude

W5: A certain scheme of phases was repetitively applied

W5: Contributions of others inspire further ideas after work in solitude after finding new ideas
  have become difficult

Integration of communication with work on shared material

W3: Integration of comments into diagrams as a mirror of the communication (beside changes
  of the diagram)

W5: Extra information space which contains organizational hints (to dos, etc.)

W4: Oral explanations of a contributed item are sometimes too lengthy to be transcribed

Support of role dynamics and varying mode of collaboration

W4 : Assigning roles such as documenters, modelers, those who ask question vs. those who
  answer them; those who try something out vs. those who observe it

W5: Splitting into subgroups of two or three to allow people to be more active

concrete empirical background of the facilitation collaboratory (ModLab) for creativity workshops. In the course of creative meetings, the interactive wall of the lab has to support several tasks which are roughly outlined in Table 4.2. The background and overall goal of the meeting has to be presented ("need for change"), the collected ideas have to be documented, the structuring of them and the building of synergies have to be supported and, finally, the selection of appropriate proposals must be facilitated.

It was also possible to assess the usefulness as well as usability of the technical support for collaborative creativity in relation to concrete workshops which were run in the ModLab. They dealt with the following topics:

W1: Marketing – how to disseminate advertising material: in a 3 h workshop the goal was to find possibilities of how to use a magnetic bookmark-clip for marketing purposes. In a first phase, the properties of the magnetic bookmark were listed as well as all the different possibilities to use it. In a second step, a list of marketing activities was listed. During the first phase, about 16 participants worked in solitude while during the second phase the results of a mutual conversation were noted down by a facilitator. Onenote™ was used to collect the ideas.

W2: How to define socio-technical systems: about 8 participants provided larger text paragraphs as definitions for the term "socio-technical system." Pictures were included. Relating the definitions to each other was also tried out. The discussion was accompanied by a meta-reflection about what is needed to make the convergence of the definitions easier (ca. 1 h, OnNote™).

W3: Vision of a project on Ambient Assistant living: A process model was used to outline the steps and goals of a project. The model was developed and presented with the SeeMe-Editor (Herrmann 2009) and the contributions of the 12 participants were annotated as comments into the model.

W4: Tagging and process modeling: The workshop presented a prototype with which process models as well as their elements can be tagged (Prilla and Herrmann 2007). The ten participants started with reasoning about different aspects of how a concrete process model can become relevant in the future. On this basis, four different aspects of the prototype's functionality and usability were evaluated and completed in four iterations. The participants used OneNote™ to complete questionnaires; results of the discussion were documented with electronic sketching and bubbl.us, a web application for brainstorming.

W5: How to build synergies between ideas: The workshop with nine participants had two brainstorming phases: the purpose of the first was to generate rich exemplary material: a huge number of ideas for functions which can be provided by handhelds of the future. The task of the second phase was to develop ideas of how to deal with such a set of collected items; it started again with a brainstorming, the results were clustered in subgroups; afterwards a meta-reflection started on how the used procedures and tools could be improved.

The workshops revealed several problems with the usage of the large screen and the applied software tools (Fig. 4.2). These problems and the need for improvement which can be related to them provide a further basis for the derived heuristics. The goal is to describe and refine the heuristics on a level which supports usability evaluation as it is – for example – described by Cockton et al. (2002). The purpose is not to use them as guidelines for implementation, but as rules of thumb for experts who

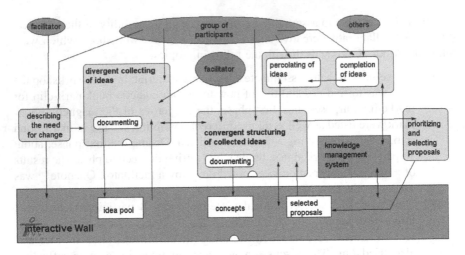

Fig. 4.2 Tasks in the context of creativity workshops using the interactive wall

have to evaluate systems. General usability testing aims at criteria such as effectiveness, efficiency, and user satisfaction. By contrast, the proposed heuristics are focused on issues such as the quantity and quality of new ideas, flexible switching between playfulness and efficiency, and synergy between various proposals, etc.

4.3 Dimensions and Barriers

The literature and the interviews reveal that there is a variety of characteristics and dimensions of collaborative creativity which have to be taken into account to derive design heuristics for CSCW support.

There is a differentiation between certain degrees of creativity: incremental vs. deep creativity (Shneiderman 2002); solving a problem vs. creating new questions and problems; finding a new solution which is immediately acknowledged vs. turning the whole problem around and handling it in a way which provokes *startlement* (In08) as well as concerns. In cases of breakthroughs, *it is hard for people to understand what is going on* (In11), and more communication becomes necessary and has to be supported. Since really deep creativity is a rare phenomenon CSCW-support should reasonably follow Shneiderman's focus on incremental creativity when developing concepts for technical support. However, CSCW-concepts should take into account that the deeper the creativity of a proposal is, the more reactions, questions, challenges, and concerns it will provoke (In11).[2] Creativeness can be assigned to products or to processes, *where the latter one tends to be more subjec-*

---

[2] Chat logs reveal that creative ideas provoke comments and responses by almost all participants (In11), while ordinary contributions usually only get one reaction.

tive (In12). The interviewees mostly refer to the processes when they characterize creativity. Creativity can be seen as something *that always happens – like experience of flows, breakthroughs, enjoyment of new ideas* (In13). However, it may be difficult for people to be creative *since they may not have time* (In02) and it is frequently necessary to stay in a pragmatic mode to get things done efficiently (In13). Therefore, it is a crucial challenge to *design tools which balance the tension between efficiency and creativity* (In13).

To describe the variety of characteristics and dimensions of collaborative creativity we refer to Vandenbosch et al. (2001) who differentiate between theories explaining the creation of ideas which variously refer to

Personal characteristics
The contexts in which ideas flourish
The processes by which ideas develop

4.3.1 Personal Differences

With respect to collaborative creativity it is decisive that some people can *only be creative while they communicate* (In01) while others prefer to work in solitude to be able to generate ideas, and can only afterwards communicate their contribution to collaborative creativity. This work in solitude is seen in connection with staying at home (*to be undisturbed and to have space to think about,* In02) or writing (In05). People who work in solitude may *come up with surprising solutions* (In01) when several ideas or discussion threads have to be merged. These people *build complex constructs of thoughts which are very solid* (In01) – but some of them may be *path-related* and have difficulties undoing what they already have achieved (In13). Creative people can be *analyzers* or *synthesizers* (In01). Similar to the comparison between communicative creativity and work in solitude, we have *multitaskers* who switch between different streams of thoughts and are willing to be interrupted (In01) vs. *people staying within a single flow* (In02) of working on a task or idea. Another dimension compares scanners who browse through data and are open-minded towards all kinds of associations and serendipity effects when researching vs. searchers who are pragmatically and exclusively focused on the well-defined problems they have in mind. Furthermore, people have different ways of expressing themselves; some of the interviewees characterize themselves as writers (In08), while others favor *sketching* (In05).

Since collaborative creativity draws its strength from combining different perspectives and stakeholders, the technical support has to offer a means to support all of the different types of personalities and their coming together. Furthermore, many people do not clearly represent one of the two poles of the pairs describing the dimensions above. They may meander between these opposed characteristics being triggered by individual rhythms or external circumstances, and the technical support has to react to these alternations. A bridge also has to be built between different professional fields: meetings and interactions between – for example – software-engineers, physicians, managers, and architects may lead to inspiring solutions for healthcare problems but have to deal with different styles of thinking, ranges of vocabulary and expression, types of knowledge, etc.

4.3.2 Contextual Aspects

We found that the settings in which creative collaboration takes place make a difference. We roughly differentiate between the following situations:

*Creativity in Everyday Work as a Primary or Secondary Task*Continuous communication about the design of new products or services, and work on these tasks can be the main characteristic of a job. Creativity is then the primary task and is integrated in the organizational structures and processes at the workplace. A typical example is IDEO's (In08) demonstration of the redesign of the shopping cart within 1 week (cf. Kelley 2001). In this context, individuals are able to take and exercise control over their own working environment – this is one of the factors which enhances creativity (Hewett 2005). By contrast, creativity becomes a secondary task if it is an employee's job to fulfill some routinized tasks or well-planned project activities which are fixed in a contract, and if he or she is additionally responsible for being aware of new ideas with respect to customer needs or ways for improving routines or technology. These employees are expected to communicate their ideas to others and to stay in discussion with them about their proposals – however, this communication is usually interrupted by the primary task and only takes place sporadically.

*Seeding*An artifact like a document, a certain kind of software, or a prototype is given to a group to continuously inspire them and to be an object of reflection and ongoing improvement. The artifact can serve as a boundary object between different perspectives and can be a nucleus of creative work and back-and-forth iteration. New ideas can concern the improvement of the artifact, new ways of using it or transforming its usage into a new context, and so on. The artifact can have the potential to replace a promoter's continuous communication about a new idea. The whole process can be considered in close correlation with Fischer et al.'s (1994) concept of "seeding, evolutionary growth and reseeding." While seeding triggers a process of divergence, the reseeding requires a preceding phase of convergence (In06).

Workshops or a Series of Workshops imply the possibility for a retreat from everyday work and are helpful if intensive communication is necessary for creativity. They imply the risk of the context of the workplace (e.g. typical constraints) being partially neglected (In06). Creative design tasks which need individual work and deliberate thinking are usually accomplished by a series of workshops, so that the time between them can be used to deal more extensively with complex issues. Workshops are usually facilitated, and larger groups are more difficult to facilitate than smaller ones (In01). The huge body of available creativity techniques (cf.

Greene 2001; Maiden et al. 2004) is mostly dedicated to workshop situations and proposes different phases, strategies of facilitation, and methods to encourage the participants to be open-minded toward unusual ways of thinking (e.g., forced relations (Hender et al. 2002)). Group Decision Support Systems or meeting support systems are mainly designed to support creative activities in workshops.

Collaborative Writing is a typical activity in the field of academia. Meetings – which are usually not supported by an extra facilitator – alternate with phases of concentrated individual work. Writing is considered as a creative process *where thinking emerges while people write (In05)*. There are different patterns such as:

(a) Doing collaborative research and then delegating the process of writing and merging of ideas to a single person
(b) Doing research, developing the structure of the paper, and then delegating sections of the text to individuals
(c) Sitting together discussing, then writing small portions of text, gathering and merging them, going on with writing

A specific challenge is the coupling of sketching and writing.

Learning Within a Constructivist Paradigm (In11) Places where learning is possible will support creativity (In09). Students can be triggered to be creative by the kind of tasks they are asked to work on. In the context of Computer Supported Collaborative Learning (Stahl 2008), math tasks which do not have a clear, single solution are used, and then the students are asked to reflect on their way of finding a solution. Groups of three to four dislocated students use a tool where references can be made between chat contributions and sketches on a shared whiteboard. A series of chat sessions takes place which is not explicitly facilitated. The degree of creativity can be influenced by the number of chats in a series, by the number and length of time periods after which the students are asked to think about their proceeding and to document it, and by exchanging the documentation with other groups. This case makes clear that an appropriate balance has to be found between the four activities: thinking, communicating, documenting, and reflecting (meta-cognition). Technical support is needed to switch between these activities and to make one aware of whether and when switching is appropriate.

The five constellations reveal that the appropriate technical support for collaborative creativity has to take into account the differences between the underlying situations, such as creativity as a primary vs. a secondary task, facilitated or non-facilitated meetings, short-term creativity vs. long-term collaboration, interaction between individuals vs. interaction between groups, etc.

4.3.3 Processual Aspects of Creativity

The literature differentiates between phases of creative work. The roughest differentiation compares a divergent phase with a convergent one. During divergence, a huge number of ideas should be produced which have to be merged and sorted out in the phase of convergence. Maiden et al. (2004) refer to Poincare and apply a scheme of preparation, incubation, illumination, and verification to run workshops of creative requirements construction. They also point out Osborn's differentiation between mess finding, data finding, problem finding, idea finding, solution finding, and acceptance finding. Shneiderman (2002) starts by citing Couger (1996) (opportunity, delineation, problem definition; compiling relevant information; generating ideas; evaluating, prioritizing ideas; developing and implementation plan). Finally, he proposes his own scheme (collect, relate, create, donate).

The interviews reveal that the interviewees do not reason about their creative collaboration by referring to a scheme of sequenced phases. This is mainly due to the fact that they collaborate spontaneously without previously prepared facilitation. This spontaneous interaction works well in smaller groups – in their context, improvisation is appropriate while it can rapidly lead to chaos within larger groups (In01). The interviewees emphasize the relevance of iteration by going back and forth including jumping between different kinds of phases, in particular between divergence and convergence. This iteration resonates with playing, applying trial-and-error strategies, and producing variations. CSCW-concepts should take into account that the deeper the creativity of a proposal, the more reactions, questions, challenges, and concerns it will provoke (In11).

The interviewees usually differentiate between two kinds of activities in the course of collaborative creativity. On the one hand they emphasize the relevance of *playfulness* (In02), *emotionality and improvisation* (In05), *resonance with one´s own feelings* (In05), *high degree of engagement* (In08), and *flow* where *the rest of the world falls away* (In02) referring to Csikszentmihalyi (1996). Creativity has a very personal dimension: "*It is not only about understanding science it is also a part of understanding me* (In05)." Playing and iteratively going back and forth is correlated (In08) to a crucial and typical creativity goal: producing a huge number of variations on the available concepts, ideas, and their elements. On the other hand, the role of *thorough, deliberate, scientific thinking* (In05) is stressed, as well as the need for structured, coordinated activities if *a larger number of participants or contributions has to be dealt with* (In01), if people *are dislocated and do not know each other very well* (In04), or if *documentation and meta-reflection* (In11) is required.

Both types of activities (playing around vs. systematic thinking) are distributed over the phases of divergence and convergence. Supporting divergence is considered as easy while convergence is regarded as difficult (In01). Collaboration has a specific importance since an individual is not able to add enough context to the description of an idea so that others can understand it (In06) – constant querying is necessary (In06) as is challenging and asking for explanations (in08).

Furthermore, it is pointed out that the back-and-forth iteration must finally lead into a phase of *pragmatism and focusing* (In10) so that the creative process can be successfully completed; the atmosphere of *open-endedness must be completed by efforts of writing* (In05) or documentation to consolidate the results. A specific tension is described: The pragmatic phase has to be planned (otherwise one spends a lot of time straying from the path in focus) and the start of the planning needs a critical mass (In06) of ideas. However, a consolidation must also take place under the condition that the phase of open-endedness at some point ends, leaving only a basis of incomplete information (In02).

Other phases between which a smooth transition should be possible are:

Conversation vs. Work on Shared Material (In01)With respect to conversation, the interviewees mention that it covers the proposing of ideas to others, challenging the ideas, explaining ideas and giving arguments, and starting negotiations about proposals. Creativity happens within conversation: While talking a third concept emerges from the contributions of the communicators (In01). Discussions are considered as important since they can bring up new solutions which were not around before (In09). One interviewee emphasizes the importance of discussions which represent a very loose form of brainstorming (In09) while another one (In02) mentions the relevance of brainstorming rules such as guaranteeing everyone a voice. By contrast, work on shared material means building on artifacts to which everyone can contribute modifications and which mirror new ideas. The documented results of a brainstorming can be considered as shared material (In01). Ideas can be integrated into artifacts so that they will not be forgotten (In011). The availability of shared material covers collaborative experimenting, or trying things out (In01). With respect to work on shared material, communication is considered as interrupting (In02). However, focusing on material makes conversation partly dispensable; communication channels can become redundant (In01). To develop new ideas, in some situations discussion is needed while others need repositories (In09) (as a kind of shared material).

Coming Together and Going Apart (In05)It is pointed out that intensive group interaction and work in solitude repeatedly alternate. Being together is needed for creativity to collect information (In05). The success of collaboration also depends on whether a group of people forms an appropriate mix ("to find the one person I have a mind melt with (In05)"). Being together covers differing patterns; for example, someone triggers others with a proposal and they develop it further or the contributions of others trigger someone to be creative (In11). From time to time, people want to have a retreat to start undisturbed thinking (In01) or to let ideas percolate (In04). This work in solitude can also happen in the same room where a workshop is located. Or it can be necessary to go out on *field work (In08), or to contrast the new ideas with the situation in the workplace (In06).

Synchronous vs. Asynchronous Interaction (In02)In synchronous phases one expects conversation and work on shared material to be highly interrelated. In asynchronous phases, maintaining this interrelationship becomes more difficult and a higher degree of coordination is needed. In this case, time can be used for going on with thinking within the group's problem space or for leaving the problem space and dealing with other tasks. Switching the task can be considered as an unsolicited interruption, or as an advantageous source for fresh ideas and inspirations. This distinction between two types of activities during asynchronous phases is important for adjusting the CSCW-support of collaborative creativity.

Content related vs. Coordinative Communication (In02)Coordination frequently punctuates the conversation about the actual problem. In synchronous phases it is expected that conversation and work on shared material be highly interrelated. This dense interrelationship is a success factor for the back-and-forth iteration which is typical for creativity. Therefore – for instance – it is reasonable to offer referencing between a shared whiteboard and chat contributions. However, in asynchronous phases, maintaining this interrelationship becomes more difficult – the degree of playfulness is reduced and the conversation on the actual problem is punctuated with coordinative acts of communication. Consequently, the distinction between content-related and coordinative communication has to be taken into account to provide means for smoothly switching between them.

4.3.4 Temporal Aspects of Creativity

The different phases and activities of the collaborative process are distributed over a time line. Somehow it has to be more or less collectively decided when a step back – to reconsider a proposal or a result – should take place or when a group separates and when it comes together again. The interviewees mostly suggest that these switches are event-driven or triggered by the conditions of the problem space (In06, In13). However, people do also tend to sense whether the time of a switch is appropriate or not. The feeling relates to their inner rhythms.[3] We assume that switching between different phases is also influenced by people's rhythms which are formed by their individual ways of working and thinking. With respect to CSCW-support we see the problem that on the one hand flexible and playful switching between the described activities is a constituent of creativity while – on the other hand – this switching has to comply with the participants' individual rhythms which can be very unequal and hard to synchronize. Within so-called socio-technical walkthroughs (STWT, Herrmann et al. 2004a) we found that some participants felt uncomfortable when we switched from intensive discussion to documentation, while others appreciated this switch since it gave them the opportunity to catch up.

If people *are really engaged*, time restrictions are overcome – *it can happen at any point at any time* (In08). Completing a creative task does not comply with long pauses (*"I have to keep it hot"* (In13)). *There are cultures where* one has *to have a certain speed otherwise* one cannot *be part of* (In02). By contrast, moving on too quickly can also become a problem in particular when people are opening up – *"the time you give people to open and share is really, really important – there might be a body rhythm for trust building, it is about the emotional trust building between*

---

[3] The concept of rhythm and its relevance for CSCW was early outlined by P. & T. Johnson-Lenz and Johnson-Lenz (1991).

people (In08)." It can be observed that the cycles, e.g., between separating and coming together, become shorter when developing a concept comes to an end or when a deadline is approaching (In01).

4.3.5 Psychological Barriers – Individual Level

Many problems are caused by the limitations of human memory. Santanen et al. (2004) suggest that the limited working memory makes it difficult to have different aspects of the problem space in mind and to build manifold and unusual combinations. It is important to stay within the same problem space but to be able to consider and to integrate various solution spaces (In08). To handle this limitation, people build semantical chunks which again guide their thinking and may limit their flexibility. The interviewees did not describe the kind of problem which could be related to a limited capacity of having new, exceptional ideas.

However, they did mention problems which can be related to the long-term memory: they forget ideas or cannot find their notes on ideas, or – if they find them – they do not understand them since they cannot remember their context (In08). Creative people tend to produce and to collect a huge amount of notes which lead to an idea overload (In06, In12) and which have to be reorganized from time to time (In08, In09). It is difficult for some people to start a pragmatic phase of focusing and consolidation (In08), if they know that there might be some of their ideas around which have not yet been sufficiently taken into account.

4.3.6 Psychological Barriers – Collaboration Level

With respect to collaborative creativity, those psychological barriers come into focus which are relevant on the group level – "… *other people can really be obstacles to your own thinking or they can greatly facilitate your creative thinking* (In13)." One important aspect is the phase of ideation (divergence) where as many good ideas as possible have to be generated. It turns out that working in groups for this purpose may prove less effective for various reasons (Diehl and Stroebe 1987; Santanen 2005): "Production blocking" may occur because people wait for a turn to speak. While waiting they may forget some ideas before they can report them; they may not generate new ideas while listening to others, or while trying not to forget their own. Free-riding occurs when people stop trying to generate their own ideas, but rely on others who are able to make contributions. A further problem is the fear of being evaluated by others (evaluation apprehension). All in all, it is possible that people stay within the boundaries of a certain type of idea which was voiced at the beginning of a brainstorming session (cognitive inertia, cf. Briggs and Reinig 2007), Furthermore, there are barriers which became apparent with so-called hidden-profile experiments (Stasser and Stewart 1992): If someone does not know the knowledge profile of another and therefore does not actively ask them for the needed information, one is not open-minded toward integrating unexpected information. The experiments reveal that items of information delivered by others receive more attention the more the recipient is already familiar with them – new information is usually neglected in the decision process. Wittenbaum et al. (2004) give an overview over the hidden-profile experiments and the possible explanations of the results. With respect to technical support it becomes clear that the permanent visualization of information and ideas which are new for others is helpful to bridge the time span which is needed to become familiar with new ideas.

In those workshop situations where brainstorming is electronically supported and leads to a huge amount of gathered items, it is hard for the participants to provide a reasonable synthesizing of the collected ideas. Therefore, most meeting support tools offer a means of prioritizing and sorting out items. However, this process is affected by the hidden-profile problem: the ideas which receive the highest scores are mostly those which are already familiar to the voters – and the really valuable new ideas are possibly sorted out. Thus, collaboration support for creativity workshops should emphasize the clustering of ideas and the relationship building between them (In01). Another way to overcome the hidden-profile problem is to assign certain roles to the participants or to make them switch between several roles (In13).

The interviewees reported a further problem which is related to collaboration and motivational issues: The context of the ideas of others and their deeper insight may not be properly understood (In08). This problem increases within dislocated collaboration if people do not know the context from which an idea originates, or the context in which it might be useful. A breakdown in understanding may happen (In11), which can prove to be an obstacle, but also a source for creativity. Diversity of viewpoints and perspectives enriches collaborative creativity; however, the opposite will happen if people are *focused on differing problem spaces* (In08), such as how to impress a manager vs. how to improve a product.

Some people are just not used to collaboration or are not aware of the limitation of their capacities for collaboration (In01). For example, they are not attentive to the conversation until a final decision has to be made – and then they start to challenge the achieved results (In01). It can also be difficult to find an appropriate task share: some of the participants should just stay within the perspective of their own field and should contribute information which is new to the others; other participants may have the task to transcend the borders of their domain to be able to integrate and to melt the presented perspectives (In13).

Another problem may be caused by undesired interruptions (Mark et al. 2005) which may suppress creativity (In03) while intentionally sought interruptions can have a positive effect by leading to inspiration or giving opportunities for a *brain feed* (In12). At least in the open-ended, more playful phases of divergence, time pressure is counterproductive to creativity as is the attempt *to manage* (In02) creativity – creative processes cannot be controlled from the viewpoint of a dominating center (In06). Another barrier to creativity occurs if people share a competitive attitude where they frown upon those among them who easily change their mind. This attitude impedes new, unusual ways of thinking and may lead to fragmentation in the group process (In07).

To overcome problems on the collaboration level the following hints can be helpful:

Social capital (In02) is needed which can be supported by *group formation* which *has to take place first* (In06). A shared problem sphere (In08) and a shared goal (In06) have to be identified and agreed upon.

An atmosphere of trust is needed where *everyone has a voice* (In02), no one dominates, and where the contributions and behavior are not the subject of judgment (In08).

On the basis of such an atmosphere, challenging the ideas of others must be possible and acceptable, *allowing irritations and directness, as well as pushing the boundaries* (In08).

4.3.7   Technology-Related Barriers

One of the interviewees put it this way: *The great irony is that although we work in CSCW we use almost nothing of that sort* (In04). The interviewees mention some reasons why they do not use elaborated CSCW-features much to support their collaborative creativity:

Different participants often use very different tools. If it comes to more specific tasks, they may have different platforms, or reside behind firewalls which make an exchange via more sophisticated media difficult (In04). People expect that the tools which are used during collaboration to *integrate with the rest of their world* (In13).

The few tools which are commonly available often do not offer the features and level of effectiveness one is used to in the context of individual work (In04). One does not like to transform material between the formats of different tools (In13).

Installing new tools on everybody's site consumes too much start-up time. *"That I know that other people have much the same stuff on their home base is enabling cooperation* (In04)."

Tools take you in a certain direction (In04) which is not always compatible with what you actually want. "I think the risk is if information technology is developed only to support efficiency – you know getting through the papers quickly – then that would be awful – because we don't want that – we don't just want to be efficient we want to be creative – so it has to do both (In13)."

Some types of communication support, such as video conferences are too stiff (In02), turn taking is too awkward (In08) or they are simply not cognitively lightweight enough.

The established word processors are not feasible for converging ideas (In05) or not flexible enough to arrange information flexibly (In06) which may explain a preference for power points in some companies (In04, In07).

4.4 Design Heuristics

There is a wide range of aspects which can be supported by technical functionality in the course of collaborative creativity. The interviewees' statements can be categorized and condensed by developing a set of design heuristics.

We propose an underlying scenario of workshops as a background for the development of these design heuristics. The concept of the workshop is mirrored in Fig. 4.1. During the workshops, the participants work together on representations of their ideas and contextual material, and phases of communication and isolated thinking alternate. In between the workshops, they compare the new concepts with the constraints of their daily work and may have time for deeper reflection. Collaboration with others can be asynchronously continued.

To make the heuristics more complete and understandable, we also draw on corresponding topics in the literature and on the experience of five workshops as described in the methodological section. Table 4.3 gives an overview of how the experience with the workshops (see Section 4.2 for the numbers W1–W5) has contributed to the heuristics. Table 4.3 lists the statements of the interviewees. Neither list of statements has the function of justifying the developed heuristics, but to disclose the exploratory sources of suggestions which lead to them.

We do not argue for the development of a particular platform or suite of tools, but we do outline the requirements which should be met by those tools being used or developed for the purpose of supporting collaborative creativity. Usually, design criteria should be as specific as possible with respect to certain domains or to the characteristics of the user. However, in the case of heterogeneous creativity workshops, the aim is to include many different domains and types of persons – therefore the heuristics and the corresponding technical functions of collaboration support have to be domain-independent. This is mainly achieved by keeping the formulation of the heuristics on an abstract level – concrete hints or examples for implementation are mainly used as illustration. These domain-independent, abstract heuristics are not conceived as guidelines for concrete software development but mainly for evaluation and for supporting decisions between several options. Usability testing is another area where this kind of domain-independent heuristics is applied.[4]

---

[4]An example of these kinds of heuristics is the seven dialogue principles of ISO9241-10, such as suitability for learning, error tolerance, controllability, etc.

Table 4.3 Interviewee statements as background of the heuristics

Supporting the larger picture – visualization of rich material

In01: It is a deficit if the meeting room and its software facilities do not support collaborative writing of text

In01: It must be possible to bring in material, captured ideas – photos, hand sketches, etc. ... the representation of the "subject" is crucial

In01: PowerPoint helps to present logical and spatial structures

In01, In02: The relevance of anonymity ... group gets a drift, if some authority reacts to an idea with "oh yeah, that's what I think is right"

In02: An appropriate means for self-expression is needed

In02: Incompleteness: Important since it is a part of being open ... ambiguity is important - variation of fringes

In05: "I organize text graphically" – no appropriate tool for that

In06: Sometimes I initiate e-mail conversations – and it is nearly impossible to overview the results ...

In08: Public large screen - helps to share context since they are very informal and very conversational, they help to make random connections, there is a physical, social shared context that already exists that gives us a fabric for building a conversation

In08: You never take the sketch pad away - you give them a place to go and sketch out new ideas,

In11: Having a whiteboard to make a summary - using the whiteboard as a pinboard; a continuous opportunity to make notes about what is going on.

In12: It must be possible to recognize the larger pattern

In13: Storyboarding, screen shots, mock-ups that all works well with computer

Malleability of shared material and stimulation of variations

In01: Directness is important when the result of modifications are mirrored

In01: It must be possible to manipulate shared material without destroying it

In02: Everything which makes people more playful is a good thing

In04: Actually you want to play with things, but there is no kind of good support for this

In06: You need a large screen to be able to move the items around

In08: Putting dynamic comments over - such a layer is really important –

In08: The malleability of the artifacts - when we start at a drawing board, we know it is a mutual object; however at the distance, when I draw a box, you cannot know whether it is shared or not, the box seems too perfect. ... I don't know whether I am allowed to mess with it or not ... the mutability of objects isn't really clear

In08: The human strength of visually spotting the difference should be more supported! Doing deltas, complex concepts are easier to understand by showing little differences!

In08: End-user generated meta-data, start annotating in content ... post-its are better than note book ... I try to move the post-its around - a kind of spatial problem

In08: Methods for back and forth prototyping; simulation;... embodied in the prototype are a whole lot of hypotheses

In12: Translating temporal into spatial relationships, increases comprehensibility

In13: Creative attitude ... to look at what's around me and try to combine it and to recombine it

Support of convergence within evolutionary documentation

In01: Convergence is either provided by individuals or it happens in a group session but needs a lot of time ... so that sufficient clustering is usually not possible

In01: The advantage of chat is that communication + documentation happen in one step

In05: This was written, rewritten, and rewritten again [and the history should be visible, TH] ... we used the tracking feature

In05: It should be easy to link things - like hypermedia but in a much more subtle way

(continued)

Table 4.3 (continued)

In06: Could there be a groupware feature which reminds me that certain conversation threads that I have initiated have lost my attention?

In08: When people do knowledge management they capture the things, since they are easy to capture, but they don't capture the insights

In08: I am more a clusterer than a mapper, first you have to get categories then you can start doing relationships

In09: The problem is not about having a lot of ideas but to get back to them

In11: A third media is added - a wiki which is used for documentation and is shared by all the groups ... documentation as a meta-level task

Smooth transitions between different modes of creative collaboration

In01: There are breakout-phases in meetings which have to be anticipated ... The larger the groups the stricter the planning and control for going through several phases

In01: When chatting I can easily retreat for some minutes and quickly resume into the collaboration when returning afterwards

In02: After having the idea it can become more structured, with milestones, etc. implementation and execution of the idea

In02: Maybe there is a convention where you can tell people that you just need some time 5 min chat may be semi-synchronous - depends on social conventions – as long as people are still there, there is a kind of awareness going on

In05: Being in a retreat but still having access to the resources

In08: It is not sensible that only one person draws

In08: Concept of translucent boards - the mutability of the object is clear

In11: In one chat someone said - let us take 5 min - and then they came back

Integration of communication with work on shared material

In01: Brainstorming tools translate brainstorming into shared material ... shared material is the core of knowledge management

In02: There must be a lot negotiation ... there just has to be a channel with which they communicate - exactly about shared material

In04: Instant messaging for giving things back and forth [as support for coordination, TH]

In05: We used the tracking feature to comment

In05: Writing a section + IM ... see that section in tandem with the conversation"

In06: To provide artifacts which can be commented on by everybody

In06: If there are several comments in the paper, or even if changes to the overall structure have been made, it rapidly becomes confusing

In08: Turn taking is really screwed up, the mutability of objects isn't really clear

In11: When you found things ... you could bookmark them and you can make notes ... collective referencing ... and you can have tables and little spreadsheets ... shared diagrams

In13: With too many comments in a document it gets hard to see the forest for the trees

Support of role dynamics and varying modes of collaboration

In01: For being creative, splitting large groups into subgroups is essential

In01: Division of roles between multitaskers, associative people, who bring in ideas, and those who investigate the potential of the ideas more systematically

In02: Role games with avatars ... avatar is just a character ... if you create a character that is not exactly you but similar - that brings play in again.

In12: People having different hats - playing different roles [to overcome the position-driven negotiation]; support role play; [role playing as a means to support variation]

In13: Roles that are one of the big things that mitigate the hidden-profile problem

4.4.1   Supporting the Large Picture – Visualization of Rich Material

One of the interviewees' main messages was that the various types of contributions and manifold ways of representing them (e.g., writing or sketching) must be visualizable and composable. The interviewees emphasized that every participant needs an appropriate means of *self-expression* (In02), and that it must be possible to recognize the larger pattern (In12). Exclusive focusing on a certain type of representation, e.g., the hierarchical relationship building of the mind map method (In08) is insufficient.

Therefore, supporting the building of a larger picture is a reasonable heuristic (cf. Conklin 2005). An electronic medium for creativity support has to visualize and combine all participants' contributions and display the available information space to a large extent with the identical visual representation for all participants, preferably on a large screen. It should allow them to flexibly insert all kinds of ideas, opinions, illustrating material or contextual background, and it has to provide anonymity (In01, In02). Therefore it is important for the collaborative interaction that:

The representations of ideas or additional information for contextualization can be easily captured and inserted and freely ordered.

Different types of vocabulary or symbols as well as varying diagrammatic notations can be used and combined.

Varying types of media such as oral utterances, sketches, pictures, video, diagrams, and text can be used, integrated, and related to each other.

Different degrees of explicitness, formalization, vagueness can be chosen.

Different degrees of details: overviews and abstract representations are possible, temporal hiding[5] of details is supported, and the simultaneous presentation of subsets of minutiae can be chosen.

Manifold means for expressing relations are offered such as arcs, highlighting, coloring, Venn diagrams, typed relationships, etc.

Differences and commonalities between the visualized ideas can be easily recognized at one glance; dissent should be particularly comprehensible (Farooq et al. 2005).

The display of individual contributions is anonymous, but the possibility for person A to recognize which items were contributed by him or her is however maintained.

Some typical examples which achieve partial compliance with this design heuristic are the Envisionment and Discovery Collaboratory, EDC (1, Arias et al. 2000) or the i-land environment (Streitz et al. 1999). With an interactive large screen a large

---

[5]Hiding certain information temporarily (e.g., the identity of a contributor) helps the avoidance of problems such as free riding, evaluation apprehension, cognitive inertia, or motivational pressure toward group uniformity (Santanen 2005).

quantity of brainstorming contributions can simultaneously be made visible and readable. Contributions can easily be related to each other by geometrical nearness, while other graphical means (such as arcs, coloring, Venn diagrams) are restricted to what current software tools provide. This limits the possibilities to express synergy.

4.4.2 Malleability of Shared Material and Stimulation of Variations

The interviewees consider *malleability* (In08) or *openness* (In05) of the material – which represents design concepts – as essential for dynamic idea generation. The variability which is achieved with these features is required by the interviewees with respect to the *playfulness* (In02) they assign to creativity, or the relevance of *going back and forth* (In08). It is suggested that changing the modes of presentation (e.g., *translating temporal relationships into spatial relationships* (In12)) increases comprehensibility and helps to solve problems.

We know from our workshop experience that participants must be invited to make changes and should not need to be afraid that these changes may have destructive effects. The more perfect the representation of a solution appears the more reluctant they are to modify it.

The jointly available representations must be modifiable and malleable in manifold ways. This includes

The free rearranging of elements with respect to their order or geometrical placing, e.g., to organize text graphically (In05)

Archiving, highlighting, or inserting of (new) elements as well as recombining the relations between them

Easy modification of elements and direct mirroring of changes and visualizing of resulting differences

The switching between different modes of representation; support of translating one mode into another (e.g., handwriting into digital text, mindmaps into text, etc.)

The obvious indication of those subsets of elements which are expected to be modified, or the proactive indicating of elements that have to be reconsidered

The enabling of "what-if" or "what-else" scenarios of modification to support experiments without losing material

The possibility of conducting joint modifications simultaneously; this can be supported by offering different layers to every participant which represent their proposals for change and can be flexibly hidden or shown (Lu and Mantei 1991)

Malleability can be increased by offering tangible objects (Arias et al. 2000). The use of handwriting or hand sketching also extends the modifiability of shared material (Guimbretière et al. 2001).

On an interactive large screen, contributions can easily be geometrically arranged, but only by one person who interacts with the wall – e.g., with OneNote™. Collaborative and simultaneous modification of clusters by two or more persons is currently not supported. This deficit limits the possibilities of synergy building.

4.4.3 Support of Convergence Within Evolutionary Documentation

Extensive phases of divergence by creating ideas via brainstorming or by varying the collated information lead to a huge amount of items and documents. To achieve final concepts, the possible synergy between the ideas has to be identified and exploited, and the contributions have to be merged and condensed. The interviews revealed that this phase of convergence is a time-consuming process and is not sufficiently supported (In01, In06) by current groupware functions. In particular, reducing the set of ideas by prioritizing them has to take place without excluding valuable contributions or possibilities of merging them. Therefore, continuous and evolutionary documentation has to accompany the phase of convergence. The results, as well as the process of achieving them have to be directly available within the workshops as well as after them. This includes:

The possibility for simultaneous clustering and documentation of relationships
– either collaboratively or individually

Managing a deliberate process of prioritizing items which includes the directing of attention toward neglected or conflicting aspects (items should be brought into the foreground if they have been neglected[6])

Unobtrusive support for collaborative documentation which should happen as a concurrent task which requires as little extra attention as possible and therefore avoids unnecessary interruptions

Inclusion of conversational threads and hyperlinks to the related contextual background material that helps us to understand the documentation and avoids the need to complete it with explicit explanations

Ensuring that changes and the process of convergence are traceable[7] and can be a subject of going back and forth along the time line (cf. the bridge tool, Farooq et al. 2005)

Communication and reasoning about changes, prioritizing or sorting things out should be documented and visualized, e.g., by means of dialogue mapping (Conklin 2005)

---

[6] This requirement can be derived from the context of "hidden profile" experiments (Stasser and Stewart 1992).

[7] Most interviewees (e.g., In08) mentioned that the most popular word processor's tracking function does not sufficiently make the history of the merging of ideas comprehensible.

Examples of groupware functions which support this heuristic are rating or voting (Limayem 2006). They help to identify priorities within group decision support systems. Grouping and clustering can be supported with mind maps. However, they have the disadvantage of promoting a hierarchical structure (In08). The experience with the workshops revealed that continuous documentation is essential for supporting synergy building but has to be as unobtrusive as possible to avoid production blocking (cf. Diehl and Stroebe 1987).

4.4.4 Smooth Transitions Between Different Modes of Creative Collaboration

The interviews make apparent that collaborative creative work includes a manifold of different activity and collaboration modes and varying preferences of the participants: phases of divergence and convergence alternate, people separate and come together, co-located meetings are followed by dislocated cooperation and vice versa, and collaborative work alternates with work in solitude as well as simultaneous with asynchronous activities (even within the same room). Between these modes, and the functions assigned to them, a smooth transition is required[8]:

A facilitator should be supported to define phases of collaborative work, to increase the awareness of the current phase type and to switch easily between the phases.

People must be enabled to contribute to a solution or a concept by thinking it through in solitude without being disturbed – that means without receiving hints about what others are doing, communicating, or observing.

An intermediate mode is offered between individual, retreated thinking and active collaboration. Within this mode, participants can easily resume the collaboration with others on the basis of available information about what has been discussed and worked upon while they were absent, and they receive continuous awareness clues about what is going on so that they can flexibly decide and switch between working in solitude and being involved in collaboration.

Flexible switching between synchronous or asynchronous communication and work on shared material needs awareness functions which support the re-synchronization and merging of individual work on shared material, as well as the mutual solving of replication conflicts.

When others have retreated or need a retreat, this should be signaled unobtrusively.

---

[8] These requirements also help to achieve a balance between the advantages of nominal and interactive groups (Santanen 2005) and to switch flexibly between different ideation techniques as described by Nov and Jones (2005).

The experience with workshops revealed that the continuous inspection and modification of artifacts needs a kind of documenting which is unobtrusive but which also has to clarify that all of the participants' contributions have been taken into consideration. If complete documentation is too awkward the usage of indicators which give visual clues of intentional incompleteness can be a reasonable compromise (Herrmann 1997).

A negative example is that the available video conferencing systems (In02) or media spaces do not provide sufficient signals about people's switching their attention focus between communication and retreated working on the problems to be solved. Face-to-face meetings with the described large-screen application can be equipped with laptops and wireless connections. This supports switching between retreated and public work and helps avoid the production-blocking problem (Santanen 2005).

4.4.5 Integration of Communication with Work on Shared Material

From the viewpoint of the interviewees, conversation and joint work on shared material are not sufficiently integrated. For example, it should be possible to *see it as a tandem* (In05) when people are jointly changing a text and are communicatively reasoning about these changes in the case of collaborative writing. Documentation builds the bridge between communication and mutual work on shared material. The playfulness of creative sessions requires light-weight, poorly structured communication on the one hand, while its continuous documentation requires discipline and compliance with prescribed conventions on the other. With the help of technical support it should be unnecessary *to develop certain conventions before the communication can start* (In02). The following features can support the integration:

Documented threads of discussions and brainstorming can be transformed into malleable shared material.

Providing the possibility of bi-directional hyperlinks between documented communication threads and (possibly modified) parts of the shared material, or links between shared material and contextual background information which has an explanatory function.

Supporting deixis which helps to relate a communication channel (e.g., chat, audio) to the shared material.

Joint editing of shared material and the arguments and negotiation which accompany it should be seamlessly integrated with tracking and commenting functionality.

Smooth insertion of recorded oral utterances or handwritten annotations, etc., into the shared material.

Making coordinative communication as easy as possible or unnecessary; the structure of the medium which represents the material should mirror the structure of the communication, e.g., turn taking (those who speak are also allowed to edit an element).

While Wikis are an example of how people can combine knowledge from
different perspectives into shared material, it is also an example of insufficient integration of communication (In02). "Concert chat" is a typical
example of how joint editing and communication are intertwined (cf. Wessner
et al. 2006).

4.4.6   Support of Role Dynamics and Varying Modes
of Collaboration

During a creative process it can become necessary for the participants to switch
between different roles and for the mode of the collaboration to be adapted, e.g.,
by switching to work in subgroups. Playing varying roles make people more
open-minded (In02); asking them to sustainably bring in certain positions may
help to overcome the hidden-profile problem (In13). People should be able to find
those roles with which they can develop their creative power. Within small
groups, creative collaboration can be more probable (In01). Specific support
should be offered for:

Switching between different modes of collaboration should also allow the partici-
     pants to switch between different roles; the role of a facilitator who supports
     the transition between the different phases should be particularly supported.
An extra role which is in charge of the documentation and which can easily be
     taken over
Making various constellations of task sharing possible by providing a means to define
     the underlying task-related roles and to coordinate switching between them
Promoting people to view a problem from different perspectives and positions
     by offering them various roles which can be played
Switching between various types of collaborative constellations such as parallel
     work in solitude vs. in the whole group, work in subgroups of different size;
     facilitated vs. non-facilitated collaboration, structured vs. unstructured with
     respect to phases or explicit roles

The essential features for this kind of support can usually be found within knowledge
management systems. With respect to role dynamics, the possibilities are mostly
restricted to access rights. More elaborated concepts for dynamic role definition
and taking are described in (Herrmann et al. 2004b).

4.5   Related Work

While the above-described heuristics aim toward collaboration, earlier work on
creativity tools (Shneiderman 2000 or Hewett 2005) is focused on human–computer
interaction. An NSF-workshop on creativity support tools in 2005 provides 12

design principles (Resnick et al. 2005); one of them entitled "Support Collaboration." This principle generally states that tools are needed which support the integration and iteration of the contributions of team members with their differing strengths and talents. The above-proposed heuristics – to which we refer with the letters (A) to (F) in the following paragraphs – attempt to detail this principle. A very early paper of Lu and Mantei (1991) identifies five areas of design requirements for collaborative drawing and idea management by designers: *Work Allocation, Design Integration, Design Ownership, Design Recall*, and *Space Sharing*. These factors mainly refer to work on shared material. *Work allocation* is needed to prepare task sharing for work in solitude while the *integration* helps to melt the individual results – both are needed to support *continuous documentation* (heuristic C) and *smooth transitions* (Heuristic D). With ownership someone can claim control of what happens to his/her contributions. Earlier ideas or versions of the shared material can be recalled – this corresponds to the documentation need (heuristic C). And the space-sharing factor proposes the possibility of layers for each individual (heuristic B – *malleability*).

Comparable with the above-described heuristics, Hailpern et al. (2007) present a list of six requirements. Requirements such as keep *multiple design ideas visible simultaneously (R1)* and *shared ideas should always remain in the collective consciousness (R4)* do positively correlate with the "larger picture" heuristic. *Allow rapid access to personal and shared designs (R5)* can be related to the need for continuous and complete documentation. In the context of smooth transition between modes (D), the requirements *provide clearly delineated personal and group spaces (R2)* and *allow multiple levels of sharing (R3)* – which mainly mirrors access rights – are of interest since they indicate the states between which transitions are reasonable. A difference to our findings can be seen in the requirement that the result of individual work phases should not be immediately visible to others (since its producer may feel unsure about its value) while we assume that it does not matter whether such results are visible to others or not, as long as the individual work remains undisturbed. The appropriateness of these two options may depend on the degree of trustfulness which underlies the specific constellation of creative work.

Furthermore, Briggs and Reinig (2007) propose six recommendations (numbered as R1–R6 by TH) for the design of ideation processes within their *Bounded Ideation Theory* approach. The integrating of contextual information into the *larger picture* (heuristic A) may support *sense-making to overcome* the *understanding boundary (R2)* and allow for the visualization of *interventions* which help *make a task more open-ended (R1)*. Switching between *lower- and higher-level concepts to overcome cognitive boundaries (R3)* can be supported by *malleability* (heuristic B); the *smooth transition between various modes* (heuristic D) supports *flexible interventions to increase diversity of stimuli(R4)*, and helps to *minimize outside distraction (R5)* or to *use formal and informal breaks (R6)*.

The above-proposed heuristics (A to F) go beyond current ideation theory since they address features for collaboration support instead of platforms and tools such as EBS or GSS. These features allow a group a varying degree of interaction on a continuum between work in solitude and the simultaneous collaboration of several participants. It is reasonable for psychological research on ideation to compare the effect of clearly distinguished different treatments (e.g., collaboration constellations), while the proposed heuristics focus on flexibly mixing various modes of collaboration support. Furthermore, the support of the heterogeneity of teams is more explicitly emphasized than is usually the case in studies on ideation.

Further hints are included in the work of Farooq et al. (2005) who emphasize the relevance of supporting the attention for dissent and of Farooq et al. (2007) who emphasize the relevance of awareness. It is plausible when Shneiderman (2007, 22) suggests that collaboration-oriented tools such as Eclipse, JDeveloper, Wikipedia, Blogger, Slashdot, Flickr, Youtube may have a positive influence on social creativity. However, these tools have still to be improved from the viewpoint of the proposed heuristics and the underlying opinions of the interviewees.

4.6 Conclusion

CSCW-support for collaborative creativity in heterogeneous teams cannot be aligned with a certain domain or type of user. Such an approach would be inadequate because of the huge variety of potential participants and constellations and the easily neglected relevance of routinized activities. Since the creative collaboration may take place in meetings where the participants bring their own laptops, or may be continued asynchronously, the provided tools should be applicable in diverse IT-infrastructures – preferably via web-applications – without requiring intensive preparation. The proposed heuristics can be used to facilitate creative collaboration, to improve CSCW-features and to inspire further research. It is of particular interest to evaluate and compare existing systems or features and to find out which of them comply better with the need for creative collaboration in heterogeneous teams. On this basis it may become possible to extract those features from existing systems – in particular research prototypes – which can then serve as role models.

The design heuristics can be applied to design creativity workshops as sociotechnical processes to achieve improvements with respect to:

Increased quantity and quality of ideas
More possibilities for playing around and going back and forth.
Increased convergence and synergy between the ideas.
Supporting convergence as a mutual endeavor where several participants contribute to the melting of ideas turns out to be one of the most relevant challenges to improve collaborative creativity.

The heuristics differ from existing usability criteria and CSCW-design guidelines because they do not focus on effectiveness and efficiency, but have to take playfulness and open-endedness into account. Further consolidation of the heuristics should be undertaken since they are only substantiated on an exploratory basis. Further steps can be to conduct experiments or surveys which include a large number of experts from different fields and then challenge their comments on the heuristics.

References

Arias, E., Eden, H., Fischer, G., Gorman, A., Scharff, E. (2000). Transcending the individual human mind—creating shared understanding through collaborative design. *ACM Trans. Comput.-Hum. Interact.* 7, 1. 84–113.

Briggs, Robert O. and Reinig, Bruce A. (2007). Bounded Ideation Theory: A New Model of the Relationship Between Idea- quantity and Idea-quality during Ideation. *HICSS 00.* 16ff.

Cockton, G., Lavery, D., & Woolrych, A. (2002). Inspection-based Evaluations. In J. A. Jacko, & A. Sears (Eds.) *The Human-Computer Interaction Handbook.* Mahwah, NJ, LEA. pp 1118–1138.

Conklin, J: (2005). *Dialogue Mapping.* Wiley, Chichester.

Couger, D. (1996). *Creativity and Innovation in Information Systems Organization.* Danvers, MA. : Boyd and Fraser.

Csikszentmihalyi, M. (1996). *Creativity: Flow and the psychology of discovery and invention.* New York: HarperCollins.

DeSanctis, G.; Gallupe, R. B. (1987). A Foundation for the Study of Group Decision Support Systems. *Management Science, Vol. 33,* No. 5. 589–609.

Diehl, M. and Stroebe, W. (1987). Productivity Loss In Brainstorming Groups: Toward The Solution Of A Riddle. *Journal of personality and social psychology 53.* 497–509.

Farooq, U., Carroll, J. M., and Ganoe, C. H. (2005). Supporting Creativity in Distributed Scientific Communities. *Proceedings of Group'05.* New York: ACM Press. pp 217–226.

Farooq, U., Carroll, J. M., and Ganoe, C. H. (2007). Supporting Creativity With Awareness In Distributed Collaboration. In *Proceedings of the 2007 international ACM Conference on Supporting Group Work.* GROUP '07. New York: ACM Press. pp31–40.

Fischer, G., McCall, R., Ostwald, J., Reeves, B., and Shipman, F. (1994): Seeding, Evolutionary Growth And Reseeding: Supporting The Incremental Development Of Design Environments. *Proceedings of CHI94.* New York: ACM Press, pp 292–298.

Fischer, G., Scharff, E., & Ye, Y. (2004). Fostering Social Creativity by Increasing Social Capital. In M. Huysman, & V. Wulf (Eds.) *Social Capital and Information Technology,* Cambridge, MA: MIT Press. pp355–399.

Greene, R. T. (2001): A Garbage Can Model of Creativity – the Four Cycle Model – Derived from a Model of 42 Models of Creativity. *Journal of Policy Studies No. 11,* Sept. 1-204.

Guimbretière, F., Stone, M., and Winograd, T. (2001). Fluid Interaction With High-Resolution Wall-Size Displays. In *Proceedings of the 14th Annual ACM Symposium on User interface Software and Technology* (Orlando, Florida, November 11–14, 2001). UIST '01. New York: ACM Press. pp21–30.

Hailpern, J., Hinterbichler, E., Leppert, C., Cook, D., and Bailey, B. P. (2007). TEAM STORM: Demonstrating An Interaction Model For Working With Multiple Ideas During Creative Group Work. *Proceedings of the 6th ACM SIGCHI Conference on Creativity & Cognition.* New York: ACM Press. pp193–202.

Hender, J. M., Dean, D. L., Rodgers, T. L., Nunamaker, J. F. (2002). An Examination of the Impact of Stimuli Type and GSS Structure on Creativity: Brainstorming Versus Non-Brainstorming Techniques in a GSS Environment. *Journal of Management Information Systems,* Vol. 18. Issue 4. 59–85.

Herrmann, Th. (1997). Communicable Models for Cooperative Processes. In: M.J. Smith, Salvendy, G. and R. J. Koubek (Eds.). *Design of Computing Systems. Proceedings of the Seventh International Conference on Human-Computer Interaction.* San Francisco, California, USA. Amsterdam: Elsevier. pp285–288.

Herrmann, Th., Hoffmann, M., Kunau, G., and Loser, K.-U. (2004a). A Modeling Method for the Development of Groupware Applications as Socio-Technical Systems. *Behaviour & Information Technology. March–April 2004, Vol. 23.* No.2. 119–135.

Herrmann, Th., Jahnke, I. and Loser, K. (2004b). The Role Concept as Paradigm for Designing Community Systems. In: F. Darses; R. Dieng; C. Simone; M. Zackland (eds.): *Cooperative Systems Design.* Amsterdam: IOS Press. pp 163–178.

Herrmann, T. (2009). Systems Design with the Socio-Technical Walkthrough. In B. Whitworth & A. de Moor, (eds). *Handbook of Research on Socio-Technical Design and Social Networking Systems*. Hershey, PA, USA. IGI Global. pp 336–351.

Hewett, T.T. (2005). Informing the design of computer-based environments to support creativity. *International Journal of Human-Computer Studies 6*. 383–409.

Johnson-Lenz, P., Johnson-Lenz, T. (1991). Post-mechanistic Groupware Primitives: Rhythms, Boundaries And Containers. *International Journal of Man-Mach. Studies*. 34, 3, 395–417

Kelley, T. (2001). *The Art of Innovation*. New York: Doubleday

Limayem, M. (2006): Human versus automated facilitation in the GSS context. *SIGMIS Database* 37, 2–3 (Sep. 2006), pp 156–166.

Lu, I. M. & Mantei, M. M. (1991), Idea Management in a Shared drawing Tool. *ECSCW'91: Proceedings of the second European Conference on Computer-Supported Cooperative Work*. Amsterdam: Kluwer. pp 97–112.

Maiden N.A.M., Manning S., Robertson S. and Greenwood J. (2004). Integrating Creativity Workshops into Structured Requirements Processes, *Proceedings of DIS'2004*. Cambridge, MA: ACM Press, pp 113–122.

Mamykina, L., Candy, L., and Edmonds, E. (2002). CollaborativeCreativity. *Communications of the ACM, 45* (10). New York: ACM Press. pp 96–99.

Mark, G., Gonzalez, V. M., and Harris, J. (2005). No task left behind?: examining the nature of fragmented work. In *Proceedings of CHI '05*. New York: ACM Press. pp 321–330.

Nov, O. & Jones, M. 2005. Creativity, Knowledge and IS: A Critical View. In *Proceedings of the 38th HICSS*. Washington, DC, 44.2: IEEE Computer Society. DOI= http://dx.doi.org/10.1109/HICSS.2005.176 [X04]

Nunamaker, J.F., Dennis, Alan R., Valacich, Joseph S., Vogel, Douglas, and George, Joey F. (1991). Electronic meeting systems. In: *Communications of ACM 34*. New York: ACM Press. 40–61.

Prilla, M. and Herrmann, Th. (2007). Semantically Integrating Heterogeneous Content: Applying Social Tagging as a Knowledge Management Tool for Process Model Development and Usage. *IKNOW 2007*, Graz. 16–24.

Resnick, M., Myers, B., Nakakoji, K., Shneiderman, B., Pausch, R., Ted Selker, T., and Eisenberg, M. (2005). Design Principles for Tools to Support Creative Thinking, In *Creativity Support Tools*: Report from a US National Science Foundation Sponsored Workshop.

Rittel, H. and Webber, M. (1973). Dilemmas in a General Theory of Planning. *Policy Sciences, 4*. 155–169.

Santanen, E. L., Briggs, R. O., and Vreede, G. D. (2004). Causal Relationships in Creative Problem Solving: Comparing Facilitation Interventions for Ideation. *Journal of Management of Information Systems. 20*, 4. 167–198.

Santanen, E. L. (2005). Resolving Ideation Paradoxes: Seeing Apples as Oranges through the Clarity of ThinkLets. In *Proc. of the 38th HICSS*, IEEE Computer Society, Washington, DC, 16.3. DOI= http://dx.doi.org/10.1109/ HICSS.2005.521

Shneiderman, B. (2000). Creating Creativity: User Interfaces for Supporting Innovation. proceedings of *ACM TOCHI, 7* (1). New York: ACM Press. pp 114–138.

Shneiderman, B. (2002): Creativity Support Tools. *Communications of the ACM*. 45, 10, 116–120.

Shneiderman, B. (2007): Creativity Support Tools: Accelerating Discovery And Innovation. *Commun. ACM* 50, 12. New York: ACM Press. 20–32.

Stahl, G. (2008). Social Practices Of Group Cognition In Virtual Math Teams. In S. Ludvigsen, A. Lund & R. Säljö (Eds.). *Learning in social practices. ICT and new artifacts – transformation of social and cultural practices*. Pergamon. Retrieved from http://GerryStahl.net/pub/cmc.pdf.

Stasser, G. & Stewart, D. D. (1992). Discovery of hidden profiles by decision-making groups: solving a problem versus making a judgement. *Journal of Personality and Social Psychology. 63*, 426–434.

Sternberg, R.J. (Ed.) (1999). *Handbook of Creativity*. New York: Cambridge University Press.

Streitz, N. A., Geißler, J., Holmer, T., Konomi, S., Müller-Tomfelde, C., Reischl, W., Rexroth, P., Seitz, P., and Steinmetz, R. (1999). i-LAND: An Interactive Landscape For Creativity And Innovation. In *Proceedings of the CHI'99*. New York: ACM Press. 120–127.

Vandenbosch, B., Fay, S. and Saatçioglu, A. (2001). Where Ideas Come From: A Systemic View Of Inquiry. *Sprouts: Working Papers on Information Environments, Systems and Organizations, Vol 1*, Issue 2 (Fall). 109–131.

Wessner, M., Shumar, W., Stahl, G., Sarmiento, J., Mühlpfordt, M., and Weimar, S. (2006). Designing an online service for a math community. *Proceedings of the 7th international Conference on Learning Sciences* (Bloomington, Indiana, June 27 to July 01, 2006). International Society of the Learning Sciences. 818–824.reference to be inserted:

Wittenbaum, G. M., Hollingshead, A. & Botero, I. (2004). From Cooperative to Motivated Information Sharing in Groups: Moving Beyond the Hidden Profile Paradigm. *Communication Monographs, Vol. 71*, Issue 3, September 2004. 286–310

Chapter 5
Designing for Collective Interaction: Toward Desirable Spaces in Homes and Libraries

Peter Gall Krogh and Marianne Graves Petersen

5.1 Introduction

Collective interaction happens often in everyday life, e.g., when two people coordinate their actions to carry a heavy object together; when children share a keyboard playing a PC-game together, e.g., one controlling a character, another his weapons; or when, for safety reasons, it is required that there are two people working together when dealing with nuclear explosives. For a number of years we have researched in collaborative systems for libraries, museums, and homes and as such we are part of the move of CSCW systems out of the workplace and into new domains investigating the characteristics of these domains and how to design them. What is striking in all domains is that despite the huge potential in supporting interaction between colocated people, most systems are designed for individuals or for connecting people who are not colocated:

> New technologies have been used increasingly within museums and galleries, both as interpretation devices and as interactive exhibits. At the same time, among museum professionals, there is growing recognition of work in cultural psychology concerned with the relevance of social interaction for learning. Whilst these ideas are recognised and respected, technologies for museum visitors continue to be designed predominantly for a lone user in isolation; they are rarely designed to support opportunities for interaction between visitors to an exhibition (Hindus 2001: 2).

Our own research has illustrated how libraries throughout the world have done tremendous efforts in making their services available over the Internet, which in many cases has resulted in decreasing number of visitors in the physical library. As a consequence, the social space in the physical library has taken a turn toward a supermarket-like atmosphere. Interviews with library visitors and librarians suggest that this is a result of serving the individual user rather than providing a space for

P.G. Krogh (✉)
Alexandra Institute, Århus, Denmark
e-mail: peter.krogh@alexandra.dk

M.G. Petersen
Aarhus University, Denmark

D. Randall and P. Salembier (eds.), *From CSCW to Web 2.0: European Developments in Collaborative Design*, Computer Supported Cooperative Work, DOI 10.1007/978-1-84882-965-7_5, © Springer-Verlag London Limited 2010

social gatherings, activities, and public awareness (Ludvigsen 2005). In line with the work presented here, Hindmarsh et al. (2005) also identify the potential in designing to encourage interaction between people as a largely overlooked issue in current interactive systems. Similarly, homes are very often places where people live together, and research has documented that, "in homes, people are concerned first and foremost with other household members, followed by family members outside of the household and then, less importantly, friends and other relationships such as those of shared interest groups" (Hindus 2001: 327).

Despite this, when looking at systems developed for the home domain there has been a strong interest in connecting individuals, who live apart, e.g., supporting people in "virtually living together" (Wadley et al. 2003) or supporting "the feeling of being together" (Sharp et al. 2006) rather than developing engaging settings for people who are actually colocated (Petersen and Grønbæk 2004).

As argued by Dunne (1999), technology is never neutral; that is a matter of design. "Paradoxically, user-centeredness is not just figuring out how people map things, it absolutely requires recognizing that the artifacts people interact with have enormous impact on how we think. Affordances, to use Norman's term, are individually, socially and culturally dynamic. But the artefacts do not merely occupy a slot in that process, they fundamentally shape the dynamic itself" (Dunne 1999, p. 32). As argued above we find from our research into the domains of home, libraries, and museums that there is a largely unexplored design space around collective interaction, and this is a problem since the artifacts shape our way of thinking and being and many of our current IT platforms are unsuitable for sustainable social situations of colocated people. Laptops and PCs have moved much of our work away from the physical visible surroundings creating demand for a multitude of awareness technologies. Mobile phones have taught us to call people rather than places – parents no longer have the type of awareness of children's contacts and friends they once had as calling the household has become less common and is replaced by calling the child itself. Mp3-players (and the walkman before that) have enabled and fostered mobile playing, storing, and cataloging of music.

What we would like to propose, framed by the concept of collective interaction, is a shift of interest from "what it is that I/you want?" to "what desirable place or situation are we forming together?" A source of inspiration in thinking about and designing desirable spaces is the tradition of architecture and design. We have earlier drawn upon architecture in investigating the inherent sociality of architectural concepts such as streets and plazas when designing interactive floors for colocated people (Ruyter and Aarts 2004). Contrary to the individualized orientation of the most current technology platforms, architecture has a long history of shaping social situations through shaping the form and atmosphere of the physical environment. As can be seen from the cases we present in the following, this has been a source of inspiration in our development of the concept of collective interaction.

Our focus on instrumentalizing collaboration is well in line with an emerging interest in co-experience, which are shared and cocreated user experience (Hindmarsh et al. 2005), whereas Forlizzi and Batterbee (2004) for instance analyze co-experience in situations that are not restricted to colocated situations. Moreover, in their research they do not take a design-oriented perspective, focusing merely on how designs per se support co-experience. We are inspired by their notion of co-experience and we share the criticism they further in challenging the individualistic perspective often adopted in the whole experience agenda. Our work represents a design-oriented approach to co-experience, in that we see collective interaction as an approach to designing for co-experience. We restrict the discussion here to situations where people are colocated.

Triggered by the motivations discussed above, we have developed a number of interactive systems exploring new ways of developing engaging settings for people who are colocated in libraries and homes. This has been a process, which has lasted a number of years and has influenced a number of research projects. The concept of collective interaction has developed from this process starting out with an overall concern for the missing focus on designing engaging spaces for colocated people to become gradually more refined into an interaction model, which directly informed the development of new concepts and prototypes. Thus we have developed the concept of Collective Interaction and designed a set of prototypes based on this concept in the domains of libraries and homes.

Based on our experiences with the prototypes we suggest that the interaction model can be a vehicle and an attractive path into designing for playful activities in domains beyond gaming. The model of Collective Interaction offers an alternative approach to be explored when designing technologies in situations of colocated people. It is the result of exploring what connects these people, how might IT facilitate people being together? As discussed above, few interactive systems are designed to support collective interaction, in the sense we propose it here.

What we offer in this paper is an interface model, which can serve as an instrument in designing for collective experiences, and some example concepts, which can provoke ways of thinking about Collective User Interfaces. We start out by presenting the model of Collective Interaction, building upon an earlier interaction model for shared group displays (Tollmar et al. 2000), but depicting a closer collaboration model than this model depicts. We outline related research and related design concepts and prototypes. Next we describe two cases of designing for the proposed interaction model. We outline the design rationales behind the prototypes, discuss and reflect upon use experiences from their applications in real-life contexts. Based on these experiences we discuss the qualities of collective interaction. We discuss pros and cons of Collective User Interfaces, and put this model in a wider perspective discussing its relation to architecture. We propose that the field of architecture has a lot to offer in the direction of development of future exemplar collective interaction systems. We discuss potential application areas before we conclude and point to future work.

5.2 Collective Interaction

Collective Interaction takes departure in colocated users negotiating a shared goal for the interaction and sharing the interaction mechanisms for achieving the goal. Collective Interaction is a matter of instrumentalizing collaboration such that the actual, physical interaction with one application involves collocated cooperation. Collective Interaction does not imply an ideal of efficiency, but rather an ideal of extended sociality beyond the actual interactive system, sociality by the system rather than through the system. Apart from the obvious seriousness in safety systems Collective Interaction exhibits playful aspects that facilitate communication among colocated people beyond what can be experienced in game-like environments.

Single-display groupware (SDG) (Tollmar et al. 2000) has been proposed as an interaction model, focusing on designing to support collaborative work among collocated people. In the SDG model, each user has a separate input channel, and all users share an output channel. Stewart et al. (1999) define input and output channels as channels that provide logically independent input to the computer and output to the users. They focus on keyboard and mouse in combination as one logical input device and output in the form of a display. In SDGs, users may independently provide input to a system, whereas in our model of Collective Interaction, we propose a closer collaboration model than the SDG depicts. SDGs and Collective Interaction can be seen as two strands within the overarching concept of Sharable Interfaces (Stewart et al. 1999). Collective Interaction, as defined here is when users share not only the output channel but also the input channel. We define Collective Interaction in the following way: Collective Interaction is when multiple and collocated users share both one logical input channel and one logical output channel. The input channel may consist of a number of interaction instruments, which are logically coupled in the interaction. Thus Collective Interaction requires more than one user for controlling and taking full advantage of the system. Through their interaction and negotiation, the users must actively coordinate their actions toward a shared goal (Fig. 5.1).

The purpose of a collective interaction system is to provide means for people to negotiate a shared goal. The actual use of the system can either be to achieve the goal or tease one another by working against and prohibiting the achievement of the goal.

We can further draw upon Bardram's use of activity theory (Bardram 1998) to illustrate the difference between the SDG interaction model and the cooperative interaction model. Based on activity theory Bardram identifies a three-level hierarchical

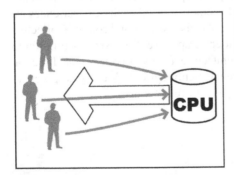 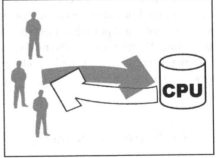

Fig. 5.1 *Left*: Single-display groupware interaction model [0]: colocated people have each their independent input channel and share one logical output channel. *Right*: Collective User Interfaces model: colocated people share one logical input channel and one logical output channel

structure of a collaborative activity and uses these levels to distinguish between different forms of distributed collaboration in work situations. The three levels are coordinated, cooperative, and co-constructive levels of activity.

Coordinated activity is when "[individuals] are gathered together to act upon a common object, but their individual actions are only externally related to each other. They still act as if separate individuals, each according to his individual task" (Engeström quoted in Bardram (1998)).

Cooperation is a mode of interaction in which the actors focus on a common object and thus share the objective of the collective activity, instead of each focusing on performing their assigned actions and roles. "The important difference between coordinated and cooperative work is the common objective, which enables the participants in the distributed activity to relate to each other and make corrective adjustment to own and other's actions according to the overall objective of the collective activity" (Bardram 1998).

The third level is co-constructive activity. This kind of collaborate activity is more radical, and rare in the daily flow of work-activities. It implies reconceptualizing both organization and interaction in relation to people's shared objects.

For our purpose here, we apply Bardram's level of cooperation to denote the cooperation around the shared objective. We are not suggesting, that there is a one-to-one correspondence between level of collaboration and interaction model. Level of collaboration can only be studied in concrete situations, and in the case where people for the first time select and experimentally adopt a system based on the cooperative interaction model, they may be collaborating on a co-constructive level, even though it is a SDG-based system. However, we do suggest that inherently, the SDG interaction model lends itself toward coordinate interaction (where people have different foci and different goals) whereas the Collective Interaction model necessarily implies some kind of negotiation of a shared goal, as the interaction itself involves negotiating the physical actions of different people. Thus by nature, the SDG interaction model lends itself more toward coordination, and the Collective Interaction model toward Bardram's cooperative level. This is exemplified in recent research, which has investigated means for avoiding interference between users of SDGs (Winther 2006). On the contrary, the intention behind Collective Interaction is to establish means for bringing people together and to let them establish common goals or engage in playful activities, which necessarily involve interfering with one another.

To sum up the key characteristics of Collective Interaction:

1. Collective Interaction involves users actively collaborating and negotiating their concrete interaction.
2. Collaboration is instrumentalized.
3. The interaction itself invites for human–human interaction beyond what is in the interface – potentially deviating discussions from what is displayed.
4. The spatial organization of people induces expectations of use and contributes to the active collaboration.
5. A shared goal is established on the basis of sharing responsibility and negotiating control and contribution of interaction.

6. Establishing shared goal through negotiation is essential both in order to achieve it and in order to challenge and thereby tease other participants.
7. The interaction may be asymmetrical, in the sense people take on different roles, but the efforts of all participating are accounted for and valued in the use of the system.

Obviously the application of Collective Interaction has its limitations, and as we discuss later, there are both advantages and disadvantages to such a model.

5.3   Related Work

In the following, we outline how our work is a design-oriented approach to shaping experience in colocated social contexts, and how this is well in line with a demand for looking into social experiences, which has been raised in the experience design area. Further, our work complements emerging design concepts addressing such experiences.

5.3.1   Co-Experience and Cooperation

Forlizzi and Battarbee have proposed co-experience partly as a criticism of the highly individualistic approach to experience design (Forlizzi and Batterbee 2004). They offer a framework for understanding different types of experiences in relation to the design of interactive systems. In their framework, co-experience is one type of experience, namely user experience in social contexts (Forlizzi and Batterbee 2004). They further argue that interactive technology can play an important role in supporting co-experience. We sympathize with this approach and their focus on how technologies per se can support co-experiences, but our interest is to investigate how we can design technologies that *invite* co-experience by their design. Our thesis is that Collective Interaction is one means among others in this direction.

Ludvigsen (Ludvigsen 2005) also introduces a framework of interaction in social situations. He suggests this framework as providing a scale of engagement ranging from at the lowest level "distributed attention" where the only thing shared is the presence in the space, virtual or physical. "Shared focus" is where the situation develops a single focus shared among its participants. "Dialogue" in turn is where people invest themselves and their opinions in a dialogue visible to all participants. Finally, "collective action" is the socially most engaging interaction. This is where participants are working collaboratively toward a shared goal. Ludvigsen (2005) argues that such collective experiences are often remarkable experiences, which stand out and are remembered. In line with Forlizzi and Batterbee (2004), Ludvigsen makes no distinction between collocated social experiences and social experiences that are mediated by digital or virtual spaces. In our research we focus on colocated users and we find the frameworks operational in qualifying the type of experiences we aim to design for, namely co-experiences or in Ludvigsen's terms collective actions, but in our case, in colocated situations.

5.3.2 Related Design Concepts

In the physical world, we see a number of examples of collective interaction. In its simplest, physical form collective interaction can be found in, e.g., the seesaw at children's playgrounds. Participants establish level of agreement in terms of how rough the game is to be played, but knowing the impact of and from the system on one's own body also gives the opportunity to tease the other, e.g., by leaning backwards and while down causing the other to "sit and dry" up in the air; teasing in this case is challenging the idea of a shared goal. Interaction is negotiated and encouraged by the participants. In this way, working with or against one another, the seesaw becomes a tool to understand and practice collaboration; collaboration is instrumentalized.

There are only a few examples where interactive systems intentionally have been designed to be collective according to our Collective Interaction model. Efforts around Computer Supported Cooperative Play (CSCP) (see Böhme 1995; Krogh et al. 2004) share with our work the interest in supporting collective, and playful activities. However, much of this research focuses on collaboration in virtual environments and not on supporting play among physically colocated users. The PingPongPlus game (Ishii et al. 1999), however, is an interesting example of a collective user interface according to the above definition. This work resulted in a table for table tennis reactive using microphones, making it possible to display graphic patterns on the table in response to the balls trajectory and contact points. Here the logical input channel consists of the collection of microphones added to the table and the output channel consists of a video projector displaying the patterns onto the table. Such an application is also a collective interface in the definition we provided above. In our research, we complement this work through focusing on how more playful activities and co-experiences can be made part of other areas than classic sport activities.

Pervasive games (Petersen 2007) are also interesting because they address the issue of co-experiences. One example is mixed reality game. Here the focus is on supporting playful activities, but in these games a mix of virtual and physical communities constitute the forum for play. There are potentially further examples of collective interfaces in the area of Smart toys. For example, Zowie Playsets consisting of a physical toy with movable pieces, which are connected to a PC. Again this example is in classic play activities and the mission of this paper is to complement this research through broadening the domain in which co-experiences can be supported by technology design.

An example close to one of our own examples is Strömberg et al. (2002) who designed Nautilus, which is an interactive group game where a group of 3–6 players act as the crew of a diving bell and are sent on a mission to rescue a dolphin.

The players stand in front of a wall display depicting the underwater world. The players control the diving bell with their body movements on the floor. For example, moving to the sides results in turning to the sides, moving back and forth results in slowing or speeding up. The floor is augmented with pressure sensors to track their movements. The players can, by means of camera detection, raise the bell through rapid up and down arm movements. From an architectural perspective the set-up resembles some of the work in Petersen et al. (2005) where streets and plazas are used to identify types of use and orientation in terms of designing interactive floors, where streets provide the basis of uniform direction of attention and plazas create a cross-field for meeting and greeting.

5.4 Design Cases

In our realization of the model of Collective User Interfaces the installations are designed and structured in such a manner that they create a sensory cross-field much in line with how tables and plazas architectonically organize people as described above. In the following, we present two selected concepts from our research projects to illustrate the model of Collective User Interfaces and the design constrains it imposes on prototypes, products and choices of technology, and physicality. Both the concepts are concrete instances of collective user interfaces. They require more than one user for the practical interaction in order to take full advantage of the system, and they illustrate how users, through coordinating their actions, can operate on a shared object.

The concepts and prototypes include:

1. iFloor: an interactive floor for a library
2. Squeeze: an interactive sack-chair enabling playful engagement with digital photos in the home

5.4.1   iFloor

The intention with iFloor is to pursue a richer social environment facilitating visitors in a library in contacting one another and raise awareness that apart from librarians, other library visitors can be knowledge resources too. According to this we chose the floor as display surface in order to make it as generally accessible and sharable as possible and pursued an interaction model that is inadequate for single use and encourages contact with other colocated visitors and the involvement of several people in interacting with the installation.

The design response was an interactive Q/A floor (Fig. 5.1), with the intention to bring visitors in the library together and spurring conversation and fruitful happenstance encounters. The Q/As are pushed to the floor using individual mobile phones or email clients, and are displayed in the floor interface in an extending circular pattern pivoting on the center of the display to avoid creating a privileged viewpoint and rather making any viewing direction possible (see Fig. 5.3). For interacting with the floor and navigating between the various messages sent to the floor, visitors collectively move *one cursor*. In order to hit an area of interest on the floor, people need to coordinate their body movements around the floor. When the prototype is attempted to be operated by a single user the cursor will be attracted to the rim of the display and thereby give no chance for exploring the whole interface, whereas if two or more persons are collaborating on moving the shared cursor the different direction and strength in attracting forces is calculated into a middle-value allowing the whole interface to be explored (Fig. 5.2).

Tiny graphic strings in the interface connected the people's position at the rim of the display and the cursor providing a clue of connection and control. As the cursor rolls over Q/As in the interface, the messages enlarge and comments to questions are revealed along with a tool-tip box informing people how to ask and respond to questions. On the basis of this people negotiated where to move in order to move the cursor to a shared goal.

The floor was installed over a 3-week period in a public library setting. In the qualitative evaluation of the prototype, we found that the iFloor promoted a sort of "step stone wonder and learn process" as follows: the interface of the floor would react as soon as someone entered the tracking area surrounding the floor, the movement

Fig. 5.2 iFloor in a library context

of the cursor would attract people's attention causing one to stop and start exploring what it might be. With one person using the floor, others were attracted and soon discussions started to evolve around what the installation might be for and how it could be controlled. Furthermore, the floor display and the organization of people around the display supported quick and easy shifts between human–computer interaction and human–human interaction as one could gaze to acknowledge and chat with participants without losing contact and view of the interface in the periphery.

The prototype combines the interaction model of SDG in terms of how the content is sent to the floor, namely by using individual input channels in relation (mobile phones and email clients) to a shared output channel whereas the instrumentalization of collaboration is apparent in the interaction with the content displayed on the floor and how it is navigated by the use of one shared cursor.

5.4.2 Squeeze

The motivation behind Squeeze is to create playful means of constructing and experiencing the immediate conception and as time pass the history of a home. Squeeze consists of a house-camera and an oversized and interactive sack-chair (Fig. 5.2), which is a site for collective and playful exploration of the history of the home as captured through the pictures taken with the house-camera. An image captured by the house-camera is automatically put on display on a wall close to the "chair." When people sit/hang out/mock about in the furniture, the pictures can be explored in different ways. As explained in the following, the Collective Interaction model has guided the interaction design (Fig. 5.3).

First the whole furniture reacts on deformation through displaying more pictures at a time, as, e.g., in Fig. 5.3 where four pictures are displayed at a time. The more activity on different places of the furniture, i.e., the more people in the furniture the more pictures displayed. This is enabled by Piezo cable, which is wrapped around the furniture. The means of moving back and forth in time consists of two active zones positioned at each end of the 6 m long and malleable furniture. Thus to navigate the pictures, the participating people need to negotiate the navigation between them, potentially verbally but also to manifest it in their collective interaction with the furniture. Moreover, also in each end of the furniture, another active zone allows users to stretch and rotate the pictures through squeezing the furniture. Through distributing the controls over the larger-than-one-person surface of the furniture, users need to cooperate in the detailed physical interaction with the pictures.

Squeeze has been put on trial use in three families. The focus of the evaluation was to observe how the key characteristics of Collective Interaction might play out in the immediate use. Making the whole furniture sensitive to activity and thus to showing more pictures at a time invited, in particular the children (between 2 and 9), to act actively and cooperatively this as a shared goal. The families shifted a lot between interacting to get new and more pictures put on display and storytelling and pointing engaging with the contents of the pictures and notably each other. Due to the flexible

Fig. 5.3 The "chair" and displays of pictures on the wall investigated through collective interaction

nature of the furniture it was easy to shift positions and to face both the contents on the wall and other family members.

In general the families were intrigued by the active and embodied interaction with the pictures provided by the prototype. The distribution of controls throughout the furniture engaged all the family members to contribute to the interaction and control. However, the means for navigating back and forth, stretching, and rotating were at times also frustrating. At times it was troublesome for users to know who was navigating one way and who was navigating the other way. At this stage we hypothesize that it would have been easier to establish the kind of playful aspect, if the effect of the individual's interaction would be clear to all participants and thus easier to cooperate and negotiate on.

The Squeeze prototype combines the interaction model of SDG in terms of how pictures are taken in the home, namely by using an individual input channel (the in-house camera) in relation to a shared output channel whereas the instrumentalization of collaboration is apparent in the interaction with the sack-chair manipulating the images displayed on the wall.

5.5   Qualities of Collective Interaction

The two concepts presented illustrate how Collective Interfaces does not only provide means for exploring digital contents in interactive environments, the interface also potentially invites communication between the participants as the interaction is constantly negotiated. This means that designing collective interfaces is not only directed at providing explorative access to specific digital resources. It is also aimed at facilitating people in becoming aware of issues beyond the use of the computer, through directing attention toward other colocated people and creating a shared forum for their engagement. Thus, one of the key qualities of Collective User Interfaces is the potential for them to allow for gradual shifts between human–computer interaction and human–human interaction and thus for creating settings that bring colocated people together.

The concepts presented above suggest that interactive systems most often consist of a number of interface models and that Collective User Interfaces are rare in their pure form. Both of the prototypes presented in the above combine the interaction model of SDG for providing input to the system and Collective Interaction for navigating the content. In the Squeeze case the combination works well whereas the use of mobile phones for providing input in the iFloor case is regarded as cumbersome. At this point we hypothesize that though the concepts involve users shifting between interaction models it is not the shifting that is the primary cause of breakdown. We see it as an issue of designing a coherent level of accessibility and anticipated use efforts across the models concerned. Where the iFloor prototype is immediately and effortlessly accessible for navigation, the Squeeze prototype demands intense physical activity. New content in Squeeze is simply produced by picking up the house-camera and capturing an image, whereas sending input to the iFloor causes the user to step out of the interaction loop around the floor and concentrate on punching in and sending a text message. Normally sending text messages is considered easy, but in combination and comparison with the effortless access to the floor it was experienced too cumbersome. This indicates that when designing interactive systems involving two or more interaction models the level of anticipated user efforts and accessibility in interaction should be considered carefully in a holistic view of the total system.

Combining different interaction models makes it possible to outweigh the intended advantage of the specific model against the intended characteristics of the situation we are designing for. The advantage of Collective Interaction consists primarily of the potential in shaping co-experiences, and in bringing people together in new ways, opening up for embracing more ludic opportunities and embedding these in everyday life (Gaver 2002). Instead of offering an efficient way of exploring materials, the interaction model provides means of negotiating interests and supporting serendipitous and playful navigation. The disadvantage of this model of interaction is of course that it is potentially inefficient and imprecise.

Collective Interaction encourages people in establishing a shared goal of interaction. As indicated in the cases, cooperating on a shared goal also provides room for individuals to break the rules, teasing and preventing others from reaching the goal.

However, both for teasing and collaboration, shared awareness of controls and what they do are criteria of success. The prototypes of iFloor and Squeeze encourage sharing responsibility, both on the level that any participant is needed, affects the system, and in the sense that all should be willing to react upon request of others in terms of doing specific actions to achieve a shared goal or the goal defined by one of the participants; thus in this way the systems instrumentalize interaction.

Moreover, the concepts illustrate the potential of this interface model in supporting more playful access to materials. It directs the attention of the users from solely focusing on accessing the contents of the system to explore how to evoke the materials, how to make it easy or hard for others to access them, thereby creating a means for teasing one another. That is, the model becomes an instrument to design for homo ludens.

In terms of aesthetic experience the concept of Collective User Interfaces also ties up to the ideals and conditions for Aesthetic Interaction (Petersen et al. 2004). As indicated in the concept of Squeeze prototype Collective User Interfaces implies the possibility for providing new relations to the displayed digital material and in this way potentially shape aesthetic experiences around the material. The physical arrangement of people and the actions taking place on Squeeze body is designed to provide an intimate setting for browsing multimedia content potentially flavoring the perception and thereby providing the basis for a renewed relationship to the displayed material.

As the concepts illustrate, the possibilities to embed sensor and actuator tech nologies in the physical environment and in this way design interactive spaces and furniture, open up for new challenges and possibilities to design for shared experiences among collocated people. It supports collective exploration of the materials instead of having co-experiences through in turn watching others being active. iFloor and Squeeze both exemplify how these large-scale interactive surfaces hold a rich potential for designing for collective interaction and co-experiences. The large scale and the distinct physical qualities, combined and augmented with digital qualities, point to the potential in learning from physical design and architecture.

A critical issue in shaping co-experiences is to determine how users collaborate physically and virtually to create shared emotions and experiences. The above concepts point to some interesting issues in particular around the physical collaboration. Comparing the cases illustrates that there is a need to consider the intended physical configuration extremely carefully, and ground the design in the characteristics of the specific context. That is, squeeze is designed for a home context; people sit rather closely, almost intimately closely, which would not be appropriate amongst strangers meeting in a public library. However, in the home, this may be a welcome opportunity for more intimate situations in an otherwise distributed and hectic life.

The concepts presented are in physical terms large interactive systems providing physical room for several participants. IT systems consciously designed for Collective Interaction take in spatial considerations as they facilitate several collocated people to interact simultaneously. Architecture is not primarily concerned with the individual user, but with how spaces and places facilitate collective use. Collective Interaction shares characteristics and qualities with architecture and interior design as these disciplines too provide frames and settings for people's social life; promotes and invites for various ways of being, playing, and working together, as McCullough (2005) argues: "*Architecture serves the body not just the gaze. It is not just perceived it is inhabited.*" Collective Interaction may potentially be a shared design subject between the traditions of human–computer interaction and architecture as it draws extensively on the design knowledge from both traditions. However, more work is needed to determine the applicability of the interface model in larger contexts such as city plazas; what design challenges, constraints, and possibilities will emerge if a range of Collective Interaction interfaces were deployed as the primary model of interaction for, e.g., an exhibition?

In a sense, architecture can be considered the oldest tradition for designing "collective interfaces." In architecture rooms and buildings are made to nurture specific social relations whether that is office design, interiors of bars, or classrooms. Architecture, when successful, makes people aware and appreciative toward societal values as well as guide behavior based on cultural conventions. Cultural conventions are what in McCullough's work is denoted "embodied predispositions." This notion is much in parallel with Dourish' (2001) notion of "embodied interaction," promoting that physical and social aspects along with our cognitive background is what shapes human abilities and the perceived context.

In the library setting of the iFloor people potentially become aware of each other as resources of knowledge, nurturing the conception that it is not only the librarians one can benefit from asking in the library but also the other visitors. In exhibiting such qualities a Collective Interface can be regarded as an architectural element, in the sense that it stages a social setting, provides the background, and invites people to meet tuned by the content and the qualities accessible through the interface.

Supporting or challenging people through design are typically not an either/or but rather a both/and. However, while much CHI design has favored the support of current practices, the approach promoted here leans toward challenging habits and thereby nurturing increased consciousness and appreciation of serendipitous encounters, everyday practices, and values.

5.6   Potential Application Areas

As suggested above, Collective User Interfaces are useful for some purposes and futile for others. Based on our experiences with the application of Collective Interaction, we hypothesize a range of potential application areas for Collective User Interfaces and propose these for promising areas of future applications of Collective Interaction.

5.6.1   Games and Sport

We have already seen how Collective User Interfaces are emerging within games and sport activities [0], and due to the potential of shaping engaging and playful activities among colocated people we expect to see more concepts in these domains.

5.6.2   Homes

As discussed in the motivation, homes are often places where several people who care for one another are colocated, and there seems to be a lack of design concepts taking advantage of this situation. Recent advances around interactive tables [0, 0] are a promising direction in this respect, and with the design of Squeeze we are trying to suggest other ways of embedding technology into playful, collective settings targeted for the home. Hopefully, the Collective User Interfaces model can serve as a driver for more developments in this direction.

5.6.3   Teambuilding and Multidisciplinary Design Teams

Activities where people need to collaborate toward common goals and get to know one another across disciplinary boundaries seem to be an interesting potential application area of Collective User Interfaces.

5.6.4   Training and Learning

Training and learning activities seems to be another domain in which the negotiation and shared forum of Collective User Interfaces seems to be applicable. In fact, in the evaluation of the iFloor prototype [0], a group of student teachers had an idea of using it as a means of teaching because of its synergetic effect between play and serious content. This idea is currently taken up in the development of the iFloor concept for the school domain, which has resulted in the further development of the floor.

5.6.5   Public Libraries, Museums, Theme Parks, etc.

We have already seen a few examples of the application of Collective User Interfaces in the domains of museums, e.g., ifloor [0] and Nautilus [0]. Again the opportunity to bring people together in collective exploration of materials and collective activities makes this potentially an interesting interface model in these environments.

5.6.6   Safety Critical Systems

A more special application of Collective User Interfaces is for controlling safety critical systems, e.g., where the negotiation is needed due to security reasons and not qualities of serendipity and learning, etc., for instance, when two people must each press their button simultaneously, in order to launch a missile.

5.7 Conclusion and Perspectives on Future Work

Provoked by current trends in technology development and grounded in design cases, we have pointed to the prospects of designing for social experiences amongst colocated people. We have coined a model of Collective Interaction to complement previous work and we have suggested this as a concrete vehicle in designing for social experiences, and we put this model in perspective with respect to experience frameworks and architecture.

Through providing examples of Collective Interaction concepts for the home and a library context we suggest that this model can encourage interaction design for social experiences in domains and situations that benefit from playful approaches. In particular, the instrumentalization of cooperation shows promise in learning environments such as schools and museums where collaboration and human–human interaction is required if not mandatory for accessing and understanding complex concepts consisting of intertwined entities reacting upon one another. Finally, we suggest that the discipline of architecture has much to offer, when designing for collective interaction and atmospheres for collaboration, as architecture provides a long tradition for spatially arranging and encouraging social settings.

Collective User Interfaces may potentially be a shared design subject between the traditions of CHI and architecture as it draws extensively on the design knowledge from both traditions. However, more work is needed to determine the applicability of the interface model in larger contexts such as city plazas; what design challenges, constraints, and possibilities will emerge if a range of Collective User Interfaces were deployed as the primary model of interaction for, e.g., an exhibition? And further, much can be learned through looking in more detail at how the tradition of architecture can contribute to developing future collective user interfaces.

We recognize that Collective User Interfaces rarely will be stand-alone installations. We identify SDG as a neighboring model of interaction, and further investigations into how other user interfaces models may complement Collective User Interfaces are needed. In terms of interaction modalities the examples promoted here are all based on bodily interaction and visual display forms. It will be interesting to explore further what other modalities might be applicable within this model. Also more exemplar concepts and mechanisms for negotiating interaction will contribute to further establish and qualify the model. Finally, further exploration and evaluation of the interface model in different domains will contribute to qualify its strengths and weaknesses beyond what we have achieved based on our limited number of cases and evaluations.

References

Bardram, J. E. (1998). *Collaboration, Coordination, and Computer Support: An Activity Theoretical Approach to the Design of Computer Supported Cooperative Work*. Ph.D. Thesis, Daimi PB-533.Aarhus: Aarhus University.

Böhme, Gernot (1995): *Atmosphere. Essays zur ein neuen Ästhetik*. Frankfurt a. M: Suhrkamp Verlag.

Dourish, P. (2001). *Where The Action Is: The Foundations of Embodied Interaction*. MIT Press

Dunne, A. (1999) *Hertzian Tales*. RCA Press.

Forlizzi, J., and Batterbee, K. (2004) Understanding Experience in Interactive Systems. *In Proceedings of DIS 2004*. ACM Press. pp261–268.

Gaver, W. (2002) Designing for Homo Ludens. *i3 Magazine*. June. pp 2–5.

Hindmarsh J., Heath C., Vom Lehn D. and Cleverly J. (2005) Creating Assemblies in Public Environments: Social Interaction. *Interactive Exhibits and CSCW. Computer Supported Cooperative Work '05*.

Hindus (2001). Casablanca: designing social communication devices for the home. *Proceedings of the SIGCHI conference on Human factors in computing systems*. Seattle, Washington, United States. pp325–332.

Ishii, H., Wisneski, C., Orbanes, J., Chun, B., and Paradiso, J. (1999) PingPongPlus: Design of an Athletic-Tangible Interface for Computer-Supported Cooperative Play. In *Proceedings of CHI 1999*. ACM Press.

Krogh, P.G., Ludvigsen, M. and Lykke-Olesen, A. (2004). "Help me pull that cursor" – A Collaborative Interactive Floor Enhancing Community Interaction. In *Proceedings of OZCHI 2004*, 22–24 November. University of Wollongong, Australia. CD-ROM. ISBN:1 74128 079.

Ludvigsen, M. (2005) Designing for Social Use in Public Places – a Conceptual Framework of Social Interaction. In *Proceedings of Designing Pleasurable Products and Interfaces. DPPI 05*. pp389–408.

McCullough, M. (2005). *Digital Ground*. MIT Press, Cambridge, Massachusetts, USA.

Petersen, M. G. (2007). Squeeze: designing for playful experiences among co-located people in homes. In *CHI '07 Extended Abstracts on Human Factors In Computing Systems* (San Jose, CA, USA, April 28 – May 03, 2007). CHI '07. ACM Press. pp 2609–2614.

Petersen, M. G., Krogh, P., Ludvigsen, M., and Lykke-Olesen, A. (2005) Floor interaction: HCI reaching new ground. *Proceedings of CHI 2005*. Portland, Oregon, USA.

Petersen, M. G., and Grønbæk, K. (2004). *Interactive Spaces: Towards Collaborative Structuring and Ubiquitous Presentation in Domestic Environments. In Proceedings of OZCHI*, Nov. 2004 Wollongong, Australia. CD-ROM. ISBN:1 74128 079.

Petersen, M.G., Iversen, O., Krogh, P. and Ludvigsen, M. (2004). Aesthetic Interaction – A pragmatic aesthetics of interactive systems. In *Proceedings of ACM DIS2004*.

Ruyter, B. de, and Aarts, E. (2004). Ambient Intelligence: Visualizing the future. In *Proceedings of AVI*, ACM Press. pp 203–208

Sharp, H., Rogers, Y. and Preece, J. (2006). Interaction Design: beyond human-computer interaction. 2nd edition. John Wiley & sons

Stewart, J., Bederson, B. B., and Druin, A. (1999) Single Display Groupware: A Model for Co-present Collaboration. In *Proceedings of CHI 1999*. ACM Press. pp 286–293.

Strömberg, H., Väätänen, A., Räty, V. (2002) A group game played in interactive virtual space. Design and Evaluation. In *Proceedings of DIS 2002*, ACM Press, pp 56–63.

Tollmar, K., Junestrand, S., and Torgny, O. (2000) Virtually Living Together. In *Proceedings of DIS'2000*. ACM Press, pp. 83–91

Wadley, G., Gibbs, M., Hew, K., Graham, C. (2003) Computer Supported Cooperative Play, "Third Places" and Online Videogames. In Viller, S., Wyeth, P. (Eds.) *Proceedings of OZCHI 2003*, pp. 238–241.

Winther, I. W. (2006) To home oneself. (Hjemlighed) Danish Paedagogical University Press.

Chapter 6
Between Casual Commitment and Cross-Media Articulation: The Faith of the Napkin

Susanne Bødker and Anja Bechmann Petersen

6.1 Situating the Study of the Napkin

Since the mid-1990s, newspaper companies have faced dramatic challenges due to stagnation or decline in the consumption of traditional media (12), new types of production technology, and new types of products. At present, media companies worldwide struggle with a new challenge called cross-media production: the integrated production of news stories to multiple media platforms (paper, TV, radio, etc.) (13). Digital materials make it possible to produce content for several different media platforms, and the different strengths of the media further support new forms of news coverage that cross these platforms. The very recent explosion of blogs and video podcasting are new examples adding to the family of products and ideally, the reporters become storytellers who choose the most suitable media for their story. The reality, however, is far more complicated: The Danish media company Nordjyske Medier was a local newspaper that has now diversified and produces daily news for radio, TV, web, a daily newspaper, and several additional products. All production is gathered in one location, where reporters produce news stories to be distributed in the various media. The editorial staff of all media is placed literally in the middle of this location. We carried out an empirical study of cooperation and planning at the media company (1; 5). The company used a production planning system in place, called the Napkin. The Napkin was not used very much, it was heavily criticized by reporters and it was at the point of being replaced by a different planning system, which was better integrated with the production system (11). This system, too, was later abandoned. This has motivated us to understand better the processes of planning and articulating the cross-media production and how information technology supported such cross-media production.

The media company was producing a daily newspaper, news for two radio stations, a 24 h news TV channel, web pages, and additional products such as a free newspaper

S. Bødker (✉) and A.B. Petersen
Aarhus University, Denmark
e-mail: bodker@daimi.au.dk

D. Randall and P. Salembier (eds.), *From CSCW to Web 2.0: European Developments in Collaborative Design*, Computer Supported Cooperative Work, DOI 10.1007/978-1-84882-965-7_6, © Springer-Verlag London Limited 2010

and mobile alerts. The newspaper contained national and international news as well as sections on lifestyle, sports, etc. It had sections for local areas: the city and the districts surrounding it. The newspaper had one daily edition being printed at night. The radio produced hourly local news for the two channels along with longer background news. The TV broadcast its first news production early every morning, and the broadcasts ran as a loop with updates twice before lunch. Individual stories were reedited or replaced, but there was no live anchor person in the studio. The remainder of the day was spent producing 20 min newscasts for the evening. The web editors published available news as they occurred.

Reporters producing news stories were physically and organizationally placed in contents groups. Each group had a group leader coordinating the daily work. A media editor had the responsibility for filling the "space" of each medium, be it newspaper pages or the radio news time slot. The media conductor maintained the general overview and coordinated stories across media platforms (1). Physically, the acting media editors and media conductor were placed in the center of the building, called the Superdesk, which was also the location of the formal meetings of the editorial staff.

The management of the media company had a vision that focused on gaining a larger share of the market through high-quality cross-media stories. Telling stories first, independent of media, producing versions for the different media types afterwards, would enhance quality and quantity of media products while reducing the cost. The media company focused both on providing diversified products to consumers on more media platforms and on new ways of coordinating and dividing work in the organization. We studied the media company, when it was in the midst of a change process aimed at realizing this vision.

This part of the empirical study was carried out mainly in the spring of 2005. It focused on coordination and orchestration of cross-media production, specifically the role of the physical space and work arrangement, organizational roles, and coordinating artifacts.

The study combined interviews, questionnaires, and counting methods with field-note-based observations. These were carried out over a period of 7 months and consisted of full-day observations of activities in various locations, in particular the Superdesk and the location of all contents groups. We followed people responsible for different media (two media conductors, one media editor from each medium, and a couple of group leaders). We carried out 35 qualitative interviews and 43 follow-up questionnaires with journalists and managers. A year later we carried out observational studies of three cases of news coverage: a soccer match, a local news story, and a cross-media event called "fat loss fight" lasting half a year. We followed the journalists that produced the news stories on the soccer match and on the local news story and the production of the cross-media event "fat loss fight" was studied through one observation day, a 2 h in-depth interview with the project manager and internal document registration on the planning and coordination of the project. Furthermore, we tried to register the news products that came out of the production on five different media platforms to see the "result" of the process.

In 1, we focused on the roles of cross-media production, in particular that of the media conductor; in 5 we analyzed the relationships between time rhythms and place; in

(Petersen 2006a) the role of Internet in the cross-media products and work was analyzed; and in (Petersen 2006b) cross-media as strategy for innovation and change is analyzed. The study of the Napkin and related technologies was carried out through a combination of specific qualitative interview questions concerned with how ideas and stories were accounted for and communicated between reporters and editorial staff; focus on the use of the Napkin in the observations in the groups of contents, and when following editorial staff; and a situated demonstration of the Napkin by two daily users.

These activities were documented in interview summaries, verbal field reports, notes and screen dumps. Our analysis methods included qualitative readings of specific interview questions and field notes. In particular we focused on contradictions and tensions between statements, or between what interviewees said and what we had noticed in our observations. In this paper we occasionally use quotes from the material to illustrate the points of the analysis.

6.2   Conceptual Framing of the Analysis

Journalistic work processes and Computer Supported Cooperative Work (CSCW) have been in focus when 2 and 8 described how the daily news production is two-sided: On the one hand, news production is about informing readers about what happens in the world with appropriate timeliness and judgment of importance. On the other hand is the internal production process-oriented side, focusing on the resources at hand and the internal deadlines. The ongoing tension between these two sides (5) was used to focus on internal and external media rhythms, and how they collided with cross-media rhythms.

In an activity as multifaceted as cross-media news production, there is a high degree of division of work, and many rules and procedures to make possible the daily production of newspapers, TV broadcasts, etc., independent of the persons working on a particular day. Though producing the substance for these media products is the primary activity, there is a lot of articulation work going on, secondary activities that it takes to, e.g., divide, allocate, coordinate, schedule, mesh, and interrelate the individual work (16). In some instances, this articulation work is separated out, to have its own purpose; in others, it is integrated with the primary activity. Since the Napkin is an instrument that supports articulation, these classical CSCW definitions help further place its roles in relation to division of work, allocation of jobs, coordination and scheduling of jobs.

The Napkin (Fig. 6.1) was named after the habit of reporters making notes on random materials, e.g., napkins, and was intended for registration of assignments, events, and loose ideas. The idea was to provide the media conductor and the planning meetings with overviews of available ideas and stories, and to help reporters plan and share stories. When a reporter wanted to file an idea in the Napkin, he would either put a particular event into the calendar, e.g., as a reminder of a major sports event, an election, etc.; he would file a "timeless idea," an idea that could be picked up anytime; or he would file a set of deliverables, in which case he also had to

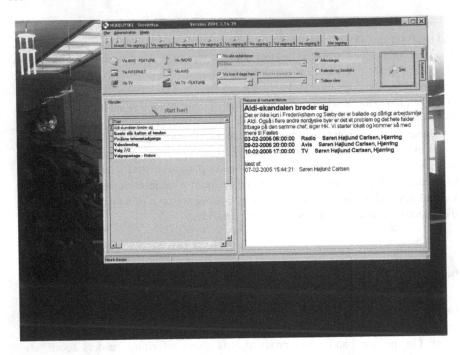

Fig. 6.1 The Napkin

choose which media he planned for and which deadlines. The Napkin allowed the
reporter to retrieve an overview of his own ideas and deliverables. Furthermore,
it was possible for group leaders, media editors, and media conductors to retrieve
overviews of all stories proposed by a particular group, or all stories proposed for
a particular medium on a particular day, or in a particular time period.

Instruments, in the general understanding from activity theory, have a (shared)
externalized form and are more or less well integrated in the daily routines of the
users. Acting subjects use instruments to create an outcome out of materials (3), at
the same time as these or other instruments are used in articulation in terms of
communication among collaborators and of dividing work between the collaborators
who create the full outcome of the activity. In the media company these instruments
exist in a complicated web where it rarely makes sense to look at one at a time.
The Napkin is one of these instruments. In this paper, we are particularly concerned
with instruments of articulation across multiple media production processes. From
our perspective, the production technologies for the various media are the instruments
of the primary activity of producing various media products, whereas the Napkin,
along with the Superdesk (Fig. 6.2), is an instrument of the secondary activities of
articulation work.

This separation matches 2 external and internal side of the production, and the
notion of product and production process-related rhythms that we developed in 5.

Fig. 6.2 Superdesk planning meeting

6.3   The Napkin in Cross-Media Production

Reporters were physically and organizationally placed in content groups. A group leader was coordinating the daily work of the group, and these contents groups can be seen as instruments of dividing work and allocating substance focus at an overall level. Each story was furthermore planned as part of the ongoing production schedule of several media products. The stories had to be completed to fit the deadlines of each particular media. In addition, each story had to arrive at the consumers to cover events, appropriately and timely.

For each media, a media editor was responsible for filling the "space" of the particular media product, such as the newspaper pages or the radio news time slot, by allocating, co-coordinating, scheduling, and meshing the stories. Each media had its own instruments, some more elaborate than others. For example, TV used an application called Newsjoiner to coordinate, schedule, mesh, interrelate, and carry out the production. Newsjoiner integrated the articulation and production of television news, once the stories had been planned for TV.

The media conductor maintained the general overview, coordinated stories and versions for the different media platforms. Planning, coordination, and evaluation of the media products took place through a combination of meetings, the walking and talking of the media conductor, and the plans that got conveyed to the media conductor through the planning system, the Napkin. The Napkin is primarily used for reporters to publish their ideas and plans for the editorial staff to see. While media conductors were walking, media editors stayed in the Superdesk. Here formal meetings of the editorial staff took place, as well as many less formal encounters (5). The daily structure of meetings among the media conductor, the media editors, and the group leaders supplemented the allocation, coordination, scheduling, and meshing work of the media conductor, since the media and the contents got a chance to meet at the meetings.

Collaboration around particular stories and events took many different forms, which are illustrated by our three cases: the soccer match, the budget cutbacks on child care, and the "fat loss fight" event.

The soccer match is played once every week, and a prescheduled news event (17) was very routine-based. New ideas were not discussed at all in this kind of news production. However, there was a standard way of doing soccer production across media, as we shall return to.

The local news story was produced in collaboration between more reporters, as in our instance, one reporter covering newspaper and radio and another reporter covering TV in collaboration with a photographer. This kind of news was less routine-based and predictable. The story evolved into different versions aired first on radio, TV followed up, and newspaper versions were made for the next day. The reporters needed to coordinate among themselves both the news angles and the different media versions.

The larger cross-media event was planned, over a longer period of time for a longer production period. The "fat loss fight" theme was planned half a year in advance and started with an idea from a reporter. It was developed into a carefully planned news series rolled out in all media over half a year. The cross-media news event covered advertisement and trailers for the event (in weekly newspapers, outdoor, trailers, flyers, radio, TV, etc.), preplanned stories (in radio, TV, website, and newspaper), events arranged by the media company in collaboration with the local authorities (weight measuring of contestants, presentations by psychologists, dieticians, athletes, and chefs, competition with prizes), and events organized by others, incorporated in the planning (e.g., running competition). The event was highly dependent on both planning between marketing department and reporters, between media platform versions, and between the media company and external partners.

We return to these three cases and their planning and cooperation needs.

6.4   What Was the Problem with the Napkin?

In the following, we pursue the Napkin and its role in producing and articulating cross-media production. We focus on three tensions reoccurring in many forms in our empirical studies, and we use these tensions to discuss why the Napkin failed its role at the media company, and what it would take to better support the articulation of cross-media production.

6.4.1   Personal Plans and Editorial Overview

Observations and interview statements point out that the Napkin was simply not used, and that there were many more ideas proposed and stories planned among the reporters, than accounted for in the Napkin. Registering a story in the Napkin was not integrated with the actual writing of the story or with other articulation instruments. One reporter, who also acted as media editor, complained: "*I don't use the Napkin. It is no good that things aren't integrated, you need to work in both the Napkin, Word and mail at the same time.*" A second media editor explained how the Napkin simply was not used enough, and how there were too many stories not accounted for in the Napkin.

In the interviews, reporters stated that they regarded the Napkin as extra work without anything in return, except for complaints. The reporters pointed directly to Grudin's dilemma of who does the work and who benefits from it (9). As an alternative to not filing stories in the Napkin, some reporters signed up stories for 1 day later than their actual intended deadline. That way, they would avoid being held accountable for missing a deadline. This is a way of optimizing their own behavior to avoid problems that contrast with what editors need from them to fill the newspaper pages, television slots, etc., and points to another of 9 dilemmas, the prisoner's dilemma.

At the time of our study, the Napkin was being replaced by a different planning system integrated with the production system. This system, too, demanded reporters to sign up ideas that could be turned into stories and events that needed follow-up. However, the system included media flexibility through which it was possible to integrate with the newspaper production system as well as with sound and video (11). The system allowed stories to be formed based on one or more ideas, and the assignment of responsible reporters to the story. As this new system, too, has been abandoned, it is unlikely that integration with the production technology as such would solve this dilemma. Instead the above analysis points out that what is needed is an instrument that would give individual reporters and editors more benefit from the work that they put into using the shared system, helping editors create overview.

6.4.2   Storytelling or Idea Generation – What Gets Articulated?

Management's vision for the reporters was to become storytellers rather than newspaper or TV reporters. To become a storyteller independent of media, or at least one that thinks story before media, seemed in contrast to the way reporters generally thought stories and media together, while considering whichever alternative versions of a story were suitable for other media. In one interview, the editor-in-chief pointed out that initially it was an indicator of quality that a story would appear in all media. However, they no longer looked at quality that way.

The groups of contents shared the responsibility for a particular topic such as sports. The groups shared ideas and planned their work in group meetings. From interviews with management we understand that the intent was that reporters got to share stories and take over ideas from one another through the Napkin. However, from interviews with reporters and observations of actual group meetings we found that reporters rarely took over stories and ideas from each other, whether the ideas had been filed in the Napkin or not.

In the Superdesk meetings, the media conductor headed planning and evaluation and took charge in prioritizing the different stories: Which stories will be useful and entertain the readers (listeners/viewers) on any given day? In general, there was always lack of stories for TV, and the prioritizing did not run smoothly. Several interviewed reporter talked about how, once it was clear that one was planning a particular story for the newspaper, "*the vultures arrived*" (as one of them called the media editors) to grab bites for the other media as well. As a result of TV's struggle to find enough stories, the Superdesk meeting often turned into a brainstorm meeting where ideas were picked up from, e.g., the Napkin, and reshaped into something that could fulfill such needs. Many reporters strongly indicated that they did not like the fact that others (i.e., the Superdesk) picked and chose among their ideas without their own participation. Neither did they like that some of their ideas were totally ignored, and that the Superdesk or the media conductor came up with other stories for the reporter to work on. The Superdesk meetings had this rather casual and noncommitted way of dealing with the ideas of the reporters, which is in contrast to the way reporters saw their contribution, as commitments to producing a particular story for particular media at a particular time.

The reporters saw themselves as producing and completing stories, rather than generating ideas. It seemed inappropriate for them to register several stories in the Napkin at a time when the story was mainly a loose idea. Furthermore, it seemed self-contradictory to many reporters to register an idea to the Napkin, that they would later, after the meeting in the Superdesk, be asked to complete, or not. Proposing the idea in the Napkin did not help complete the story, and the proposal did not become a plan until it had been through the hands of the media conductor.

The Napkin mainly supported the reporter's individual anticipation of what and how (title, deadline, etc.). When reporters complained about the way the Superdesk handled their stories, they indicated that the editorial staff did not understand the motivation behind an idea or a story. And they often lacked motivation in the other direction; when they were told to produce a certain story for a certain medium, they did not understand why. For all reporters and editorial staff to become part of articulation and production of the total cross-media product, they needed to see their own role and their shared contribution to all of the media products and processes. Reporters needed to understand better how their particular stories fitted in with other stories in the particular media product. In the Napkin, there was no way for the reporter to motivate the idea or place it in context of other ideas, themes, or stories. From this perspective, the existing articulation of ideas or stories needs to be supplemented with a better, and two-directional, way of motivating ideas and stories. Also it is insufficient to focus on singular stories. In particular the overview of contents of each media product that was mainly held by the media conductor (see 5) would provide a better motivational context for reporters, if it were available to all.

6.4.3   Casual Commitment or Visibility for All?

One reporter pointed out what happens when one makes something public, lasting and to be accounted for that is really only an ephemeral idea (10). When reporters wrote something into the Napkin, it was there for them to use in their planning here and now, but it was also there for everybody to see days and weeks later. She found it nice to use the Napkin for her own planning, but less appropriate that plans became public. The Napkin primarily broadcast ideas of the reporters to other reporters, media editors, group leaders, and media conductors. Feedback on these ideas, either in terms of new ideas or precise production plans, came to the reporters through other means. The media conductor made rounds to introduce reporters to their ideas (5), and to adjust the ideas of the reporters to the plans of the media conductors. In those encounters with the media conductor, the reporters also told about ideas that were not necessarily accounted for in the Napkin. Similarly, group leaders utilized their own meetings and talks with reporters to make overviews and plans (on paper) that they brought and adjusted in the Superdesk meetings. One of the content group leaders even told that she had invented an overview mechanism of her own as a portable alternative to the Napkin. This addressed such elements as top stories, page number, TV, radio, and the reporter responsible for the story in question. She printed the form and brought it with her to Superdesk meetings in order to keep track of the different media stories.

The process of making commitments public in one direction was a problem in several respects: The feedback was individualized and lacked tool support; the actual cross-media plans were not public, they were decided in the Superdesk meetings without the participation of reporters, and brought out of the meetings through the walking and talking of the media conductor, the group leaders, and the media editors. The visibility of commitments was not matched with a similarly public and firm commitment from the editors.

Only the media conductor really had the overview, and hence the control of delegation and feedback. Not even the Superdesk meetings had a shared overview of products, how they were scheduled, how stories were anticipated to fit in; nor of the current actual production status of the different media. The Napkin was never designed to provide this, and accordingly, it needed to be supplemented with a way of feeding back overview and product plans from the editorial staff to the reporters. The overall cross-media articulation was mainly carried out by the media conductor, while walking the building (5). Similar to what 2 noted, it seemed necessary for a technology like the Napkin to move beyond the desktop and become mobile; to follow the media conductor as he moves, or the group leaders and reporters as they attend their activities in the Superdesk. This would perhaps reduce the feeling of double work experienced by the reporters and editors? The overview would also need to be shareable in the meetings, which basically means that the overview must come in different forms that may migrate, e.g., between small mobile technologies, and larger, shared displays in the Superdesk and elsewhere.

6.4.4   Different News, Different Needs

So far, much of the focus regarding the Napkin has been on the cooperation between the reporter and the editorial staff. However, our three cases show that news production comes in many different forms that are heavily connected to planning and cooperation and hence, the Napkin.

Our three cases demonstrate how news production needs are very different in terms of planning and coordinating according to the kinds of news in question. The prescheduled (17) news, e.g., the soccer match can be characterized as follows: A match is played once every week, with a well-defined beginning and end – there will be a result and hence, something to report no matter what. Reporting is routinized, and quite schematic. Specifically, there was a standard way of doing soccer production in the company and the need for a coordinating, planning, and idea sharing through the Napkin or any other IT system was very limited. Reporting was done mainly on site. The reporters did not actively relate to the challenge of versioning for different media platforms because they were primarily producing for one medium each (one newspaper reporter, one for radio, and one for the web). Hence, new ideas are not discussed in this kind of news production.

Local news stories were produced in collaboration between several reporters doing, e.g., coverage for radio, TV and newspaper. In the case studied, one reporter was bi-medial, producing for newspaper and radio, whereas the other was covering the story for TV in collaboration with a photographer. Even though this kind of news production, targeting on governmental budget cutbacks, was routine work for the journalists it was less routine-based than the soccer match because they did not know how the story would evolve. The particular story evolved into different versions aired first on radio, TV followed up, and newspaper versions were produced for the following day. The reporters needed to coordinate among themselves as to which angle was covered for the different media versions. The reporters spent a great deal of time researching the story, booking TV equipment, phoning people for interviews, and preparing a main interview for TV. They had to keep each other updated on the process. This was not done in the Napkin but through email messages and mobile phone. The development of different news angles was not supported well enough in the Napkin to support planning and coordination of this kind of news story, which was quite different from the "pipe-lining" between reporter and media editor, mainly targeted by the Napkin.

The larger, cross-media event, the "fat loss fight," was planned to take place over a longer period of time. It was planned half a year in advance, initiated by one reporter.

The carefully planned news series was rolled out in all media over a half-year period. Trailers and advertisement for the event were prepared for weekly newspapers, outdoor posters, flyers, radio, TV trailers, etc. Preplanned stories were brought in radio, TV, on the company website, and in the morning newspaper. Events were arranged by the media company in collaboration with the local government; e.g., the weight measuring of contestants and competitions with prizes. Furthermore, events initiated by others, were incorporated into the planning. Such events included a fat burn run. The entire cross-media event was highly dependent on planning and coordination between marketing department and reporters, between media platform versions, and between the media company and external partners.

It is not surprising that the Napkin did not support this kind of longer "news pipeline." There was no connection between the marketing department and the reporters, and the Napkin did not support collaboration with external partners. It is nonetheless interesting to understand how the team behind the "fat loss fight" put together a bricolage of tools (7), such as spreadsheets, email, paper overviews, and meeting schedules (Fig. 6.3). However, throughout the whole project period they lacked a central place to access all information and not least to sketch and assess the sequences of events and the planned collaboration.

The case studies demonstrated that there were different needs for planning and coordination dependent on the type of news productions. The needs varied according to the degree of cross-media production, the time span, and the need for explicit preplanning of the news, i.e., the routinization of task as such and the regularity of the event.

The three cases illustrate that there was a lot of planning and coordination in the media company that was neither about the individual planning of news stories, nor relating to the pipelining of individual stories to the editorial staff. It is evident that the Napkin was not made to support the more complex of these forms. Even the

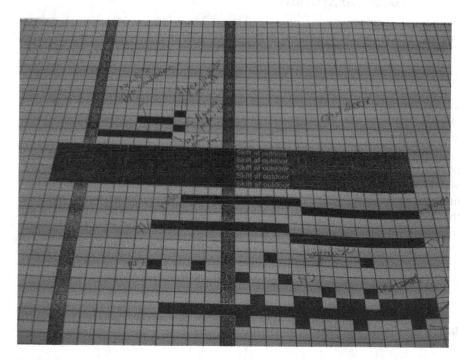

Fig. 6.3 The picture shows how the project manager planned the time line of the "fat loss fight" as a spreadsheet. The vertical lines indicate the start of the preplanned stories and the start of the user competition where the person who loses the most wins a money prize

metaphor of the Napkin does not make such promise. It is more surprising that reporters found no need for Napkin-like support in the simpler cases. However, the highly regular and standardized form of the object of attention as such, in the case of the soccer match, seemed to suffice (and work better than the Napkin) for coordination in the simplest form.

The reporters applied a clear least-effort strategy when they were pointing to the problems of the Napkin being an add-on to five different software solutions. They wanted one software system covering "everything." At the same time, they liked the fact that they had simpler systems for each media, and they demonstrated how they could skillfully integrate several ad hoc technologies in their planning.

This dilemma between integration and differentiation is well-known to CSCW. The technical complexity of integrating all news production systems into one, while making such a solution useable and shared, seems preventive, and we would not argue for such a solution. At the same time, the Napkin has turned out to be too limited and isolated, and a new balance seems necessary for a future solution. At the same time, as we shall see, the partners in planning and production are an expanding group.

6.4.5   New News Producers: Web 2.0 in Cross-Media Production Systems?

The last case study raises an additional concern regarding integration, because this kind of larger cross-media venture was a collaboration with external partners. Also as the events were unfolding, the users in the "fat loss fight" became so engaged with the concept that they demanded more of the website than intended from the media company. They wanted, e.g., an opportunity to arrange workout with each other in their local area, they wanted to be able to make a fat-loss diary of their own, and to be able to access other diaries.

This engagement and "producer" culture (6) in web 2.0 challenges cross-media production as well. If the ideas, stories, and contents were produced by the "fat loosers" and the framing only was planned by the reporters, how would a cross-media planning and coordinating system cope with this kind of openness? How would it support the ad hoc emergence of producers of news? And how would it coexist with the traditional content production supported? As the CEO of the media company stated, the news production of the future "is process-oriented rather than having a focus on products." It is not evident that experiences from the use of the Napkin would help designing support planning and coordination for these new conditions.

6.5   From Articulation to Sharing

In the case of the Napkin and cross-media news production, what it means to do the work and to benefit from it, takes on new dimensions: First of all, producing a story based on an idea was an important, but minor, part of the ongoing day-to-day production of several media products. This articulation involved many instruments in the hands of many different groups of users. The Napkin served the intermediate steps in the articulation process by *making ideas public,* in order to be managed and scheduled in various ways by the individual reporters and by editorial staff. The consecutive step from making ideas public to completing timely stories was much more informal and carried out through a number of casual encounters between reporters and editorial staff. Reporters requested *feedback* through the Napkin from this step, in terms of overview of stories and deadlines. This would give them something in return for the work of filing ideas into the Napkin. Such feedback, however, could not be generated from the information in the Napkin alone. *Overview of the current state of products and processes* was dependent on the planning of the media editors and media conductor. However, instruments to make *their* schedules publicly available lacked entirely. A better overview of all daily products as they were in the making would more profoundly motivate the work of each reporter and editor.

However, coordination also meant to make concrete, shared plans of a cross-media news production involving several reporters and editors, and even external partners and partners in other branches of the media company. This is the first place where the metaphor of the Napkin did not hold, since such planning involved much more than making individual plans visible to editors. What was needed were shared plans as the basis for negotiation over time.

The biggest and most immediate problem, however, was the one-way submission by reporters of premature ideas that they felt committed them to producing a story. Through the Napkin, these premature and sketchy ideas were transformed from "here and now" to "everywhere and forever," in the manner described by 10. While metaphorically, the Napkin indicated casual planning in the making, the visibility, permanency, and commitment of the entries in the system did exactly what Grudin warned against: making the ideas available everywhere and forever. The reference to the casual metaphorical background of the napkin did not hold in this respect either. In addition, the receivers of this made-public information allowed themselves to stay uncommitted, informal, and in private (or at least in one-to-one situations), further emphasizing the imbalance between those producing and those receiving.

The media company seemed at a crossroad: Was casual commitment a possibility? A substitute for the Napkin could either be designed to move cross-media production in the direction of increased cooperation, where better overview would be provided for all, the one-way commitment downscaled, reciprocity enhanced, and reporters more involved in the selection and choice of stories to be pursued. Or it could support a further division of work, where the emphasis was on more detailed plans, fed back from the Superdesk to reporters, and less on understanding why. While some sort of division of work would obviously be needed in a production this complicated, it is nonetheless a good question whether quality media products could come out of such a tailoristic approach to articulation.

This crossroad at the same time illustrates the problem, discussed, e.g., by 4, of the analytic separation of work and articulation work. With production processes as multiple and complicated as cross-media production, the separation of work and articulation work is conceptually problematic: something that is in one instance the job of somebody and in other instances part of the articulation. What is an appropriate level of identifying the activity as "the real job" may change: For long parts of the production, the actual stories are of minor relevance, while the totality of the media coverage is in focus. At other times the specific, timely versioning of a story for a particular media is essential, which the success or failure of, e.g., the daily newspaper may depend upon entirely. The separation is equally problematic design-wise, and our discussion points out the many ways in which it is essential to integrate the mediators of articulation with those of story and (cross) media production.

As we pointed out the pressure to make use of the most recent WWW facilities, often termed Web 2.0, further challenges several elements of the planning and coordination of cross-media production. First of all, it introduces a new group of news producers, formally known mainly as readers. These are in several respects more "wild": It is little predictable when and in what connections they become active, and their participation in the news production is not controlled by news editors or media editors. The timing and time horizon of such contributions is less predictable, and their contributions are ad hoc, and as such they cannot be planned, at the Superdesk or elsewhere. The instruments through which the editorial staff may have any kind of control of such contributions are on a different level: They may plan, and even try to boost the contributions and interactivity, but they have no means of knowing or controlling what comes out.

Acknowledgments The empirical study was carried out together with Stinne Aaløkke and Eva Bjerrum as part of the DEKAR project, sponsored by the Nordic Innovation Centre. We thank Nordjyske Medier for their participation, and Christina Brodersen, Leysia Palen, and Joan Greenbaum for useful discussions. Marianne Dammand Iversen and Dorthe Haagen Nielsen helped improve our language.

References

Aaløkke, S., Bjerrum, E., Bødker, S. & Bechmann Petersen, A. (2005). Gate Keeping or Bridge Building? – Cooperation, Learning and Boundary Working in a Cross-media Workplace. *OLKOS* Trento.

Belotti, V. & Rogers, Y. (1997). From Web press to Web pressure: multimedia representations and multimedia publishing. *Proceedings of CHI*. New York: ACM Press. 279–286

Bertelsen, O. W. & Bødker, S. Activity Theory. (2003). In Carroll, J. (ed.). *HCI Models, Theories, and Frameworks: Toward an Interdisciplinary Science*. San Francisco, CA, USA: Morgan Kaufman Publishers. 291–324,

Bødker, S. & Mogensen, P. One woman's job is another man's articulation work. (1993). In Robinson, M. & Schmidt, K. (eds.), *Developing CSCW Systems: Design Concepts. Report of the CoTECH WG4.* pp 149–166

Bødker, S. & Petersen, A. B. (2007). Seeds of cross-media production, *Journal of Computer Supported Cooperative Work,* 16(6). 539–566.

Bruns, A. (2005). *Gatewatching: Collaborative Online News Production.* New York: Peter Lang.

Büscher, M., Gill, S., Mogensen, P. & Shapiro, D. (2001). Landscapes of Practice: Bricolage as a Method for Situated Design. *Computer Supported Cooperative Work: An International Journal, 10*(1). 1–28.

Forsberg, K. & Ljungberg, F. (1998). The Organising of Editorial Work: Eliciting Implications for New IT use. In N. J. Buch, J. Damsgaard, L. B. Eriksen, J. H. Iversen & P. A. Nielsen (eds). *Proceedings of the 21st Information Systems Research Seminar in Scandinavia.* pp 223–234.

Grudin, J. (1988). Why CSCW applications fail: problems in the design and evaluation of organizational interfaces. *Proceedings of the Conference on Computer-Supported Cooperative Work*, Portland, OR. New York: ACM Press, New York. pp 65–84.

Grudin, J. (2002). Group dynamics and ubiquitous computing. *CACM 45*(12). 74–78.

Larsen, J. (2003). *Videnstyring på medier.* Center For Journalistisk Efteruddannelse, Aarhus.

Pavlik, J. V. & McIntosh, S. (2004). *Converging Media.* London: Pearson Education

Petersen, A. B. (2006). *Mediediffusion*, Centre for Internet Research. University of Aarhus

Petersen, A. B. (2006). Internet and Cross Media Production: Case Studies in two major Danish media organizations, *IJETS – International Journal of Emerging Technologies and Society*, *Vol. 4*, No. 2. 84–107.

Petersen, A. B. (2006b). *The In-betweens of Media: Multiple and Cross Media as Strategy for Innovation and Change*. PhD dissertation. University of Aarhus, Denmark.

Schmidt, K. & Bannon. L. (1992). Taking CSCW seriously: Supporting articulation work. *Journal of Computer Supported Cooperative Work, 1*(1–2). 7–40.

Tuchman, G. (1973). Making News by doing Work: Routinizing the unexpected. *American Journal of Sociology*, 79, 1. 110–131

Part III
Web 2.0 Problems and Solutions

Chapter 7
People Tagging and Ontology Maturing: Toward Collaborative Competence Management

Simone Braun, Christine Kunzmann, and Andreas Schmidt

7.1 Introduction

Competence management has received increasing attention as an implementation of a systematic approach to human resources management, e.g., part total of quality management approaches such as European Foundation of Quality Management (EFQM). Furthermore, trends such as recurring shortage of skilled workers and the anticipated demographic changes have led to an increasing awareness about employees' capabilities.

One reason for that is the fact that competencies have proven useful as an abstraction of work-relevant human behavior in a variety of contexts and across different actor groups (individual, organization, and market; see Fig. 7.1). Within an organization, competencies enable instruments for more effective resource allocation (e.g., for team staffing), knowledge management and informal learning support, and human resource development in general. They aim at making transparent individual competencies and their relationship to organizational goals. Recently, this view has been complemented by the usage of competencies in employability processes, ranging from competencies as part of e-portfolios, via competency-based curricula, to competency-driven recruitment processes.

However, especially on the level of individual employees, such approaches have so far not been able to show sustainable success on a larger scale (Schmidt and Kunzmann 2007). Piloting applications such as expert finder or expert locator systems have often failed in the long run because of incomplete and outdated data, apart from social and organizational barriers. This affects both competency profiles of the individual employee and nonadequate and often also outdated competency catalogs used as a vocabulary for the profiles.

In this contribution, we argue that a lack of participation of all employees has been one of the key problems. To overcome this, we propose a collaborative approach

S. Braun (✉), C. Kunzmann, and A. Schmidt
FZI Research Center for Information Technologies, Germany
e-mail: simone.braun@fzi.de

D. Randall and P. Salembier (eds.), *From CSCW to Web 2.0: European Developments in Collaborative Design*, Computer Supported Cooperative Work,
DOI 10.1007/978-1-84882-965-7_7, © Springer-Verlag London Limited 2010

Fig. 7.1 Use cases for competence models and catalogs

based on Web 2.0-style people tagging and complement it with community-driven ontology engineering methods.

As a first step, we analyze current approaches to competence management (Section 7.2), before describing our approach based on people tagging (Section 7.3). In Section 7.4 we describe our tool support with the social bookmarking application framework SOBOLEO and present an evaluation in Section 7.5. In Section 7.6, we briefly compare our approach to the state of art and conclude with a brief summary and outlook.

7.2 Competence Management Approaches and Their Problems

7.2.1 Competence Management Approaches in General

Traditionally, competence management approaches are conceived as top-down instruments (see, e.g., Berio and Harzallah 2005; Biesalski and Abecker 2005) and are based on controlled vocabularies in the form of competency catalogs. In such approaches, a small expert group models such competency catalogs and thus defines

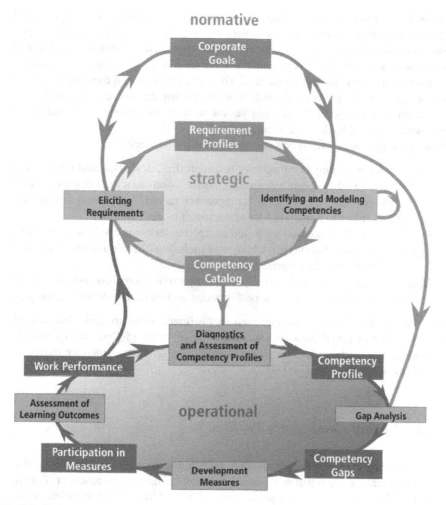

Fig. 7.2 Reference model for closed-loop approaches to competence management

the vocabulary at irregular intervals (usually less often than yearly) or even as a one-time activity without scheduled updates. This catalog is then provided to the lower management and the employees to provide, update, and apply requirements and competency profiles.

As noted by Schmidt and Kunzmann 2007, this method usually leads to communication and coordination problems between strategic and operational level. They have proposed a closed-loop approach (see Fig. 7.2) in which two-way communication between the different levels forms an integral part of the process. This model is designed from a human resource development perspective. On the strategic level, the competence catalog and the requirement profiles for job roles are modeled in a continuous loop, taking into account corporate goals (to ensure that the catalog and the profiles are oriented toward the future) and feedback from the operational level. The operational level uses this vocabulary to describe the actual competency profiles of the individual employees. By comparing the actual competency profile with the requirements profile, it is possible to determine a competency gap, which can be addressed by development measures. Their outcomes should then improve work performance, which provides the indicators for setting up competency profiles and also competency aspects that are not yet included in the competence catalog and thus have to be fed back to the strategic level.

As a summary, core competence management activities include:

> *Competency modeling* as the activity that identifies, describes, and relates competencies to other competencies and has the competency catalog as its result (sometimes also referred to as "competence model" – although this in some contexts refers to a meta-model of competency descriptions)
>
> *Requirements elicitation* stating which competencies are needed for a certain job role (now and in the future), which may include a differentiation in minimum requirements and development pathways
>
> *Diagnostics/assessment* as the activity of making explicit actual competency profiles of individuals based on work performance and other assessment techniques.

But even with a closed-loop approach as outlined, there are still considerable problems when putting those approaches into practice. In what follows, we will analyze the competence modeling and diagnostics/assessment activities, which are in practice the most challenging ones.

7.2.2   Getting Competency Profiles

On the operational level, the most obvious problem is getting the competency profiles. One fundamental issue is that competencies cannot be measured, sensed, or observed directly. What we can observe is performance (Lau and Sure 2002) in various forms: assessment of learning outcomes, performance in every day job activities, etc. All of these yield evidence from which a competency is usually deduced heuristically.

In practice, one can observe two approaches (Biesalski and Abecker 2005): (1) self-assessment approaches in which employees themselves are asked to provide their competencies, sometimes mediated in a second step by their superior and (2) external assessment approaches done by superiors or through formal assessment procedures.

While the latter approach is very expensive and cumbersome and thus can only be observed in limited areas, the first approach often fails because of missing motivation. This lack of motivation can be traced back to there being no immediate benefit for the employees. For instance, systems are hardly embedded in everyday work activities and have not proven their usefulness there. Or it can be even traced back to negative incentives; for instance, if you disclose your competencies, others will contact and perhaps disturb you or you will fear appearing not competent enough.

As a result, employees might downplay or exaggerate their competencies as Becerra-Fernandez (2006) reports. Often, these competency profiles also do not contain information that is of high relevance to colleagues; for instance manually updated repositories become particularly outdated (Miles and Bechhofer 2008). Thus, recent and usually very specialized topics are not yet contained in the competency catalog because of the long update intervals.

Several studies address this problem by automatically extracting profile information from data the user generates in his or her daily work; e.g., from publications (Crowder et al. 2002), documents (Reichling et al. 2007), or community contents (John and Seligmann 2006; Breslin et al. 2007). Ley et al. (2006) propose a competence performance approach that derives competencies from executed tasks. In this approach, a task competency matrix is created together with domain experts. This matrix relates a set of tasks, e.g., required for a position, to a set of competencies needed to fulfill these tasks successfully. Based on this model, the system can infer a user's competency from her successful performance of a task in her daily work.

A different approach to employee profiles starts from the purpose of those profiles for expert finding and community formation: (enterprise) social networking, e.g., LinkedIn (2009) or Xing (2009). These platforms are based on the self-promotion paradigm: People can represent themselves with a profile and indicate their connections to other users. Further, in some of these approaches, the principle of social tagging and bookmarking is transferred to people (cf. Bogers et al. 2006); for instance Xing (2009) or the NTSH (2009) allow organizing your contacts with tags. Within IBM's Fringe Contacts (Farell et al. 2007a), each employee can describe their colleagues by tagging them with key words on their expertise and interests. Thus, step by step, a publicly visible tag cloud grows characterizing the individual employee. This leverages network effects for setting up some sort of profile of the individual, and improves usefulness for the individual user of the system which, in turn, motivates to contribute. For instance, Farell et al. (2007b) could state that tagging people was used to create communities.

However, the resulting profiles lack legitimation and commitment by the organization, especially with respect to the vocabulary used. The approaches do not provide support to overcome the gap and leverage the bottom-up topics to an organizational competences vocabulary. But that is a prerequisite for organizational competence management – ranging from team staffing, via human resource development to organizational competence portfolios.

7.2.3 Competency Modeling

That points back to the issue of competency modeling for building a shared organizational understanding. If we analyze the scientific literature, a lot of attention has been paid to exploiting competency models for team staffing, applicant selection, etc., via profile matching, but little investigation has taken place into *competency modeling processes*. Existing approaches vary in terms of modeling depth (ranging from around 20 competencies (Draganidis 2006) up to several hundred per catalog), and structures used (flat lists (Cooper 2000), hierarchical structures (Schmidt et al. 2006)) a combination of context-free generic competencies, and context ontologies (De Coi et al. 2007). But all of them are based on the assumption that a small group of experts is responsible for the task of competence modeling. This ensures that the resulting catalog gets organizational legitimation and commitment. Practical experience shows the following problems:

1. Competence models are frequently outdated and do not get updated in time. Usually, competency modeling is considered to be a *one-time activity instead of a continuous improvement.*
2. Competence modeling is mainly *done on a strategic level*, or as part of central-ized function units, which lack information about operational needs.
3. The process of competency modeling is often *just too complex*, i.e., it requires modeling skills, which are not readily available in organizations. This can be compensated as part of one-time efforts, but it poses severe challenges for con-tinuous updating. The main issues here are that it is unclear where to start, and it is hard to provide templates to facilitate the modeling process.
4. When applying the competence catalog, employees encounter the problems such as (1) they *cannot understand the meaning* of competency labels (because they were not part of the modeling process – so it is language of someone else), (2) they *do not find the relevant topics* (what is interesting for them), which particu-larly applies to emerging topics, and (3) if they find something, it is not at a *right level of detail.*

All of these lead to the perception that competence management is actually just another administrative exercise because it is not part of vital organization processes.

7.3   Approach

Based on these fundamental problems, we could easily argue that competency mod-eling as such is the wrong path as the essential assumption that competencies are an adequate and practical model to reduce real-world complexities does not hold. But the situation is not as bleak if we analyze the problem from a semantic perspective (see also Table 7.1 for a semantic differentiation of the most typical use cases):

In the collection of different use cases for competencies, there are different requirements for the *level of detail* of competence modeling and profiles. Aligning corporate strategies with employee competencies is by nature on a highly aggregated level, while team staffing or targeted human resource development requires fairly specific competencies.

Similarly, *precision* for the competency notions is not always required in the same way. While anything with a direct impact on employee salaries and/or career opportunities needs a sound foundation, this is not the case for infor-

Table 7.1 Semantic differentiation of the most typical use cases

Use case	Requirements	Notions
People finding	Timely inclusion of	Interest
Finding help on a problem	emerging topics	
Community formation		
		Experience
Team staffing	Sufficient level of detail	Experience
Application selection	in combination with	
Matching requirement	relationships for	
and actual profiles	similarity measures	Competency
		Potential
Training planning		Competency
Human resource development	Sufficient level of detail,	Learning
Identifying development needs	corresponding to the	outcomes
and selecting measures	granularity of measures	
Learning on demand support	Fine-grained descriptions	Topics
Suggesting learning opportunities	of what is relevant for a	Competency
within the work process	certain situation	
Reward schemes	Very reliable measurements	Competency
	through key	
	performance indicators	
Career planning	Lower level of detail	(Potential)
Aligning employee competence	Small set of stable	Aggregated
development with corporate	competences	competence
strategies		

mal networking activities as part of expert finding or community formation. In the latter case, it is sufficient to know about interests or experiences, which can, but definitely do not need to, relate to competencies.

On the assessment side, *formal* (and thus objective and reliable) competence *assessment* can only be made for a small subset of competencies. Only for these we can define a sufficiently reliable set of key performance indicators. For the others, we need to rely on less formal procedures (like self- or peer assessment) anyway.

On the other hand, if we are not focused on formal assessments, we will find that there are *indicators* for competencies *everywhere*. Each single indicator is not very reliable (e.g., task performance can depend on a lot of environmental factors, which can be accidental), but the combination of a multitude of those indicators can provide good approximations (as the wisdom of the crowd principle claims).

As a summary: It appears that the observed problems can be partially traced back to the narrowed perspective which takes the use case with the highest requirements for formality, level of detail, and precision as the base standard. Our approach, which we will present in the next section, takes a differentiated approach, which allows for following a Web 2.0-style participatory approach to competence management.

7.3.1 General Considerations

To overcome the problems sketched in Section 7.2, we propose a collaborative competence management approach, which combines Web 2.0-style bottom-up processes with organizational top-down processes: Web 2.0 oriented bottom-up processes allow every employee to participate and contribute with low usage barriers; i.e., by tagging colleagues; the organizational processes take up and guide these bottom-up developments toward organizational goals.

This requires bringing together the following elements:

Bottom-Up Collection of Opinions About Individual Competencies Instead of cumbersome (top-down) processes to assess an employee's competencies, we make use of the "wisdom of the crowd" effect and collect the collective view of the community of employees on the competencies of the individual. Therefore, we need to empower the employees to describe each others' competencies in an easy and task-embedded way.

Freedom to Evolve Competence Vocabulary Employees need to be enabled not only to state their opinion on who has which competency, but they have to be enabled to modify the vocabulary for stating those opinions as well. Otherwise, we do not exploit the ability of bottom-up processes to detect new trends.

Shared Vocabulary for Comparability Competencies usually have an integrating function in the enterprise, bringing together strategic and operational levels, and human resources, and performance management aspects. This means that competencies are not limited to an individual or to a group, but these notions have to be shared by the whole organization (in the ideal case): in consequence we cannot do without a shared vocabulary.

Legitimation and Commitment by the Organization If competencies are to play an important role in diverse organizational processes, ranging from team staffing, via human resource development process, up to organizational competence portfolio management, it is important that resulting competency profiles and competency catalogs are not only derived from the "wisdom of crowd," but have also the commitment of the organization. This is a main difference to the open world of the web of individuals. Major decisions depend on the appropriate identification of competencies and competency profiles so that the organization must *decide* at some point to which extent it relies on the result of collective bottom-up processes and to which extents it defines certain binding aspects.

As a summary: The key idea is that we cannot do competence management completely without an agreed vocabulary (or ontology), i.e., the competency catalog. But we have to make the process of evolving this catalog more collaborative and embedded into its actual usage (e.g., while tagging other employees). Likewise, we do not conceive competency profiles as self-descriptions, but rather as results of collective judgments of others (cf. Farell et al. 2007b)

7.3.2 Ontology Maturing Process for Evolving Competence Catalogs

We approached this problem as a collaborative ontology construction problem. The conceptual foundation is the Ontology Maturing Process Model (Braun et al. 2007) (based on a more general Knowledge Maturing Process (Schmidt 2005)). The Ontology Maturing Process Model (see Fig. 7.3) is based on the assumption that ontologies, i.e., competency catalogs, cannot be formalized in a single activity. They are rather the result of continuous negotiation and collaborative learning processes that take place when applying the ontologies. The model structures the process of evolving competence ontologies into four phases:

Emergence of Ideas By employees annotating each other with any topic tag, new topic ideas emerge. For instance, they describe a recent or very specialized topic. These topic tags are individually used and informally communicated.

Consolidation in Communities A common topic terminology evolves through the collaborative (re)usage of the topic tags within the community of employees. The topic tags are defined and refined; useless or incorrect ones are rejected.

Formalization Within the third phase, the special members of the community (usually legitimated by the organization by assigning "gardening" tasks) begin to organize the topic terminology into competencies by introducing relations between the topic tags. These relations can be taxonomical (hierarchical) ones as well as arbitrary ad hoc relations, expressing similarity (e.g., Java Programming and C# Programming). That results in new or updated competency notion, i.e., lightweight ontologies, which allow primarily for inferencing based on sub-concept relations.

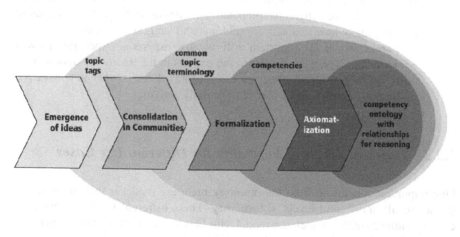

Fig. 7.3 Ontology maturing for competence ontologies

Axiomatization In the last phase, modeling experts add axioms for exploiting relationships for reasoning. This includes especially precise composition relationships. This allows and improves for complex inferencing processes, e.g., subsumption of competencies for the purpose of competency gap analysis, or competency-based selection of learning opportunities (Schmidt et al. 2006).

It is important to note that ontology maturing does not assume that the competence ontologies are built from scratch. It can be equally applied to already existent core competency catalogs that might be further developed and can be used for seeding.

7.3.2.1 Competence Ontology Maturing in Corporate Practice

If we translate this to corporate practice, we can distinguish between different roles (or levels of involvement) and expected skills:

In the first phase, we mainly rely on a large number of individual employees with little or no knowledge about competence modeling. They are mainly concerned with their task at hand and use tagging practices to find people later on more easily. They can align themselves with other colleagues through observing their tagging behavior and potentially through tag suggestions (which essentially is a system-mediated observation of the behavior of others).

In the second phase, we rely on gardeners that partially and incrementally consolidate the tags, usually focused on areas with a high volume and heterogeneity of tags. These gardeners are usually not in a special centralized function unit, but rather emerge from their peers (but can be equipped with organizational legitimation from their superiors) because of their interest and mission. They play the important role of facilitators of the consolidation process although they do not accomplish the task alone. These gardeners do not necessarily need to be experts in competency modeling, but need basic semantic modeling know-how to discover problems and suggest solutions.

For core areas, which are important to formalize, experts or expert groups will be responsible. These are similar to the experts in the traditional approaches, but as opposed to those, they are now informed about what is considered important by employees as part of their daily activities.

7.3.3   Different Levels of Formality for Different Use Cases

One important conclusion from the ontology maturing model is that the different phases result in different levels of formality. These different levels of formality coexist within a single competence model. But how can we represent these different levels of formality so that we can also exploit the information?

As part of the Professional Learning Ontology, we have developed a conceptualization of competencies that has three basic levels: topics (as weak notions),

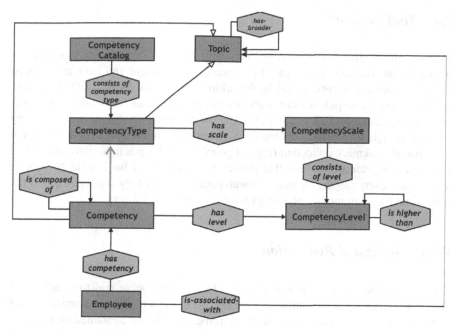

Fig. 7.4 Core part of the professional learning ontology

competency types (without differentiation), and competencies (with levels). These relate to each other as shown in Fig. 7.4.

In this way, we can (1) represent all four phases of the ontology maturing process and (2) degrade the semantics of more formal statements if needed. Especially, the latter is important for the different use cases of competence models:

Topic Tags As many Web 2.0 sites show (2007), tags are sufficient to provide a basic level of useful search and retrieval functionality and similarity between the tagged resources. Precise tag definition would help, but are not needed.

Competence Types For basic profile matching we need well-defined competency notions and taxonomic relationships to allow for different levels of abstraction by using broader–narrower relationships. We can also perform basic competency gap analysis (by exact matching).

Competencies (with Levels) This allows for a more extended version of profile matching as you can have different degrees of fulfillment for individual competencies. This can also form the basis for describing the objectives of learning opportunities (trainings, learning objects).

Competency Relationships If we have precise is-a semantics, or composition of competencies in the competence model, we can introduce the notion of competence subsumption (e.g., if competency X is part of competency Y, X subsumes Y. This allows for more sophisticated competency gap analysis (and competency-based selection of learning opportunities.)

7.4 Tool Support

In order to realize the Ontology Maturing Process Model for competence
management, we rely on the social bookmarking paradigm and have customized
the AJAX-based semantic social bookmarking application SOBOLEO that offers
task-embedded competence ontology development and an easy-to-use interface.
SOBOLEO (Zacharias and Braun 2007) is the acronym for **So**cial **Bo**okmarking
and **L**ightweight **E**ngineering of **O**ntologies. It supports the collaborative development
of a shared bookmark collection (e.g., of people's web pages in an intranet) and of
a shared competence ontology that is used to organize the bookmarks to people.
That means users can tag the people's web page with ontology concepts, and at the
same time they can modify and adapt the competence ontology.

7.4.1 Technical Realization

SOBOLEO consists of four major parts: (1) a collaborative real-time editor for
changing the competence ontology (see Fig. 7.5), (2) a tool for the annotation of
web pages (see Fig. 7.6), (3) a semantic search engine for the annotated bookmarks,
and (4) an ontology browser for navigating the competence ontology and the content
of the bookmark collection.

With SOBOLEO, all users create and maintain one competence ontology and
one shared bookmark collection collaboratively. If the users encounter a resource,
e.g., a colleague's profile or homepage, they can add it to the bookmark collection
and tag it with concepts from the competence ontology (see Fig. 7.5). In the case
they want to tag the resource with a topic the existing ontology concepts do not
cover (e.g., because the topic is too new or specific), the users can adapt an existing
concept (second phase of the ontology maturing process) or just use new topic tags,
without an agreed meaning (first process phase). These new topic tags are automatically added to the ontology as "prototypical concepts," reflecting the fact that it is
not clear yet how they relate to the existing concepts.

SOBOLEO provides consolidation support for the gradual formalization of these
new topic tags to competence types and competencies with levels. By providing an
easy-to-use and easy-to-access collaborative real-time editor, the users can refine
and correct concepts when they apply the competence ontology within their everyday
activities. By removing topic tags from the "prototypical concepts" container and
integrating them into the ontology and adding additional information, topic tags are
transferred into competence types and competencies with levels. In this way, the users
can easily bring topic tags to competence types and competencies with levels.

As standard and formal ontology language we use the SKOS Core Vocabulary
(Miles and Bechhofer 2008) and the SKOS Extensions Vocabulary (Miles and
Brickley 2004)

By its lightweight and intuitive language it supports handling the trade-off of having
different levels of formality and an easy understandability for non-modeling experts.

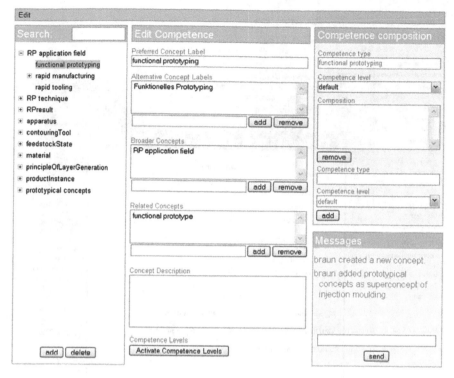

Fig. 7.5 Collaborative competence ontology editor

In this way, users can structure the concepts within SOBOLEO with hierarchical relations (broader and narrower) or indicate that concepts are "related" which supports the third process phase. These relations are also considered by the semantic search engine. That means the user can improve the retrieval of the annotated bookmarks by adding and refining ontology structures.

7.4.1.1   System Architecture

The SOBOLEO system is realized in a multi-tier architecture with four layers (see Fig. 7.7):

Presentation/Interface Tier realizes the interfaces of the application, i.e., web and service interfaces.

Application Logic Tier realizes the application behavior, e.g., semantic search logic that utilizes both ontology and documents (e.g., a person's web page).

Domain Tier manages the domain objects (user, ontology, annotation, documents) on top of the data storage.

Data Tier realizes the efficient and persistent storage of the application data.

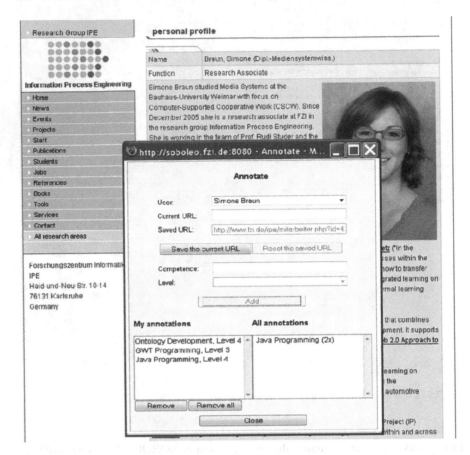

Fig. 7.6 Annotating an employees personal Web page

SOBOLEO is implemented in Java 6 on top of the Apache Tomcat 6.0 application server (http://tomcat.apache.org/).

The four tiers will be detailed in the following. The presentation/interface tier realizes the user interface of the semantic search and the ontology browser using Java Server Pages; the AJAX interfaces of the ontology editor and annotation tool are created with Google's Google Web Toolkit framework to offer real-time interactions. In addition, we provide an Atom feed interface that allows the subscription for recent changes about annotations (for a specific competence or the entire competence ontology). Using the Apache Axis2./Java 1.4.1 SOAP engine (http://ws.apache.org/axis2/) we provide web service interfaces, e.g., for the export of the competence ontology.

The application logic tier realizes the application services. For instance, the semantic search service considers subsumptions of competences, i.e., if competency k with level l_1 subsumes competency k with level l_2 because $l_1 > l_2$ then searching

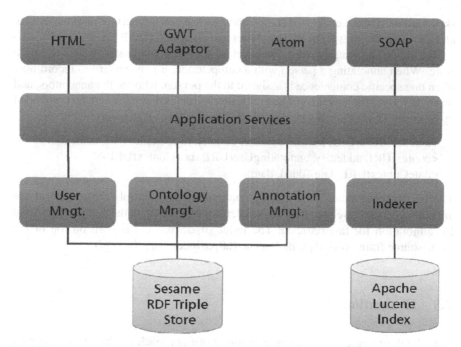

Fig. 7.7 SOBOLEO architecture

for persons with (k, l_2) also finds persons annotated with (k, l_1). This means that domain-specific reasoning is implemented within those application services, which allows from an architectural point of view the flexibility to incorporate various methods for semantic augmentation in an application-context-specific manner.

The domain tier comprises four components which manage users, ontology, annotations, and documents on top of the data storage. The user management component is in charge of, e.g., the creation and deletion of users and the provision of user data. Users are represented with the FOAF vocabulary (Friend of a Friend) 9 Brickley and Miller 2007) and stored together with the ontology and annotations in a RDF triple store using the Sesame RDF repository framework (http://www.openrdf.org/).

The ontology management component controls the competence ontology elements, e.g., checks for potential cycles produced by adding new relations. New hierarchical relations between competence types are created using skos:broaderGeneric and skos:narrowerGeneric respectively. A competence instance relation is represented by skos:broaderInstantive and the inverse skos:narrowerInstantive between a competency (with level) and a competence type:

<competenceInstanceURI, skos:broaderInstantive, competenceTypeURI>
<competenceTypeURI, skos:narrowerInstantive, competenceInstanceURI>

Between different competence instances, i.e., competencies with level, compositions relations can be defined. These are modeled using skos:broaderPartitive and skos:narrowerPartitive. Any of these relations are sub-properties of skos:broader and skos:narrower respectively (see Miles and Bechhofer 2008).

The annotation management component handles annotations storage into the triple store. When annotating a person with a competence, it is necessary to record how often one specific competence is assigned to the person, who are the annotators, and when they made the annotation. Such reification is realized using the contexts provided by Sesame. Thus one annotation is represented by three statements:

<annotatedUserURI, hasCompetence, competenceInstanceURI, contextURI>
<contextURI, addedBy, annotatingUserURI, dateContextURI>
<dateContextURI, dateAdded, date>

The fourth component is the indexer component that controls the storage of the annotated person's web page (content, url, title) together with the competences used for annotation for fast retrieval. The index of documents is built on top of the open-source framework Apache Lucene (http://lucene.apache.org/)

7.5   Evaluation

With the development and implementation of our approach we follow evolutionary prototyping within the design-based research methodology (Design-based research collective 2003). In order to test the approach of people tagging in general and to explore motivational and social aspects in particular, we conducted two field experiments. The field experiments took place in parallel with the system development and thus based on paper prototypes.

7.5.1   Procedure

Two research groups within the area of computer science were involved in the field experiments. Group I consists of 50 people from two organizations; Group II consists of 63 people distributed over four organizations where some of the people belong to both research groups. Work atmosphere within both groups is frank and friendly. People work together closely to very closely within their organizations, less closely across organization borders.

Both groups lacked awareness about the people's topics, interests, and competencies within the groups. They wanted to better exploit synergies and to know whom to ask for a problem at hand. Neither of the groups had competence management established, but it was considered to introduce such within Group I in order to improve/facilitate (a) team staffing and (b) career planning. Both groups were open to new technologies and familiar with tagging, Web 2.0 and semantic technologies (as they are doing research and software development in this area). They were not familiar with competence management.

The first field experiment (FE I) took place with 39 participants of Group I in July 2008, the second field experiment (FE II) with 38 participants of Group II in September 2008. Seventeen people participated in both field experiments. The field experiments took place in the course of each research group's internal retreat. During these retreats, people tagging was an explicit item on the agenda and task during the three days of the retreat.

We prepared paper-based posters for each group member (including nonparticipating members). Each poster showed the name and photo of the person and blank lines to write down tags. We prepared a seed list of tags. This seed list consisting of topics the people are dealing with in their daily work was meant for inspiration and stimulation of the participants to start tagging.

There was an opening presentation in order to introduce the topic of competence management and people tagging, the task, and the purpose of the experiment. The given task was:

Please tag your colleagues and yourself according to the interests you associate with them (by writing the tag on the poster).
Use whatever tag you find appropriate.
Use some from seed list, or ignore them completely.
Reuse tags of others.
Indicate also if you assign the same tag as already there (by repeating the tag or by adding a multiplying factor).

We asked the participants to start walking around and tagging and to continue with the tagging in the following 2 days. From time to time, we encouraged the participants in doing so. Compared to FE I, in FE II no time slot exclusively dedicated for people tagging was foreseen in the agenda. Additionally, due to unforeseen circumstances, the introductory slides could not be presented in FE II. The introduction took place orally but without clearly communicating the background and purpose.

At the end of each field experiment, an extended discussion session together with the participants took place. After both experiments were conducted, all members of the groups were asked to fill out a short online survey. People who are members of both field experiments were asked to fill out one survey for each. In total, 29 members of each research group answered the survey.

7.5.2 Results

Overall people tagging has been regarded as positive and useful. People enjoyed the experiments and stated that "it was fun." The participants appreciated reflecting about others' interests and competencies: "tagging people forces you to think about what you actually know about others." They liked "to learn about others" and "to get new insights" in this way, in particular about people they are not so much in contact with. With the tags it was possible to get a quick overview and to see who works in the same area as oneself or has similar, also nonwork-related, interests. The participants expressed the wish to have tool support that facilitated finding similar people or comparing people based on their tags. Concerning individual reflection, the participants enjoyed to see how others perceive them and what they associate with them.

It was stated that with single words a description is possible and that the tags "converge to the right results." However, the participants also complained that tags are sometimes not expressive enough or misleading. They indicated that having more context and semantic information would be desirable. It happened that different tags were used for the same concept even on the same poster (e.g., use of both "Personal Knowledge Management" and its acronym "PKM"). The seed list was recognized only rarely as it was not integrated into the actual tagging process; i.e., the participants forgot about the list while tagging. The participants wished to have auto-completion and suggestion support with more "semantics" during the tagging process. These issues were directly integrated into the software development process of SOBOLEO.

Another issue the participants raised was the difficulty to start tagging from scratch with a blank sheet. Here again the participants asked for support functionalities or seeding, e.g., everyone tags oneself at first. On the other hand, another group of people stated that seeing the already assigned tags biased them toward confirming these tags instead of adding new ones.

In total the participants enjoyed people tagging as a social activity, i.e., walking around, meeting other participants in front of the posters and jointly reflecting about skills, competencies, and (nonwork-related) interests.

At the same time, however, the joint reflection and discussion about other persons was also perceived as negative because it resulted in "talking about" instead of "talking with" people. This was particularly problematic in FE II where due to the missing introduction of people tagging some serious social issues arose. In FE II, a small number of participants saw people tagging as an intrusion into their privacy – they objected in particular to off-topic (nonwork-related) tags and to a small number of slightly offending tags. Interestingly even tags not seen as problematic by both tagger and taggee caused problems when read by people lacking the context needed to understand them in the playful way they were intended.

FE II has shown that it is very important to clearly communicate the purpose of people tagging, i.e., what it is intended for and why it is used and what happens with the data afterwards. It should be decided and communicated beforehand how to handle off-topic tags in general and that (even slightly) offending tags are not allowed.

Some participants of FE II also perceived the (partial) anonymity of tagging, i.e., that it was generally untraceable who tagged whom, as negative and as one reason for the high number of nonwork-related tags.

The general fear of transparency also arose as an important issue. The participants asked for more control over the tags assigned to them, i.e., that they should be able to decide which tags are publicly visible and which not. Some participants also asked for the possibility to opt out of people tagging altogether, to indicate that they do not want to be tagged, to display only self-given tags (with only them being able to see tags by other people) or to disable tags from other people.

7.6 Summary

7.6.1 Comparison to Traditional Approaches

People tagging represents a bottom-up approach to competence modeling, while classical approaches were characterized by top-down expert groups. If we compare our approach to those classical approaches to competence management, we can identify the following differences (Table 7.2).

7.6.2 Conclusions and Outlook

Our approach of collaborative competence management provides a solution to overcome the hitherto strictly top-down competence management approaches. In this way, competence ontologies can be developed that also cover less formalized topic tags and structures. This guarantees usefulness and timeliness when being applied.

The field studies have shown that it is possible to retrieve competencies from tags and that it supports reflection about individual and organizational competencies. However, they also identified important societal and privacy issues that must be addressed. Addressing these issues must be done both with respect to the introduction process and tag visibility controls. Especially the proper introduction and communication of purpose have emerged to be one of the most important issues. Therefore, a methodology for introducing and implementing people tagging should

Table 7.2 Comparing people tagging with classic approaches

	Classic approaches	People tagging approach
Modeling paradigm	Expert group modeling informed by workshops with operational departments	Participatory modeling in which expert modelers are "gardeners," consolidating bottom-up input
Modeling frequency	Rather long periods between updated	Continuous modeling
Complexity of modeling competencies and their relationships	Lack of guidance of what is important and how it relates to others	Modeling process can be informed through existing tags
Perceived usefulness	Appears to be other-directed and without immediate use for the operational level	Participation of all employees according to their needs, thus also creating a form of identification with the result
Effort of competence modeling	Requires dedicated expert groups that need to conduct and moderate the modeling process	Effort is distributed Reduced effort for involved experts

be elaborated and further research on organizational and social constraints related to culture and atmosphere as well as on implications of people tagging is necessary.

With SOBOLEO's embeddedness in everyday work activities and easy usage, employees are motivated to contribute. If users discover that a topic is missed within the ontology, they can simply add it. If they cannot find a colleague under the estimated topic or not at all, they can just add a new bookmark and tag it appropriately. These annotations we want to use in a next step for automatic profile generation.

Extending SOBOLEO's functionality for subsumption and composition support by introducing *is-a* and *is-part-of* relations as sub-properties of the broader relation introduces also higher complexity for the users; we are evaluating within the EU IP MATURE[1] how the users deal with this.

Acknowledgments This work was co-funded by the European Commission under the Information and Communication Technologies (ICT) theme of the 7th Framework Programme (FP7) within the Integrating Project MATURE[15] and by the German Federal Ministry for Education and Research within the project Im Wissensnetz.[2]

References

Apache Axis2. Apache Axis2/Java is a Web service engine implementing SOAP. http://ws.apache.org/axis2/ (accessed 2009-03-30)

Apache Lucene. Apache Lucene is a high-performance, full-featured text search engine library written entirely in Java. http://lucene.apache.org/ (accessed 2009-03-30).

Apache Tomcat. Official reference implementation for the Java Servlet and JavaServer Pages technologies. http://tomcat.apache.org/ (accessed 2009-03-20)

Becerra-Fernandez, I. (2006). Searching for experts on the Web: A review of contemporary expertise locator systems. *ACM Transactions on Internet Technologies, (6)*4, New York: ACM Press. 333–355

Berio, G. and Harzallah, M. (2005). Knowledge Management for Competence Management. *J. UKM 0(1).* 21–28

Biesalski, E. and Abecker, A. (2005) Human Resource Management with Ontologies. In: *Professional Knowledge Management. 3rd Biennial Conference, WM 2005* Kaiserslautern, Germany, Springer. pp 499–507

Bogers, T., Thoonen, W., & Bosch, A. van den (2006). Expertise Classification: Collaborative Classification vs. Automatic Extraction. *Proceedings of the 17th annual ASIS&T SIG/CR workshop on Social Classification*, Austin, TX, USA

Braun, S.; Schmidt, A.; Walter, A.; Nagypal, G. and Zacharias, V (2007). Ontology Maturing: a Collaborative Web2.0 Approach to Ontology Engineering. *Proceedings of the Workshop on Social and Collaborative Construction of Structured Knowledge at 16th International World Wide Web Conference*

Breslin, J.G., Bojars, U., Aleman-Meza, B., Boley, H., Mochol, M., Nixon, L.J.B., Polleres, A. and Zhdanova, A.V. (2007). Finding Experts Using Internet-Based Discussions in Online Communities and Associated Social Networks. *The 1st International Expert Finder Workshop, Berlin, Germany*

---

[1] http://mature-ip.eu
[2] http://www.im-wissensnetz.de

Brickley, D., Miller, L. (2007). FOAF Vocabulary Specification 0.91. Namespace Document 2 November 2007 – OpenID Edition. http://xmlns.com/foaf/spec/

Cooper, K. (2000). *Effective Competency Modeling & Reporting*. New York: American Management Association

Crowder, R., Hughes, G., Hall, W. (2002). Approaches to locating expertise using corporate knowledge. Int'l J. of Intelligent Systems in Accounting, Finance & Management, 11(4). 185–200

De Coi, J., Herder, E., Koesling, A., Lofi, C., Olmedilla, D., Papatreou, O., Siberski, W. (2007). A Model for Competence Gap Analysis. *Proceedings of 3rd International Conference on Web Information Systems and Technologies (WEBIST)*. Barcelona, Spain.

Design-based research collective (2003). Design-Based Research: An Emerging Paradigm for Educational Inquiry, *Educational Researcher, Vol 32*, No. 1. 5–8

Dittmann, L. and Zelewski, S. (2004). Ontology-based Skills Management. *Proceedings of the 8th World Multi-conference on Systemics, Cybernetics and Informatics (SCI 2004), Vol. IV*. pp 190–195

Draganidis, F. (2006). An Ontology Based Tool for Competency Management and Learning Paths. *Proceedings of I-KNOW '06, Graz, Austria*

Farell, St., Lau, T., Nusser, S., Wilcox, E. and Muller, M. (2007a) Socially Augmenting Employee Profiles with People-Tagging. *Proceedings of the 20th annual ACM symposium on User Interface Software and Technology*. New York: ACM Press. pp 91–100

Farell, St., Lau, T. and Nusser, S. (2007b). Building Communities with People-Tags. *INTERACT (2)*. 357–360

Google Web Toolkit. Google Web Toolkit – Build AJAX apps in the Java language. http://code.google.com/webtoolkit/, (accessed 2007-03-20)

John, A. and Seligmann, D. (2006). Collaborative tagging and expertise in the enterprise. *Proceedings of WWW 2006 Workshop on Collaborative Web Tagging*

Klemke, R,, Kröpelin, P., Kuth, C. (2003). Ganzheitliches Kompetenzmanagement. *Personalwirtschaft 2003(2)*. 26–31

Lau, T. and Sure, Y. (2002) Introducing Ontology-based Skills Management at a large Insurance Company. *Modellierung in der Praxis – Modellierung für die Praxis*. 123–134

Ley, T., Lindstaedt, S.N. and Albert, D. (2006). Competency Management Using the Competence Performance Approach: Modelling, Assessment, Validation and Use. In: Sicilia, M.A. (ed.) *Competencies in Organizational E-Learning*. Hershey, PA.: Information Science Publishing. pp 83–119

LinkedIn, http://www.linkedin.com, (accessed 2009-03-20)

McDonald, D.W. and Ackerman, M.S. (2000). Expertise recommender: a flexible recommendation system and architecture. *Proceedings of the 2000 ACM Conference on Computer Supported Cooperative Work*. New York: ACM Press. pp 231–240

Miles, A. and Bechhofer, S. (2008). SKOS Simple Knowledge Organization System Reference. *W3C Working Draft 25* January 2008

Miles, A., Brickley, D. (2004). SKOS Extensions Vocabulary Specification. W3C Working Draft 18 October 2004

Reichling, T., Veith, M. and Wulf, V. (2007). Expert Recommender: Designing for a Network Organization. *Computer Supported Cooperative Work: The Journal of Collaborative Computing (JCSCW), 16*(4–5). 431–465

Reinhardt, K. and North, K. (2003). Transparency and Transfer of Individual Competencies – A Concept of Integrative Competence Management. *J. UCS 9*(12). 1372–1380

Schmidt, A. (2005). Knowledge Maturing and the Continuity of Context as a Unifying Concept for Knowledge Management and E-Learning. *Proceedings of I-KNOW '05, Special Track on Integrating Working and Learning*

Schmidt, A. (2008). Enabling Learning on Demand in Semantic Work Environments: The Learning in Process Approach. In: Jörg Rech and Björn Decker and Eric Ras (eds.) *Emerging Technologies for Semantic Work Environments: Techniques, Methods, and Applications*. Hershey PA, IGI Publishing

Schmidt, A. and Kunzmann, C. (2006). Towards a Human Resource Development Ontology for Combining Competence Management and Technology-Enhanced Workplace Learning. In: Robert Meersman and Zahir Tahiri and Pilar Herero (eds.): *On The Move to Meaningful Internet Systems 2006*: OTM 2006 Workshops. Part I. 1st Workshop on Ontology Content and Evaluation in Enterprise (OntoContent 2006), *Lecture Notes in Computer Science vol. 4278*, Springer. 1078–1087

Schmidt, A. and Kunzmann, C. (2007). Sustainable Competency-Oriented Human Resource Development with Ontology-Based Competency Catalogues. In: Miriam Cunningham and Paul Cunningham (eds.): Expanding the Knowledge Economy: Issues, Applications, Case Studies. *Proceedings of E-Challenges 2007*. IOS Press

Schmidt, A., Kunzmann, C. and Biesalski, E. (2006). Systematische Personalentwicklung mit ontologiebasierten Kompetenzkatalogen: Konzepte, Erfahrungen, Visionen. In Norbert Gronau and Jane Fröming and Simone Schmid (eds.): *Fachtagung Kompetenzmanagement - Schulung, Staffing und Anreizsysteme*, Potsdam, 5.10.2006, GITO

Sesame RDF repository framework, http://www.openrdf.org/ (accessed 2009-03-20)

The NTSH, http://thentsh.com (accessed 2009-03-20)

Xing, http://www.xing.com (accessed 2009-03-20)

Zacharias, V. and Braun, S. (2007). SOBOLEO – Social Bookmarking and Lightweight Engineering of Ontologies. *Proceedings of the 1st Workshop on Social and Collaborative Construction of Structured Knowledge at 16th International World Wide Web Conference*

Chapter 8
Beyond Web 2.0 ... and Beyond the Semantic Web

Aurélien Bénel, Chao Zhou, and Jean-Pierre Cahier

8.1 Introduction

Tim O'Reilly, the famous technology book publisher, changed the life of many of us when he coined the name "Web 2.0" (O' Reilly 2005). Our research topics suddenly became subjects for open discussion in various cultural formats such as radio and TV, while at the same time they became part of an inappropriate marketing discourse according to several scientific reviewers. Indeed Tim O'Reilly's initial thoughts were about economic consequence, since it was about the resurrection of the Web after the bursting of the dot-com bubble. Some opponents of the concept do not think the term should be used at all since it is underpinned by no technological revolution. In contrast, we think that there was a paradigm shift when several sites based on user-generated content became some of the most visited Web sites and massive adoption of that kind is worthy of researchers' attention.

As computer scientists working on CSCW, we are concerned with designing software for knowledge workers that would foster participation in much the same way as Web 2.0 currently does for entertainment. In saying this, we differ from researchers who think that the future of the Web is the "Semantic Web." Contrary to those who called it "Web 2.0," we do not see how "data processable by machine" (Berners-Lee et al. 2001) could be the future of the "wisdom of crowds" (O'Reilly 2005). If semantics is important to improve Web 2.0, we think that we need a social semantics rather than a computational one.

In the first section, we will give a definition of what could be called a "social semantic Web," as compared to the Web, the Semantic Web, and Web 2.0. In the second and third sections, we will illustrate this definition with a course material sharing platform and a collaborative document analysis software, respectively.

A. Bénel (✉), C. Zhou, and J.-P. Cahier
Université de Technologie de Troyes, France
e-mail: aurelien.benel@utt.fr

D. Randall and P. Salembier (eds.), *From CSCW to Web 2.0: European Developments in Collaborative Design*, Computer Supported Cooperative Work,
DOI 10.1007/978-1-84882-965-7_8, © Springer-Verlag London Limited 2010

8.2   Toward a Social Semantic Web

The term "Socio-semantic Web" was coined by Manuel Zacklad et al. (2003) to express the view that there was another way to build a "Semantic Web" than the computational way promoted by the World Wide Web Consortium. The main idea is to provide a digital medium for knowledge workers, where knowledge models are created and updated through cooperation and debate. It can borrow concepts and technologies from both the Social Web and the Semantic Web and combines them in a new way. In the following subsections, we will see why it is a "web" and why it is both "semantic" and "social."

8.2.1   A "Web"

To define the "Web," we shall analyze how the "Mesh," an internal IT project from the CERN,[1] invented in 1990 and prototyped in 1991, became a "World Wide Web" of more than one trillion pages.[2,3]

Initially, the Mesh was created to solve the problem of the knowledge loss due to high turnover in personnel in the organization. Transmission of data between staff was difficult since the documents and other data of a project were scattered among different servers with incompatible formats, data structures, and protocols. To avoid that, Tim Berners-Lee proposed a distributed hypertext as a loose integration structure (Berners-Lee 1989). It is reasonable to argue that the rapid success of the Web was due to its three core components (Jacobs and Walsh 2004): URL, HTML, and HTTP.

A URL (uniform resource locator) provides an easy way to identify a digital "resource" anywhere in the world, may it be on the Web (independently of its format) or on other digital services (such as the older FTP and Gopher for files, NNTP for news, Prospero for directories, e-mail addresses, etc.).

HTML (hypertext markup language) makes it possible to structure a text both hierarchically (into headings, paragraphs, lists, tables, etc.), and with internal and external transverse links. With some technology (e.g., CGI), it is possible to generate a universal interface (a hypertext view) of an existing database. Moreover, having a formal network of informal nodes provides room for both computation and human interpretation. Because it is based on a URL, a link in an HTML document can point to a resource that is provided by a different community.

---

[1] CERN: European Organization for Nuclear Research, Geneva.

[2] "We knew the web was big...", from http://googleblog.blogspot.com/2008/07/we-knew-web-was-big. html Official Google Blog.

[3] The "deep Web," hidden into organizations intranets, is considered to be 500 times larger than the "surface Web" indexed by Google.

HTTP (hypertext transfer protocol) is the application protocol used between web clients and web servers. Just like FTP, it allows us to create, retrieve, and delete resources on the server with requests named "PUT," "GET," and "DELETE." The main difference is that HTTP is "stateless." Because Web browsing causes the user to visit and quit a server without known patterns, each HTTP request must be processed independently, without any knowledge of the previous requests stored on the host.

Roy T. Fielding, who was one of the coauthors of the HTTP specification (Fielding 1999), and was involved in the development of HTML and URIs, generalized the key factors of the Web success (Costello 2002) for distributed network systems and named the resulting architectural style "Representational State Transfer" (REST) in his Ph.D. thesis (Fielding 2000). In the REST architectural style, he argues, every resource should have a unique, global identifier: the URI. Its state is modified through a universal set of operations called "CRUD," (for "Create, Read, Update, and Delete") in the database community (Gregorio 2004), the mapping of CRUD onto HTTP command is: POST, GET, PUT, and DELETE, respectively.[4] Another principle of a "RESTful" design is to "link things together" (Tilkov 2007), so that it is possible to navigate from one resource to another, simply by following the links.

In order to have a hypertext network as distributed, robust, and versatile as the Web, we decided to define a RESTful protocol for the Socio-semantic Web (Zhou et al. 2006).

8.2.2   A Web Which Is "Semantic"

Using a Web search engine reminds us that there is a huge difference between what can be stored and processed by a machine (character strings), and the meanings that people write, read, and look for. It reminds us powerfully that there is a semantic gap between the two.

In 2001, Tim Berners-Lee coauthored a Scientific American article announcing the "Semantic Web" program launch. His idea for bridging the semantic gap was to gradually turn the Web into "well formed" data so that machines could "understand" them and deduce responses to user queries (Berners-Lee et al. 2001). The World Wide Web Consortium (W3C), founded by Tim Berners-Lee after he left CERN then began to develop Semantic Web technologies, following a roadmap humorously called "the layer cake" (see Fig. 8.1). Layered architectures are indeed a very common way to build computer and network systems. Each layer is supposed to be built only on the layer below and to grow in complexity and specialization. Thus, the layers can be developed and standardized with a relative independence.

---

[4]It is noteworthy that there are some common misunderstandings: ignoring PUT and DELETE, and using GET even to change the state of a resource.

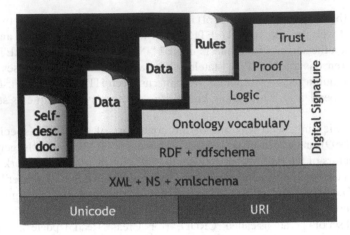

Fig. 8.1 The semantic Web architecture (Berners-Lee 2000) – also known as the semantic Web layer cake

First presented by Tim Berners-Lee at an XML conference (Berners-Lee, 2000), the cake is unsurprisingly built on Web technologies (Unicode and URI) and on XML (a tree serialization format). The next level is made from "RDF," a directed graph model, and "rdfschema" (also called RDFs), a "vocabulary" aimed at using RDF to model classes and properties.

Those bottom layers have been standardized for years. Nevertheless, after more than 80,000 research articles about the "Semantic Web" and 200,000 about "ontologies,"[5] the feasibility of the upper layers still seems unclear. The "Ontology vocabulary" is supposed to be a formal definition of the terminology used in a specific context. "Logic" refers to the automatic inferences drawn from the statements given in the lower layers. As for "proof" (explaining the courses of the logical reasoning) and "trust" (users' trust in the data), no slide was dedicated to them in the original talk, and very little has been written on them in the Semantic Web literature.

For François Rastier: "The recommendations of the W3C, reassuring enough when they are presented as being purely practical, are in fact designed to become standards"; "standards are established, and then given the status of theoretical models." François Rastier goes further: "By conveniently proclaiming the creation of Web Science in 2007, [Tim Berners-Lee] shrewdly avoids having scientific problems raised and debated outside the Semantic Web community, which is self-engendered and must therefore undergo only self-assessment." In particular, "the adoption of 'low- level' standards such as HTML, or Unicode, or even XML, in no way entails that languages of representation such as RDF or OWL should be adopted as standard, unless one merely seeks to yield easily to the attempt by the W3C to force through the 'Semantic Web'" (Rastier forthcoming).

---

[5] Source: Google Scholar on Feb. 2009.

In contrast to the slow development of the Semantic Web, breakthroughs in Web search techniques were achieved through citation analysis (Google PageRank), directories (DMOZ, also used in Google), and tags. All of these technologies use simple structures created by human authors or readers, and none uses content formalized by knowledge engineers. In order to allow for a semantics dependent on the decisions of the human subject and on the semiotic substrate, we decided to define a model allowing users themselves to enrich documents with a model of their interpretation (Zacklad et al. 2003, 2007; Bénel et al. 2001).

8.2.3   A Web Which Is Semantic and Social

The "semantic Web," as suggested above, and although it is supposed to aim at "trust," in fact has very little interest in the social dimension of the "Web." We can only wonder what sort of "trust" could be based on "proof" and "digital signatures." Socially speaking, trust is precisely what is required when there is *no proof*. A digital signature, in other words, can effectively attest that data has not been modified by someone else other than the bearer of a digital key, but it is far from being sufficient to provide trust. One might wonder with François Rastier (2009, forthcoming), what exactly the political and economical program is that is underpinned by the Semantic Web.

Conversely, "harnessing collective intelligence" is one of the main features of what Tim O'Reilly called "Web 2.0." Whether it comes from the "scientific debate" (Bénel et al. 2001), the "marketplace" (Cahier and Zacklad 2002), or the "wisdom of crowds" (Surowiecki 2004), collective intelligence can arise from a shared place where contradictory viewpoints can be expressed. In Web 2.0, this can be achieved by allowing people evaluate a resource or a person, comment a blog post, edit a wiki discussion page, or tag a resource with a free keyword. These are situations where trust is needed, and can be socially constructed little by little. Web 2.0 tools usually try to aggregate the viewpoints into an average of marks, a "cloud" of tags, or in a consensual wiki page. Because we are more interested in smaller communities, we focus on visualizations which preserve each actor's viewpoint (Zhou and Bénel 2008).

Instead of being decomposed into layers, the Social Semantic Web relies on three human and social phenomena (see Fig. 8.2):

- *Documents*, because they are *proofs* of something else, not in the manner of a mathematical proof but more in that of a juridical one; they are a testimony to be kept, evidence to be brought to bear
- *Interpretation*, because the meaning of a document depends on its authors and readers
- *Intersubjectivity*, because the confrontation between conflicting interpretations allows to us overcome individual subjectivity (Bénel and Lejeune 2009, forthcoming)

The Social Semantic Web can therefore be seen as the confluence of Knowledge Engineering and Computer Supported Cooperative Work. In the first research

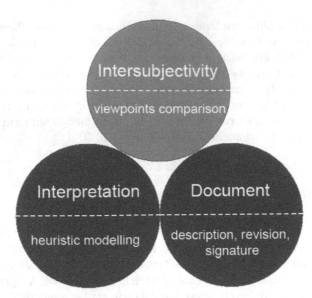

Fig. 8.2 The social semantic Web trefoil

community, there has been a renewed interest in digital documents, because of their semiotic richness compared to formal models, and their ability to be hybridized with knowledge organization systems such as thesauri, topic maps, and classification schemes (Bachimont 2003; Schmidt and Wagner 2005). In the second research community, it is known that a lot of cooperative activities involve documents and categorizations, not as "data" but as social and iterative constructs (Israel 2000). This is supposed to give actors reflexive methods and tools to help them in carrying out self-description (Herrmann et al. 2005), building maps cooperatively, expressing conflicts, comparing points of view, and assimilating or imitating conflicting interpretations (Salvador 1997). For both research communities, focusing on user interpretation is a way to adopt a pragmatic approach to knowledge and to place emphasis on practices (Schoop et al. 2006; Park 2008; Shum 2006). To sum up, an increasing amount of research work in Knowledge Engineering and Computer Supported Cooperative Work permits us to think that a more semiotic and pragmatic Web could be possible. But because it consists mainly of human and social phenomena (see Fig. 8.2), we cannot build it ourselves. We can only construct the structured writing *medium* (Goody 1986; Bachimont 2000) to let these phenomena happen.

8.3 An Illustration: Education

The project named "CogDoc" aims at providing a platform for sharing course materials (slides and audio/video records) among teachers and students from French-speaking universities related to an international and interdisciplinary research group. A prototype was made at Troyes University of Technology with *Agorae*, a web space for topic map cooperative building (Zaher et al. 2006), and *Argos*, a web service implementing our protocol for the community-driven organization of knowledge. In according with the socio-semantic Web approach, the prototype provided a space for documents, interpretation, and intersubjectivity.

8.3.1 Document

Two teachers have documented 40 course lectures (see Fig. 8.3) with their corresponding slides (one version to be displayed, one to be annotated), exercises (if any), and description (title, author, date...).

Course lectures have been primarily classified upon their universities, majors, and learning units. This catalog made of preexisting official topics can be browsed from a tab called "universities" (see Fig. 8.4).

8.3.2 Interpretation

Once the teacher or student is logged in, any course lecture screen shows a panel for tagging (see Fig. 8.5). On the top of this panel is a drop-down list of viewpoints,

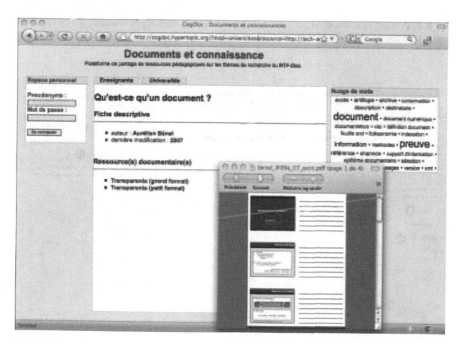

Fig. 8.3 A course lecture with its attributes and resources – agorae screenshot

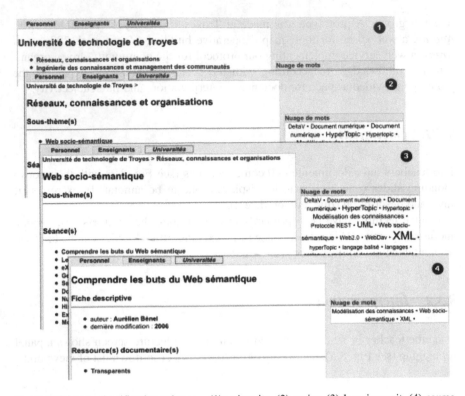

Fig. 8.4 Primary classification scheme – (1) university, (2) major, (3) learning unit, (4) course lecture

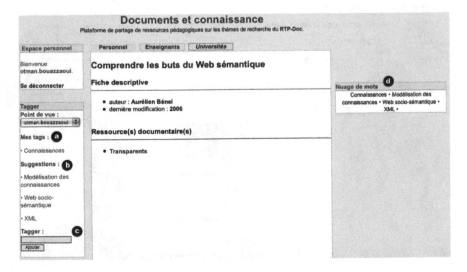

Fig. 8.5 Describing a course lecture with existing or new tags – agorae screenshot

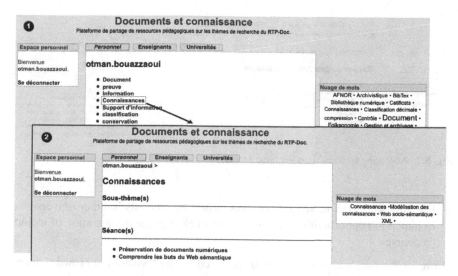

Fig. 8.6 Browsing one's tags – agorae screenshot

related to him or her. Within a selected viewpoint (see Fig. 8.5a), they are able to reuse tags assigned by someone else (see Fig. 8.5b) or to input their own (Fig. 8.5c). Then, tags can be accessed through a personal tab and be used to browse one's personal collection of course lectures (see Fig. 8.6). Therefore, contrary to the primary classification scheme, tags are unstructured and uncontrolled terms chosen by the user for his or her own use. But the more the user reuses his or her tags on different lectures, the more he or she reveals intertextual links between them, and the more he or she organizes his or her knowledge of the field.

8.3.3   Intersubjectivity

The hundreds of tags assigned by 70 students and teachers are dynamically aggregated into a tag cloud dependent on the page (see Figs. 8.3 and 8.4). To reduce misspelled or erroneous tags we filtered out tags used only once or twice from the cloud. Moreover, even if participants were incited to choose popular expressions as tags, and reuse them, the diversity was so important that we had to show only the 80 most frequent tags per cloud (and make them case-insensitive).

The resulting emergent description of courses, majors, and universities in terms of learnt knowledge and know-how is quite interesting in what it affords:

- For students to choose a university or course, to revise for exams, to communicate ideas, to evaluate course sessions, to set milestones, to express opinions
- For teachers to detect students' misunderstandings, false interpretations, or needs for discussion on certain topics

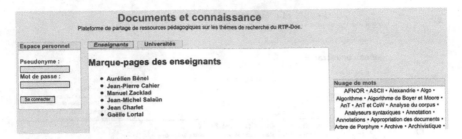

Fig. 8.7 Accessing teachers' tags – agorae screenshot

- For university staff to validate courses passed by students in other universities, to match job opportunities with majors, or to change the organization of majors or courses

However, because education cannot be replaced by the "wisdom of crowds," intersubjectivity is also featured in a more asymmetric and private mode between teachers and students. Firstly, teachers' tags can be accessed by anyone as a reference from the "teachers" tab (see Fig. 8.7). Secondly, a teacher can access the tags of any of his or her students to evaluate what they understood and grade them.

8.4 An Illustration: Research

Our second case study is about the use by art historians[6] of *Porphyry* (Bénel et al. 2006), our collaborative document analysis software.

8.4.1 Documents

In this research project, the objects of study are Iron Age vases discovered in the excavations of the cemetery of Athens called "Kerameikos." These artifacts are documented with photographs named after their storage location and inventory identifier (see Fig. 8.8).

8.4.2 Interpretation

The selected vases are particularly important for the understanding of the history of ancient Greece, since they are supposed to be from a short period (called

---

[6]Pr. Jean-Marc Luce and his master students (CRATA Laboratory, University of Toulouse II, France).

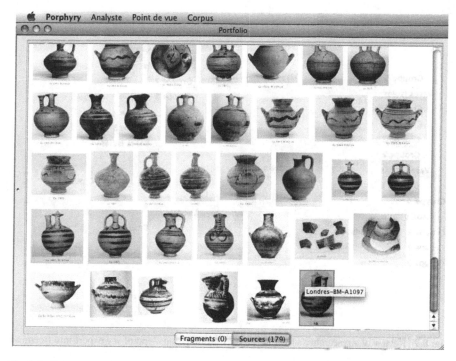

Fig. 8.8 Vases photographs named after their storage location and inventory identifier – porphyry screenshot

"submycenaean") between the end of the Mycenaean civilization and the beginning of the Greek "dark ages." Indeed, invasions and external influences are supposed to have impacts on vases styles, progressively making forms simpler and patterns more geometric.

A recent monograph analyzed stylistic features of each vase, and then gathered them into new coherent stylistic groups. In order to review this research work, Jean-Marc Luce used our software (see Fig. 8.9) to model "how [the author], himself, classified it"[7]: "I haven't followed his analysis, all his headings. I just put the groups."[8]

Then, to initiate master students to research, he asked each of them to analyze the stylistic features of one type of vases (see Fig. 8.10):

"The tool is interesting for several reasons: [...] it introduces them to ceramics study; [...] it teaches how to 'decorticate' and then recompose everything. When they do a dissertation on it they are 'driven', they are forced to do a rigorous work."[9]

---

[7] "Comment lui l'a classé."

[8] "Je n'ai pas suivi son analyse, toutes ses rubriques. J'ai juste mis les groupes."

[9] "L'outil est intéressant à plusieurs titres: [...] introduire à l'étude de la céramique, apprendre à tout décortiquer puis recomposer. Quand ils font leur mémoire dessus, ils sont cadrés. Ca les oblige à faire un travail rigoureux."

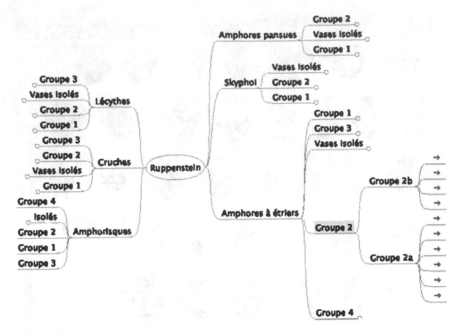

Fig. 8.9 Review of a researcher's hypotheses on stylistic groups – porphyry export into freemind

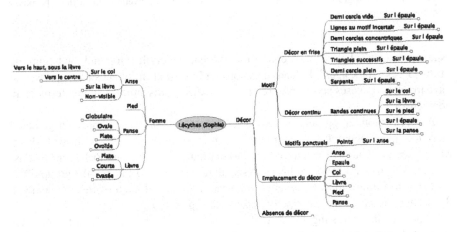

Fig. 8.10 Masters student's analysis of stylistic features – porphyry export into freemind

Whether or not the tool really "drives" students, it seems to be through a dialog with their professor that they learn:

1. How to identify a feature on a vase?
   Professor: "It is not a checker pattern. Zoom in."[10]

---

[10] "Ce n'est pas un damier. Grossissez davantage."

2. How to name a feature?
Sophie: "I didn't know how to name it."
Professor: "Generally, one says ..."[11]

3. How to build a group?
Professor (to the observer): "That's what one learn: combining features to get groups as coherent as possible."
Professor (to Sophie): "Your systems are rather compatible, but not always coherent."[12]

4. How to interpret a group?
Professor: "Patterns are diverse. It is made by hand. It is the most ancient phase."
Sophie: "It's indeed what it seemed to me."[13]

8.4.3 Intersubjectivity

By comparing the viewpoints expressed in the new monograph and in an older one, the professor was able to guess that one of the innovations was to consider several vases (see Fig. 8.11) as being from a transitional phase ("groupe 4") to a later period rather than being submycenaean. Another innovation consisted in considering vases (see Fig. 8.12) formerly tagged as from the end of the mycenean period ("HRIIIC récent") as, more properly, submycenean ("groupe 1," "groupe 2").

Another use of viewpoints comparison was to confront Masters students' interpretation and those of senior researchers. Even if the analysis by Sophie was incomplete and perfectible, the vases she described as having a flat paunch ("panse plate") and a short lip ("lèvre courte") appeared to be exactly what the specialist considered to be the oldest group (see Fig. 8.13). Moreover, she successfully identified features (oval paunch, flat lip, triangles, or circles patterns) which were sufficient criteria to assign a vase to the more recent group. Indeed, as a Masters student, comparing one's viewpoint with those of senior researchers' should not be seen just as a way to get correct answers, but as a way to take part in the sense-making process followed by specialists, a way to get involved in the "on-going science."

8.5 Conclusion

This paper introduced the "Socio-semantic Web" as an alternative to the Semantic Web and Web 2.0. In contrast to the Semantic Web, it is not interested in formal semantics, but in semantics dependent on the human subject and on the semiotic

---

[11] "Je ne savais pas comment l'appeler. — En général, on dit ...."

[12] "C'est ce que l'on apprend : combiner les traits pour avoir des groupes aussi cohérents que possible. – Vos systèmes sont assez compatibles mais pas toujours très cohérents."

[13] "Les motifs sont diversifiés. C'est fait à la main. C'est la phase la plus ancienne. — C'est bien ce qu'il me semblait."

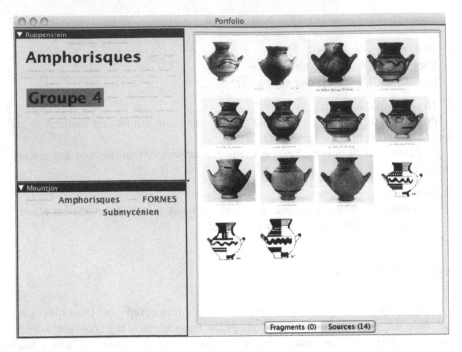

Fig. 8.11 Submycenaean or transition to the next style? – porphyry screenshot

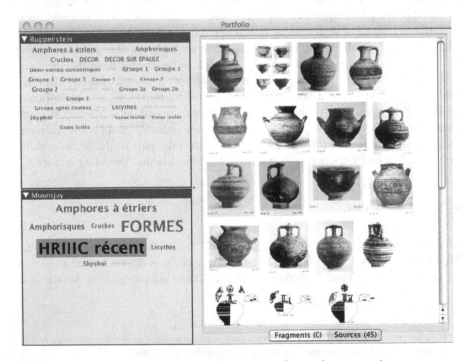

Fig. 8.12 End of mycenean or beginning of submycenean? – porphyry screenshot

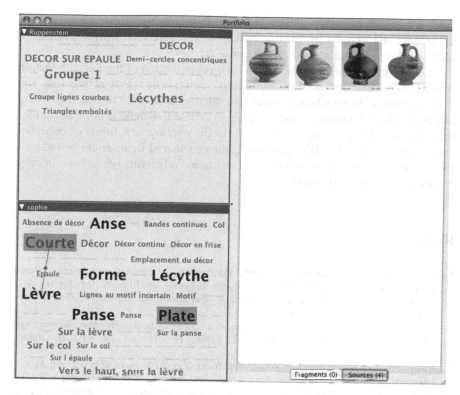

Fig. 8.13 Does your stylistic features define a group? – porphyry screenshot

substrate. Similarly to what Web 2.0 does for entertainment, it aims at fostering people's participation in knowledge work. In this trend, software design relies on three human and social phenomena:

- Documents, because they are proofs of something else, not in the manner of a mathematical proof but more in that of an evidence to be kept and brought
- Interpretation, because the meaning of a document depends on its authors and readers
- Intersubjectivity, because the confrontation between conflicting interpretations allows to overcome subjectivity

Software prototypes complying with this approach have been tested on different domains[14] (archaeology, sociology, civil society, and engineering). In this paper, we focused on two iconic sense-making activities: education and research. In the first illustration, by fostering the intersubjective description of content by students and teachers, a simple course material sharing platform has been turned into a digital

---

[14] See our community wiki: http://www.hypertopic.org/

space for collaborative knowledge building. In the second illustration, allowing researchers and Masters students to model and compare their own hypotheses to established ones prepared them for scientific debates.

As illustrated by the applications, the main contribution of the Social Semantic Web would be the introduction of 'viewpoints', consciously managed by actors. This would emphasize hyper-singular knowledge, micro-communities of practice, making conflict explicit, comparison and competition. While this trend is not free of risks, it nevertheless brings great opportunities for discovering new forms of collective intelligence on the Web. Divergent viewpoints on shared items could be indeed a trade-off between unrealistic extremes: positivism and relativism, tyranny and anarchy, dogmatic discourse and chaotic din.

References

Bénel, A., Calabretto, S., Iacovella, A. (2006): Porphyry & Steatite: Software layers for sense makers in humanities. In Harzallah, M., Charlet, J., Aussenac-Gilles, N. (eds.) *Actes de la semaine de la connaissance: Workshop on Indexing and Knowledge in Human Sciences*. Nantes, June 26–28.Volume 3. pp 72–75.

Bachimont, B. (2000). L'intelligence artificielle comme écriture dynamique : de la raison graphique à la raison computationnelle. In Petitot, J., Fabbri, P. (eds.) *Au nom du sens*, Grasset. pp 290–319.

Bachimont, B.: Meaning and indexing : Which issues for multimedia documents? In Gabbouj, M., ed.: *International Workshop on Content-Based Multimedia Indexing* (CBMI). (september 2003)

Bénel, A., Lejeune, C. (2009) Humanities 2.0: document, interpretation and intersubjectivity in the digital age. *International journal on Web-based communities* (forthcoming).

Bénel, A., Egyed-Zsigmond, E., Prié, Y., Calabretto, S., Mille, A., Iacovella, A. and Pinon, J.M. (2001). Truth in the digital library: From ontological to hermeneutical systems. *Proceedings of the fifth European Conference on Research and Advanced Technology for Digital Libraries [ECDL]. Number 2163 in Lecture Notes in Computer Science*, Berlin, Springer Verlag. pp 366–377.

Berners-Lee, T. (1989). Information management: A proposal. Technical report, CERN

Berners-Lee, T. (2000). Semantic web on XML. *XML 2000*, Washington, DC (December 6 2000).

Berners-Lee, T., Hendler, J. and Lassila, O. (2001). The semantic web. *Scientific American (May 17)*

Cahier, J.P., Zacklad, M. (2002). Towards a 'knowledge-based marketplace' model (KBM) for cooperation between agents. In Blay-Fornarino, M., Pinna-Dery, A.M., Schmidt, K., Zaraté, P. (eds.) COOP, IOS. pp 226–238.

Costello, R.L. (2002). *Building web services the REST way.* – xFront website. http://www. xfront. com/REST-Web-Services.

Fielding, R. (1999). Hypertext transfer protocol. *Technical report, IETF* (June 1999)

Fielding, R.T. (2000). *Architectural Styles and the Design of Network-based Software Architectures*. PhD thesis, University of California, IRVINE

Goody, J. (1986). *The Logic of Writing and the Organisation of Society*. Cambridge University Press

Gregorio, J.: How to create a REST protocol XML. com website. http://www. xml. com/pub/a/ 2004/12/01/ (December 2004)

Herrmann, T., Thomas, G. and Loser, K.U. (2005). Socio-technical self-descriptions as a means for appropriation. *Workshop on Supporting Appropriation Work: Approaches for the 'reflective' user.*

Israel, R. (2000). Classification schemes: Some genesis and maintenance issues. *Workshop on Cooperative Organization of Common Information Spaces*. Copenhagen (August 2000)

Jacobs, I. and Walsh, N. (2004). *Architecture of the world wide web*, volume one (December 15)

O'Reilly, T. (2005). What is web 2.0: Design patterns and business models for the next generation of software. *Social Science Research Network Working Paper Series*

Park, J. (2008). Topic maps, dashboards and sensemaking. *Fourth International Conference on Topic Maps Research and Applications (TMRA).* pp 11–29

Rastier, F. (forthcoming, 2010). Web Semantics *vs* the Semantic Web? The problem of keyness. In M. Scott and M. Bondi (eds.) *Keyness in text*, Amsterdam: Benjamins.

Schmidt, K., Wagner, I. (2005). Ordering systems: Coordinative practices and artifacts in architectural design and planning. *Computer Supported Cooperative Work 13.* 349–408

Schoop, M., de Moor, A. and Dietz, J.L. (2006). The pragmatic web: a manifesto. *Communications of the ACM 49*(5) (May 2006) 75–76

Shum, S.B. (2006). Sensemaking on the pragmatic web: A hypermedia discourse perspective. *1st International Pragmatic Web Conference.*

Surowiecki, J. (2004). The Wisdom of Crowds: Why the Many Are Smarter Than the Few and How Collective Wisdom Shapes Business, Economies, Societies and Nations. New York: Doubleday.

Tilkov, S.: A brief introduction to REST. – xFront website. http://www. xfront. com/REST-Web-Services. (December 2007)

Zacklad, M., Bénel, A., Cahier, J.P., Zaher, L., Lejeune, C., Zhou, C. (2007). Hypertopic : une métasémiotique et un protocole pour le web socio-sémantique. In Trichet, F., ed.: *Actes des 18eme journées francophones d'ingénierie des connaissances*, Toulouse, Cépaduès. 217–228.

Zacklad, M., Cahier, J.P., Pétard, X. (2003). Du web cognitivement sémantique au web socio sémantique: Exigences représentationnelles de la coopération. *Web sémantique et Sciences humaines et sociales.* (May 2003)

Zaher, L., Cahier, J., Zacklad, M. (2006). The Agoræ Hypertopic approach . In Harzallah, M., Charlet, J., Aussenac-Gilles, N. (eds.) *Actes de la semaine de la connaissance: Workshop on Indexing and Knowledge in Human Sciences.* Nantes, June 26–28.Volume 3. pp 66–70.

Zhou, C., Bénel, A. (2008). From the crowd to communities: New interfaces for social tagging. In: Proceedings of the eighth international conference on the design of cooperative systems (COOP'08).

Zhou, C., Bénel, A., Lejeune, C. (2006). Towards a standard protocol for community-driven organizations of knowledge. *Proceedings of the thirteenth international conference on Concurrent Engineering. Volume 143* of Frontiers in Artificial Intelligence and Appl., Amsterdam, IOS Press. pp 438–449.

Chapter 9
Engineering 2.0: Exploring Lightweight Technologies for the Virtual Enterprise

Andreas Larsson, Åsa Ericson, Tobias Larsson, Ola Isaksson, and Marco Bertoni

9.1 Introduction

In a traditional business partnership, the partner companies are under contractual obligation to share data, information, and knowledge through one or several information systems that the leading firm decides. In such a case, the issue of sharing "whatever needs to be shared" is settled in contracts before any action is taken, however, also giving the implications that sharing expertise becomes a heavy and time-consuming activity. In turn, it can be argued that the heavy administration affects the lead time of product development negatively since the necessary input flows are delayed. In addition, the adaptation to certain predefined collaborative information systems is both expensive and resource-consuming (e.g., educating staff to use them). Also, the system might not be adaptable to the existing internal technology structure, causing a "translation" procedure, again taking up resources. Another structure for collaboration is a network or alliance of independent partner companies. One motivation for a network structure is that the partners can join or leave it more easily. A reason for joining and staying is an implicit sense of knowledge sharing (Tomkins 2001) and access to a "win–win" environment. Furthermore, the partners can be linked by information technology, i.e., forming a virtual structure rather than a physical one. The technologies provide the channels with additional knowledge. In a best-case scenario, a company would get access to a wide range of useful competences, and in a worst-case scenario the company would be drained of its core competences. Accordingly, at least two considerations for joining a partner network can be considered. First, the resources needed to couple the technologies have to be reasonable, due to the underpinning logic of going in and out of more than one network. Second, the company has to identify its knowledge base and evaluate the prospective gains and losses of sharing its expertise.

Engineering work tasks are currently well supported by computer applications, e.g., CAD (Computer Aided Design), CAE (Computer Aided Engineering), PDM

A. Larsson (✉), Å. Ericson, T. Larsson, O. Isaksson, and M. Bertoni
Lulea Technical University, Sweden
e-mail: Andreas.c.Larsson@ltu.se

D. Randall and P. Salembier (eds.), *From CSCW to Web 2.0: European Developments in Collaborative Design*, Computer Supported Cooperative Work,
DOI 10.1007/978-1-84882-965-7_9, © Springer-Verlag London Limited 2010

(Product Data Management), and PLM (Product Lifecycle Management). CAD supports a visualization of the product, e.g., a 3D technical drawing and enables the engineers to validate the design and all changes against certain technical rules. CAE also offers a visualization of the product and focuses more clearly on simulation and optimization techniques to elaborate on, for instance, the distribution of stresses and displacements on a component in a welding process. PDM/PLM systems support the management of the entire life cycle of a product. A product life cycle is, commonly, described as going from an idea, via design, manufacture, distribution, and use to recycling; thus PDM/PLM systems manage not only product information but also customer and business information. These applications or their descriptions are not intended to be exhaustive, but rather to provide a sense of the nature of the information technology that is used in modern product-development companies.

It can be argued that one misconception of engineering work is that the very embodiment of product properties into 3D models and data structures of the above kind implies that all the relevant data, information, and knowledge have been captured and can serve as a base for decisions. Engineering work, which can be viewed as knowledge work, relies on expertise and competences that relate to the product that is being developed, i.e., the physical thing. However, knowledge work also has a social dimension, e.g., learning and experiencing. The assessment of the result from a number of distinct computer analyses, i.e., "putting two and two together," and what engineers know by experience influence many decisions in product development, but this kind of design reasoning is usually not made visible in the same way as technical product information. Of course, one constraint is that such knowledge is hard to express and consequently problematic to capture and formalize into information systems. Further, if captured and formalized into a knowledge base or expert system, the contents become "lagged" or "old" over time. The maintenance of the contents is commonly a huge effort where a number of engineers are struggling to keep it up-to-date. Traditional kinds of systems insist on a similar approach, and a drawback is that the practice contributes to a situation where the content of the systems and the enhancement of it are separated from those who deal with the knowledge generation processes in their daily, regular work activities. In general, this describes a knowledge *management* perspective, where the focus is on reuse of knowledge, and the information system is used to monitor and control the process.

Another view is a knowledge *sharing* view, where the focus is to spur and nurture knowledge creation (Ackerman et al. 2003) and, accordingly, the supporting technologies should also enable experiences, design reasoning, and lessons learnt to be shared. In engineering collaboration, such support seems to be lacking in the commonly used information systems. However, lightweight technologies are used by people interacting, generating, and sharing knowledge over the Internet. In this chapter, we will make the assertion that lightweight technologies can have a serious potential when it comes to effectively sharing knowledge between actors partaking in product development in a virtual context. Thus, the purpose of this chapter is to highlight opportunities, describe the possibilities, and discuss the ways in which lightweight technology can be adapted to be supportive in a business-to-business network.

Proposing lightweight technologies, e.g., wikis, tag clouds, and mashups, in an industrial context is sometimes controversial; we would like to clarify our intentions in this chapter. First, note the word "adapted" in the purpose above. This means that we will explore what can be *learnt* from lightweight technologies, *discuss* the potential for an industrial application, and suggest *modifications* that need to be done. Second, we make a distinction to the commonly used technologies, e.g., CAD/CAE/PDM/PLM, by calling them "heavyweight"; this is not done to favor one over the other. We like to distinguish the efforts in applying and using them. Also, we do not intend to argue for a replacement of "heavyweight" technologies; rather, we argue that both are needed and complement each other. A main point in such a discussion is that lightweight technologies are rarely considered as useful in an industrial context.

A delimitation of the scope in this chapter is that we focus on understanding the kinds of problems that occur and can occur when the intention is to share knowledge. We do not attempt to produce technical requirements for the design of a solution, nor do we evaluate the technologies. Another delimitation of this chapter is its focus on "engineers"; however, "what engineers do" is framed by a changed view on the product they are going to develop. We will present the idea of life-cycle commitments, which are one trigger for change in the traditional work of engineers. A life-cycle commitment is based on a product-development process that has the outcome of added value for customers. Accordingly, engineers take on a larger part of the intangible value creation activities when designing the physical thing. Also, the typical engineering work increases in scope and is challenged by relational complexity when collaborating in partner networks, or, as outlined in this paper, a virtual enterprise. These parts motivate the discussion on lightweight technologies, which compose the main part of the chapter. The discussion is delimited to focus on opportunities and possibilities; so while we understand the problems with intellectual property rights, the importance to clarify who owns what knowledge assets and how to both protect and share knowledge, we do not include this in our discussion.

The discussion in this paper has evolved in our research context, which includes close collaboration with industrial companies, hence also providing access to empirical cases. The aspects of knowledge – management and sharing – have provided an overarching theme for our research interest during the last 10 years. In recent time, our participation in two large research projects, have provided access to a total of nine international companies, and numerous people from these companies. For example, we have conducted a number of multiday workshops, participated in virtual meetings, made company visits to perform interviews on both a formal and an informal basis. The paper draws on data from a number of industrial development projects related to several different products in various industry segments – ranging from the development of manufacturing tools and industrial drive systems, to aircraft engines and armored terrain vehicles. So, the identification of the problematic situations has been noticed in the larger empirical context. The excerpts that are presented in this paper are transcribed from taped interviews performed at various companies. The excerpts are chosen based on their potential to represent the kinds of problems that typically are experienced when sharing knowledge and extend the offerings toward life-cycle commitments.

9.2 Life-Cycle Commitments

Framed by a Product-Service Systems paradigm (Bains et al. 2007) a movement toward extended business models is taking place in industry. Here, the term "life-cycle commitments" is used to cover the various concepts used in industrial companies. The name differs, but there are common features, e.g., an increased interest in providing "functions" rather than selling "hardware," and a general focus on providing added value to customers. A life-cycle commitment which is provided by the aircraft engine manufacturer Rolls-Royce is called "Total Care" and aims to deliver "power by the hour" in order to "improve product availability and reduce the cost of ownership by tying a supplier's compensation to the output value of the product generated by the customer (buyer)" (Kim et al. 2007).

One consequence of such life-cycle commitments is that customers and providers are taking a step closer to each other in the value chain, hence also creating long-term business relationships. This is a challenge, insofar as many consumer-product companies can reverse-engineer competitors' products in a matter of days. Another consequence of this performance-based business model means that customers pay for the result of the product use, i.e., what ultimately adds value. Further, time and material associated with repairs and overhauls are incorporated into a life-cycle commitment.

From the provider's perspective this means that maintenance becomes a cost instead of a profit. Considering that airline companies spend on average US$ 870 per flight hour in direct maintenance costs, with engines representing over 40% of that cost, it is safe to assume that the companies need to provide attractive offers that are profitable for all partners. A jet engine could be kept in service for as much as 30–40 years, and providing a function means that the functional product provider cannot longer, in the traditional sense, earn money on the once lucrative aftermarket. Also, the aftermarket is incredibly competitive even in the current situation. Essentially, to create a win–win situation for providers and customers, a life-cycle commitment has to be considered from a product-development perspective. Although many products in today's marketplace might be *sold* as functions, they are rarely *developed* with a function view, i.e., focusing on use of performance to provide perceived value.

Life-cycle commitments do, on one side, mean that the business is based on a long-term relationship. On the other side, it indicates an increased interest and incentive to collect and use information from the entire life-cycle and, in particular, make use of downstream information early on (Boart 2005). That is, information about how customers are *using* the physical product becomes vital, and the long-term horizon adds an interest to gain insights into the basic reasoning that makes the customer link the use of performance to perceived added value.

The view of a product is, from a customer perspective, holistic and encompassing (Mello 2002), while from a traditional development perspective it is broken down into a view of a service or a physical thing.

In addition to the business development processes, such a perspective makes two separate development processes discernible. A product development process for life-cycle commitments has to consider these processes in an integrative way in early development. In a broad sense, decisions concerning whether or not to provide life-cycle commitments have to be made, as well as decisions for how to technically solve the long-term provision of functions. To what extent should services be "designed-in" or "added on," and what competences and knowledge are needed for the development and the provision of use of performance. So, the scope of early product development activities rapidly changes to encompass a wider range of data, information, and knowledge that is not readily available in a traditional product-development process.

To provide an "ideal" life-cycle commitment that is capable of delivering use of performance during 30–40 years, as in the case with a jet engine, a risk- and revenue-sharing environment together with business partners is a key. In general, the formation of a joint venture can be a solution, where a structure of a network of partners supported by technologies is a specific way. Within the frame for the discussion in this paper, two main challenges need to be addressed to achieve successful collaboration, namely (1) how to effectively share relevant and valid knowledge in time and (2) how to capture and make use of it. Hence, companies need to rethink how knowledge is created and shared across the many boundaries of the global value chain.

9.3 Knowledge Sharing in the Virtual Enterprise

In the case of a joint venture, here a *Virtual Enterprise* (VE), the issue of what knowledge to share and how to share it needs to be resolved. A VE is essentially a network of independent companies, including suppliers, customers, and even competitors, that are "linked by information technology to share skills, costs, and access to one another's markets. It will have neither central office nor organization chart. It will have no hierarchy, no vertical integration" (Byrne 1993). Thus, a basic idea is that no single company in the partnership can impose their preferred way to collaborate. The idea of a network structure highlights a swift and easy way to get linked to different business partners. Basically, to impose a preferred technological way to get access spoils the idea of easily getting in our out of the network.

Defined in logical terms, not physical, the VE is based on the idea of organizations gaining access to more resources than they currently have available, without having to expand. Further, a VE is extended to encompass a network of partners and suppliers that work together to reach common goals. In this environment there is unlikely to be any single partner that can decide the infrastructure, tool set, or processes to be used.

Ray Noorda, founder of Novell, noted that companies need to simultaneously compete and cooperate, thus coining the term *coopetition* (Brandenburger and Nalebuff 1997) which essentially deals with the interplay between competition and cooperation. Partners in a VE may choose to work together with the aim to collectively enhance their performance by sharing resources, risks, and rewards – and they may, at the same time, work independently to improve their own performance and market attractiveness. For instance, two independent airline carriers, such as Singapore Airlines and Qantas Airlines, can compete against each other for landing slots, gates, freight contracts, and passengers, while cooperating to share the development cost of the Airbus A380 aircraft that are part of their current fleet expansion. On a larger scale, these companies are also part of separate airline alliances, the *Star Alliance* and the *oneworld Alliance*, which further blurs the lines between who is a customer and who is a supplier. Note that a jet engine manufacturer, such as Rolls-Royce, might develop engines to be used on both Airbus and Boeing aircraft, which are ordered by different airliners, which are partners in different airline alliances, etc. For example, the V2500 aero engine family is provided by International Aero Engines (IAE), a joint venture including Pratt & Whitney, Rolls-Royce, MTU Aero Engines, and the Japanese Aero Engines Corporation (www.v2500.com). The CFM56 aero engine product line is developed by CFM International, a joint venture between GE and Snecma (www.cfm56.com), and the GP7200 engines powering the Airbus A380 are a result of the Engine Alliance (www.enginealliance.com), a joint venture between GE and Pratt & Whitney.

Since coopetition, i.e., "collaborating with the enemy," is becoming increasingly common in the domain of global product development, being able to handle the rapid transformations in and out of a VE is critical. Each partner company in the network needs to know, in terms of knowledge sharing, what they can bring into the partnership and what they can take from it. Accordingly, a cohesive and intentional life-cycle perspective also on knowledge is needed.

9.4   The Need to Raise the Knowledge Baseline

The starting position for a heterogeneous development team consisting of people from different departments, different companies, etc., means that the team, as a whole, usually does not have a previous history of working together – there are fundamentally no "shared assumptions" of how to collaborate within the team or, in the case of new products included in a life-cycle commitment, no "shared vision'" for what to develop. Rather, there are as many assumptions and visions as there are people involved. One of the success factors in this kind of collaboration is the ability to effectively and seamlessly assemble and utilize, drawing from the different perspectives of the VE partners, their pool of resources, the various combinations of specific capabilities to be applied in the project at hand. Furthermore, there is an inevitable flux of team members over time in product development projects, so knowledge not only needs to be utilized, but also made available into a larger context than within the team.

This points out the issues of how to make structural knowledge capital out of the human knowledge capital and make it available internally and externally to make sure that knowledge assets can be effectively shared across organizational and departmental boundaries. These challenges are part of the activities to raise the knowledge baseline in joint development projects. Effective knowledge sharing is challenged by more distances than the geographical, and differences include language, culture (both "corporate" and "local"), educational background, government regulations, and time zones. There are several aspects that can impose negative influence on the performance of cross-boundary collaboration in development teams. Issues of how to build trust, rapport, and respect to bridge these differences is identified as crucial (Larsson 2005). Another crucial point when the product has a long life-cycle, as in the aerospace industry, is that knowledge assets need to be maintained for a period of time that could extend several years after the development project has been concluded. Take Pratt & Whitney's JT8D engine, for example, which has been in use since the early 1960s in different variants.

Also, the movement of data, information, and knowledge is vital for a competitive total life-cycle commitment. Knowledge from the "later" phases of the product life-cycle (i.e., production, distribution, use, maintenance, recycling, etc.) now needs to be used as a knowledge foundation in the earlier phases of the product development process. It is most advantageous to make changes at the preliminary design phase, since it will become more expensive, more difficult, or even impossible to compensate or correct the shortcomings of a poor design concept in the later life-cycle phases. So, in order to provide products that, in life-cycle commitments, truly meet the full range of the actors' demands and needs, it is highly important to investigate how downstream knowledge could be made available to all actors, to improve early-stage decision making in cross-disciplinary product-development teams. For example, the deployment of Knowledge Based Engineering applications (Boart 2005: 36) enables companies to move downstream information upstream, essentially making information of the result of later activities available at an earlier stage of development. Several iterations of "what if" studies can be conducted already in the conceptual phase, which will form a useful knowledge base from which to more accurately predict life-cycle costs, etc.

9.5 Engineering 2.0: Lightweight Technologies in Engineering

As stated in the introduction to this chapter, we make the assertion that lightweight technologies show serious potential when it comes to effectively sharing knowledge between actors partaking in product development in a VE. Here, the term "lightweight" principally means that the technologies: (1) require little time and effort to set up, use, and maintain (i.e., lowering the threshold for adopting the technologies); (2) do not impose a predefined structure (i.e., letting structures evolve over time as an almost organic response to the activities, practices, and interests of the knowledge workers that use these technologies as part of their everyday work; and (3) support informal communication also in absence of physical proximity (i.e., by capturing also the subtle, spontaneous, and multidimensional messages that characterize personal interaction).

Since this work draws its context from the fields of engineering and product development in primarily business-to-business situations, we have chosen to summarize these lightweight technologies in the term "Engineering 2.0" – borrowing from the concepts of "Web 2.0" (O'Reilly 2005) and "Enterprise 2.0" (McAfee 2006).

> One of the key lessons of the Web 2.0 era is this: Users add value. But only a small percentage of users will go to the trouble of adding value to your application via explicit means. Therefore, Web 2.0 companies set inclusive defaults for aggregating user data and building value as a side-effect of ordinary use of the application. As noted above, they build systems that get better the more people use them. (O'Reilly 2005)

The simplicity of Web 2.0 technologies offers a few key characteristics that have particular relevance for the highly distributed, highly cross-functional Virtual Enterprise. To reap the benefits of Web 2.0, companies need to (1) support lighweight programming models that allow for loosely coupled systems (i.e., in line with the loosely coupled VE network); (2) support syndication rather than coordination of data (i.e., content will flow from the bottom-up rather than from the top-down); and (3) support reuse and remixability in an open-source model (i.e., content can be used for other purposes than for which it was originally intended).

Similarly, McAfee's concept of 'Enterprise 2.0' includes "new digital platforms for generating, sharing and refinding information that are focusing not on capturing knowledge itself, but rather on the practices and output of knowledge workers" (McAfee 2006). Engineering 2.0 is specifically targeting how these lightweight technologies and approaches could benefit globally dispersed engineering teams, working in business-to-business contexts of the VE kind, where the available technology support for knowledge sharing still mainly centers around CAD/CAE/PDM/PLM systems, complemented with online collaborative workspaces and web conferencing systems to support both asynchronous and synchronous collaboration.

As noted earlier, there are a number of unique features of this emerging industry context that highlight the need for complementary knowledge sharing technologies:

1. Virtual Enterprises are "loosely" coupled networks of independent partners, established on a project-by-project basis.
2. Knowledge workers in enterprise-wide teams do not normally have a shared history of working together.
3. Knowledge workers in enterprise-wide teams do not normally have a shared knowledge base with lessons learned, best-practices, etc.
4. Knowledge workers move in and out of enterprise-wide teams as different competencies and capabilities are needed.
5. Knowledge workers in enterprise-wide teams do not normally have a shared set of technological systems to create, store, and share knowledge.
6. Development of "functions," rather than "hardware," as part of total life-cycle commitments radically changes the scope and objectives of engineering activities.

7. Knowledge workers will need to increasingly work in highly cross-functional, cross-disciplinary, enterprise-wide teams.
8. Knowledge workers will need to develop closer relationships with customers and suppliers, to better understand the desired "function" to be developed.
9. Knowledge workers will need to improve their understanding of their contribution to the overall development and product life cycles.
10. Knowledge workers will need to make their knowledge available to a much larger audience than before, and will also need to use knowledge from many more sources than before.

Due to these characteristics, our research focuses particularly on knowledge that currently resides outside of the traditional scope of product development teams. We have chosen to refer to such knowledge as "downstream knowledge," since we are mainly interested in identifying and utilizing knowledge assets that normally would not enter the scene until after a design concept has already been selected. For example, the same fundamental knowledge assets might be used for the purposes of both product development and opportunity management, but since there are different competencies involved with different goals and motivations, it is crucial to be able to share this structuralized knowledge on an adequate level of detail or abstraction depending on each particular setting.

An important aspect of these knowledge assets is that they can be found in a wide range of professional domains – both within the own company, and at customers and partners. Thus, the overall research agenda seeks to address how boundary-crossing teams across the VE can decrease the start-up time for new product-development projects by rapidly identifying and effectively utilizing a shared knowledge base from day 1 (i.e., rather than starting from "scratch"). Also, it addresses how these various teams can successfully create, share, and utilize "generic" knowledge, i.e., making sure that the knowledge assets they create are easily available to other teams in the VE, regardless of what domain of expertise they are working in.

9.5.1 From Weak to Potential Ties

It has been observed that engineers and scientists very often turn to a person for information rather than to a database or a file cabinet, and people seem to rely heavily on colleagues that they know and trust. Our research indicates that "knowing who knows" (Larsson 2005) is crucial in global engineering design teams and while that seems to be a commonly accepted feature of collaborative work, it also poses a severe threat to VEs, where this kind of "engineering know-who" (Larsson 2005) is not as easily developed as in more traditional enterprise settings. The increasing globalization and the influx of VE thinking means that engineers are working together with more people than ever before, but often with very limited knowledge of who they are actually working with, what their collaborators know, and to what extent they can be trusted. To achieve effective global design teams, it is crucial to address and deal with such issues of "social disconnectedness."

In the context of manufacturing tool development, one of our informants noted that your ability to access and try to better understand customer needs fundamentally depends on whom you talk to in the customer organization. "The customer" is more than one person, and the answers vary from person to person, and are also dependent on the bias of the person who is asking the questions. A similar problem as highlighted by an informant at the industrial drive systems company:

> Different functions meet the customer at different occasions. It is not easy to merge. Who has the complete picture? Customer value is dispersed across many different persons who have different information about the customer need. We have different persons at the customer site as well: technicians, purchasers, service-personnel, etc.

The concept of "weak ties" (Granovetter 1973) points to the value of establishing personal relationships that transcend local relationship boundaries both socially and geographically. For example, Granovetter's has indicated that a person looking for a job is, for certain professions, more likely to find a new job through an acquaintance rather than through a close friend, much because the acquaintance is more likely to move in other social circles, and is also more likely to possess other information than what you already have. So, this is particularly interesting when it comes to product-development activities, since that is a field where knowledge workers are explicitly interested in avoiding redundancy, and instead seek novelty and innovation. However, what would be the output if VEs could also better harness the power of "potential ties"? This notion includes:

> a still-larger set of fellow employees who could be valuable to our prototypical knowledge worker if only she knew about them. These are people who could keep her from re-inventing the wheel, answer one of her pressing questions, point her to exactly the right resource, tell her about a really good vendor, consultant, or other external partner, let her know that they were working on a similar problem and had made some encouraging progress, or do any of the other scores of good things that come from a well-functioning tie. (McAfee 2007)

To really harness the knowledge that is dispersed across the VE, we need to recognize that the foremost experts on your products might not be on your payroll, and that there might be "hidden experts" around the enterprise, who are willing to volunteer outside of their official job description (Mayfield 2007). Also, of course, these potential ties could be "lead-users" (von Hippel 1986), in any part of the customer network, offering their advice and experience, whether you asked for it or not. Social networking software, such as LinkedIn or Facebook, and blogs and wikis are some of the ways in which engineers can both increase the density of their weak ties, and get connected to people with knowledge and experience that is new and possibly complementary rather than well-known and possibly redundant.

9.5.2 From Personal to Public Benefit

This chapter discusses lightweight technologies for knowledge sharing, and if a technology is perceived as "lightweight" or not naturally depends on the benefits derived from using such technologies. If the personal benefits are large, i.e., if the return on investment is high enough, users might even tolerate a slow and tedious system because the results are considered worth the extra effort. Similarly, even the lowest threshold could be considered too large if the results are not benefiting the user. One could argue that one of the reasons why many projects are poorly documented is that project participants have difficulties seeing the benefits of making this extra effort to capture rationale, experiences, lessons learned, etc. The people who have to do the extra work are normally not the people who will reap the benefits.

Tang et al. (2007) performed a study on how knowledge workers in a workplace environment store and manage files on their workplace computers, to see if any social patterns could be identified for the benefit of the company. The interesting thing here, from an Engineering 2.0 perspective, is that identifying these collaboration patterns did not require any additional work by the user. These patterns fell out of the work users are already doing in managing and storing files concerning information that they care about.

When attempting to lower the threshold for knowledge sharing, this is a highly appealing concept. If what people are doing as part of their everyday work produces traces and patterns of how they create, use, and share knowledge, why not use these traces and patterns to achieve public benefits across the VE? The social effects of using social software are sometimes unintended – which is something of a paradox. Knowledge workers do not have to put extra effort into sharing knowledge across social networks, but other people in the enterprise can still make sense and use of the traces they produce. In a VE context, where the social ties between knowledge workers are relatively few and weak, or even nonexistent, to start with, the ability to derive public benefits from personal actions is very interesting. Here, the concept of a "folksonomy" (Vander Wal 2007) makes sense, much because, as opposed to a taxonomy, people "are not so much categorizing, as providing a means to connect items (placing hooks) to provide their meaning in their own understanding" (Vander Wal 2007).

This provides opportunities to find emergent vocabularies and trends, and since information tagged for personal use can benefit other users (Golder and Huberman 2005) across the enterprise, this could allow knowledge workers to find people across the disciplinary, departmental, and organizational boundaries of the VE. Rather than relying entirely on up-front decisions about where in the enterprise to look for relevant knowledge and persons, finding people who tag items the same way they do, will allow knowledge workers to find social groups based on similar interests and ways of speaking and acting, rather than based on where they are placed in the organizational chart.

Paying attention to customers' everyday internal discussions about how they use, or even modify, a product could sometimes be more useful than first-hand accounts of what the customer need is perceived to be. On this point, one of our informants working in the manufacturing tool business commented that a source of innovation could be to look at situations when their customers actually use their products in unanticipated ways:

[W]hen you look at the customers, they use certain hardware. There are situations where the customer has created the innovation by using the hardware in a certain way. Customers use the product differently than we had thought during development, and this can be an opportunity for innovation if we get to know this.

Apart from the benefits related to uncovering knowledge that you could not normally access through conventional interviews or observations, McAfee (2007) points to some interesting networking effects. As more people author, link, search, and tag information, the emergent structure becomes increasingly fine-grained: "They can make large organizations in some ways more searchable, analyzable and navigable than smaller ones, and make it easier for people to find precisely what they're looking for" (McAfee 2008). Here, concepts like tag clouds and social bookmarking could provide some of the lightweight capabilities to create public benefits from personal actions.

Lightweight technologies can also provide public benefits by increasing the common understanding of data and information stored inside and outside the organization. For instance, a document repository that contains most or all of the structured content produced by project members is typically undecipherable to people outside the project, to people who join the project after it is underway, and even to the original project members after time has passed (Grudin 2006). Since knowledge assets need to be maintained over time, it becomes increasingly important to record the contextual dimensions related to such content, since people may leave the organization, new partners may join the project, or new needs and requirements may emerge along the way. Lightweight technologies for knowledge sharing can support engineers in providing a context to the documentation stored in company databases. Blogs, for example, may be used to provide easily skimmed chronologically ordered records of the important events of a project (i.e., status changes, etc.) which may give knowledge users deeper understanding of how the work is being performed in the project and why it is being done in a certain way.

9.5.3 From Predefined to Emergent Structures

One of the defining features of lightweight technologies is that they do not impose a predefined structure to how these systems "should" be used. The intelligence of such systems is, instead, provided by users in low-threshold ways, where control is shared with users to create value. These technologies "are trying not to impose preconceived notions about how work should be categorized or structured. Instead, they're building tools that let these aspects emerge" (McAfee 2007). This means that there are no predefined roles, identities, or privileges; there are no workflow or process steps to follow; there are no specific data formats to adhere to, and there are no "required" fields to fill out. In the case of social bookmarking, people self-define their tags using words that mean something to them at the time, rather than categorizing their bookmarks according to a predefined taxonomy. For example, a customer statement that is captured in the context of a request for a maintenance engineer might be very interesting for an engineer working with concept development in the early phases of product development.

However, if categorized only according to the corporate taxonomy, that piece of knowledge is likely to stay hidden in the "aftermarket" document archives. In our work in the aerospace domain, we have discussed that the "context" of a specific engineering activity is constantly emerging. If we, for example, take six relevant context dimensions (product, activity, project, gate, role, and discipline) into consideration, we can easily assume that engineers switch roles and projects as time goes by, and that different knowledge is needed at different gates and in different projects, etc. A challenge here is to make sure that just because the context dimensions might have been defined at one point in time, the knowledge attached to a certain context might be highly relevant in other contexts. If we can assist knowledge workers in contributing to a continuously emerging "folksonomy," rather than merely adhering to a predefined taxonomy, we should be able to better support the serendipitous discovery of information or knowledge that we would not have discovered by traditional searches in the enterprise knowledge base.

The absence of a predefined structure may also help in mitigating barriers to interoperability (Chen and Doumeingts 2004), which characterizes networked organizations. Traditional heavyweight systems are typically not designed for cross-company collaboration and are difficult to integrate from a technological perspective, especially in a Virtual Enterprise situation. Moreover, such systems are typically characterized by a rigid taxonomy, which raises further barriers to interoperability from a conceptual point of view. Other barriers relate to human factors and behaviors incompatible with interoperability (Chen and Daclin 2006). The lack of an explicit definition of responsibilities and authorities in accessing, using, and maintaining these systems may constitute a strong barrier to cross-enterprise collaboration.

Lightweight technologies offer promising solution alternatives to increase the capability of networked organizations to effectively manage their knowledge assets in light of an increased interoperation. On one hand, they require little time and effort to be set up, used, and maintained and may be effortlessly aligned with related systems inside and outside of the organization. Moreover, since they do not impose a predefined syntax or semantics, they may contribute in lowering the conceptual barrier to interoperability. Problems such as polysemy, homonymy, and synonymy may find a solution over time, since the language (e.g., the folksonomy) evolves and people tend to adapt their jargon to the ones generated by others. Moreover, since lightweight technologies do not foresee predefined roles, identities, and privileges (i.e., wikis are open to authorship to all the team members) they may encourage the knowledge-sharing process in the earlier project steps, when roles and responsibilities are not yet clearly defined.

9.5.4 From Lookup to Exploration

While it is always beneficial for knowledge workers to know where to get their facts checked and their questions answered, it is not merely the Wikipedia effect we are striving for when discussing the potential benefits of an Engineering 2.0 approach. We believe that one of the most promising aspects of such technologies is that they can help knowledge workers move beyond known-item searches, fact retrieval, and question answering (Winograd 2008). In the context of product development activities of the kind described earlier, it is highly interesting to assist knowledge workers in more exploratory and investigative activities, which are "more concerned with recall (maximizing the number of possibly relevant objects that are retrieved) than precision (minimizing the number of possibly irrelevant objects that are retrieved)" (Marchionini 2006: 43).

One of our informants working with manufacturing tool development noted how the domains of product development and opportunity management were starting to become increasingly intertwined with the move toward developing "functions":

> Earlier, we talked about product properties. Now it is about demands on the result of the product in use. This is needed to sell service-intensive products. We want to acquire the needs, and then be able to translate these into the products and services that need to be created.

Moving away from the hardware-centric view of product development means that we must give engineers (and other actors throughout the value chain) opportunities for serendipitous knowledge discovery, where they can "stumble upon" relevant knowledge, where they can browse a wide variety of topics that makes sense to others, and where they can gain a deeper understanding of what knowledge other people find useful and how they choose to deploy that knowledge. When we cannot easily find a match between a well-defined "need" and a well-defined "product property," lightweight technologies could help in exploring a wide range of opportunities, from a wide range of perspectives, with very little effort.

9.5.5 From Directional to Intersectional

Sir John Rose, chief executive of Rolls-Royce PLC, talks about how Rolls-Royce outsources and offshores about 75% to its global supply chain, keeping the 25% which are the "differentiating elements ... the hot end of the engine, the turbines, the compressors and fans and the alloys, and the aerodynamics of how they are made" (Friedman 2005: 459). Rose further notes that while companies are becoming increasingly specialized to meet market demands, this specialized knowledge will only address parts of any meaningful business or social challenge, which means that innovation comes from putting specialties together in new and different combinations (Friedman 2005: 457).

Johansson (2004: 2) argues that companies need to step into the intersection of fields, disciplines, and cultures to combine existing concepts into extraordinary new ideas, which implies that we need to harness the knowledge and intelligence of people who are not "officially" on the team, who are not "supposed" to have an opinion, and who are not "familiar with" the specifics of the particular project. To us, this seems like an excellent pool of resources for innovation, if we can utilize it at a low overhead.

At Stanford University's "d.school," this integration of perspectives is visible in their ambition to create "T-shaped" people, who "maintain the depth and focus of a single discipline while adding a 'crossbar' of design thinking that drives the integration of multiple perspectives into solving real problems" (Winograd 2008). The vertical part of the T represents depth in a particular discipline and the horizontal part of the T represents a broader "empathy" when it comes to respecting, valuing, and embracing a diverse set of disciplines and perspectives. We believe that Engineering 2.0 is largely about providing lightweight technologies that facilitate the "empathic discovery" of knowledge in a wide variety of knowledge sources spread across the many boundaries of the VE.

9.5.6 From Teams to Crowds

On the web, how many people that link to a particular page is an indicator of how "good," "interesting" or "useful" that page is, but many corporate intranets do not allow their knowledge workers to create such links between the material they produce. Since a VE is a highly distributed work environment, there is a problem of achieving critical mass in knowledge creation, sharing, and discovery. While the number of knowledge workers in the enterprise might be very high, "knowing who knows" is more difficult than before due to the fragmentation and distribution of knowledge across the enterprise. As noted before intersectional innovation means that the notion of "what a team is" has to be reconsidered.

Engineering 2.0 implies that the innovation ecosystem of a VE includes "open and amorphous networks of peers" (Tapscott and Williams 2006: 257), where the people who contribute with knowledge might not be a part of the team or even the organization, and where community-developed answers and ideas play a major part. If we consider the characteristics of functional product development in VEs, we can actually see that some of the challenges of that context, i.e., related to diversity and distribution of knowledge workers, are turned into significant opportunities. To tap into the wisdom of crowds, you should keep social ties loose, keep yourself exposed to as many diverse sources as possible, and participate in groups that range across hierarchies (Surowiecki 2004). Engineering 2.0 technologies offer the potential to leverage on "spontaneous and decentralized forms of mass collaboration" (Tapscott and Williams 2006) in a self-organized way.

Flipping the "knowing who knows" concept upside-down, it is also very important, from a user perspective, to "know who *should* know." Very often, knowledge is generated in several parts of the organization, without being properly captured, stored, or shared. This often happens because people cannot recognize the value of this knowledge to others, and are not aware of which people in the organization that can be potentially interested in it. Knowing who "should know," is a crucial topic related to knowledge generation and exchange in a cross-company environment. The loose connection between the partners and the absence of personal networking is one of the main reasons that the generated knowledge may not be fully utilized in the design process.

An interesting example of how knowledge may be distributed across the enterprise and how serendipitous knowledge discovery plays a crucial role in the actual product development process has been proposed by one of our informants working in the development of manufacturing tools. Companies in the metal cutting industry are trying to reinforce their business by providing customers not only with tools and inserts, but also with the knowledge they need to use these tools in the most efficient way.

> [I]f you lower the purchase price of the tools by 30 percent, the customer will save 1 percent of the cost of the component. If he buys a better tool and increases tool life by 50 percent, he lowers the cost of the component by 1 percent. But if instead he buys a better performing tool and speeds up by increasing cutting data then he can reduce the cost of the component by 15 percent. (Abberley 2005)

Such *applications* have the aim to add value to the customer production process by providing examples of how to properly run a machining operation in the specific customer contest. Sometimes, however, customers may discover applications that are even more efficient than the ones suggested by the manufacturer.

One of the application engineers we have interviewed told us the story about a customer who has tried to adapt a turbine blade machining application to his low-power machine. The customer finally got significant improvements by radically modifying the machining settings in terms of tools, feed, and speed. After a while, a technician visiting the customer shop floor had the occasion to see the new application and to make a movie, which was then stored in a local database. After several months, a spontaneous and informal meeting held at the margins of a training session activity gave the technician the chance to talk to one of the persons responsible for application development and show him what he had found during his visit. The movie had been further analyzed by the application development engineers and stored with other relevant material in the common application database. This example underlines, on one side, the importance of serendipitous knowledge discovery, while on the other side it shows how crucial it may be to *know who should know*, in order to exploit knowledge assets at the earliest possible time.

From the metal cutting industry, we found two other examples of user-generated solutions that might more easily be put to common good through the deployment of lightweight technologies. A is an experienced product-development engineer working on insert design. He told us that, in order to rank and sort out good or bad knowledge elements, he usually renames the files contained in the common project database. After accessing a document, he typically put (+) in front of the file name if the content is particularly interesting for the project purpose, (=) if the description may be useful during the development of the new tool, or (–) if the file does not provide any crucial knowledge to fulfill the project goals.

B is a newcomer at the application development department. B has been assigned to a project that focuses on the possibility to reduce residual surface stress after turning. He started to look for people in the company who could support him with a particular X-ray analysis. Since B was new to the company, his first thought was to ask more experienced people, trying to access their network of expertise, but the effort was unsuccessful. Then he tried to make a keyword search in the corporate online contacts book. Although the contact book contained detailed people profiles, the search was not successful either, for two main reasons. First, it was not possible to retrieve information meaningful enough regarding people competences and past experiences. Second, it was difficult to find relevant people through the keyword search, since they were tagged in many different ways (using *röntgen* instead of *roentgen*, or *x-ray*, *x-rays*, *radiation*, *radiography*, etc.). In the end, B kept in touch with one of the colleagues in his former company, an expert in X-ray equipment. This colleague could refer B to other colleagues that have previously worked with the company, and these people were finally able to give B the contact information he was looking for.

9.6   Conclusions

A crucial point we would like to make here is that we believe that engineering, in the context described in this paper, is moving back and forth between "problem solving" and "prediction." When developing "functions" that are to be included in total life-cycle commitments, engineers are working with a multitude of actors across the value chain. They need to, collaboratively, figure out how to approach ill-defined problems, and in cases where it is just not possible to reach an agreeable solution, or even shared understanding about what the problem is, they need to make well-founded predictions about what a solution might look like in the future. In our opinion, "heavy-weight" PDM or PLM systems undeniably play a strong role in virtual enterprise collaboration, but we believe that their strengths in data and information management need to be complemented by more lightweight knowledge-sharing systems that are better equipped to enable an open, bottom-up, collective sense-making approach to knowledge sharing, rather than the somewhat controlled, top-down, management approach to knowledge sharing that is common in current industry practice. Both approaches are needed, but we should be clear that we also should expect highly different results from the two. One of the major problems when it comes to knowledge sharing in the VE is the absence of "shared assumptions" – about how we do our jobs; who does them; how coordination is done, etc. – and a major benefit of lightweight technologies is that they allow such shared assumptions to develop through folksonomies and other decentralized, bottom-up approaches. Further, if we pay closer attention to what documents, data, photos, and stories *really mean* to people, as opposed to what corporate taxonomies and databases they should be put into, what management thinks is most important at any given time, or what the company's product portfolio has looked like in the past – then we can start exploring the true potential of mass collaboration and peer production in a VE context.

We would like to conclude that the notion of Engineering 2.0 is something different from "traditional" engineering and product development. The organization is different, the team composition is different, the objectives are different, and the responsibilities are different. In our opinion, the technologies most suitable for effective knowledge sharing will be different, too.

References

Abberley (2005).The 15 billion dollar question! *American Machinist.* September 11 http://www.ameri-canmachinist.com/StateOfManufacturing/ArticleDraw.aspx?HBC=StateOfManufacturing&N IL=False&CID=11583&OASKEY=Issue.

Ackerman, M.; Pipek, V.; Wulf, V. Editors (2003). *Sharing Expertise, Beyond Knowledge Management.* Massachusetts Institute of Technology. USA.

Bains, T.S., Lightfoot, H.W., Williams, G. and Greenough, R. (2007). State-of-the-art in lean design engineering; a literature review on white collar lean. *Int. Journal of Mechanical Engineering, Vol.221-Part B.* 1543–1552.

Boart, P. (2005). Life Cycle Simulation Support for Functional Products. Licentiate Thesis. Luleå University of Technology. ISSN 1402-1757, ISRN LTU-LIC--05/20.

Brandenburger, A.M. and Nalebuff, B.J. (1997). *Co-Opetition: A Revolution Mindset That Combines Competition and Cooperation: The Game Theory Strategy That's Changing the Game of Business.* New York: Doubleday/Currency.

Byrne, J. (1993). The Virtual Corporation. *Business Week. Feb 8.* pp 98–104.

Chen, D. and Daclin, N. (2006). Framework for enterprise interoperability. *Proceedings of the International Workshop on Enterprise Integration, Interoperability and Networking EI2N'2006,* Bordeaux, France.

Chen, D. and Doumeingts, G. (2004). European Initiatives to develop interoperability of enterprise applications - basic concepts, framework and roadmap. *Journal of Annual reviews in Control, Vol. 27*(2). 151–160.

Friedman, T. (2005). The World is Flat: A Brief History of the Twenty-First Century. Farrar, Straus and Giroux, New York.

Golder S.A. and Huberman, B.A. (2005) The Structure of Collaborative Tagging Systems. *Technical Report, Information Dynamics Lab, HP Labs.*

Granovetter, M. (1973). The Strength of Weak Ties. *American Journal of Sociology, Vol. 78.* No. 6. 1360–1380.

Grudin, J. (2006). Enterprise knowledge management and emerging technologies". *HICSS '06: Proceedings of the 39th Annual Hawaii International Conference on System Sciences,* Washington, DC, USA. 57–71.

Johansson, F. (2004). *The Medici Effect: Breakthrough Insights at the Intersection of Ideas, Concepts, and Cultures.* Boston: Harvard Business School Press.

Kim, S-H., Cohen, M.A., Netessine, S. (2007). Performance Contracting in After-Sales Service Supply Chains. *Management Science. Vol. 53.* No. 12. 1843–1858.

Larsson, A. (2005). Engineering Know-Who: Why Social Connectedness Matters to Global Design Teams. Doctoral Thesis. Luleå University of Technology, ISSN 1402-1544, ISRN LTU-DT--05/19.

Marchionini, G. (2006). Exploratory Search: From Finding to Understanding. *Communications of the ACM, Vol. 49.* No. 4. 41–46.

Mayfield, R. (2007). Talk at PARC Forum. In the "Going Beyond 2.0" Speaker Series, http://www.parc.com/events/forum/, November 15.

McAfee, A. (2006). Enterprise 2.0: The Dawn of Emergent Collaboration. *MIT Sloan Management Review, Vol. 47.* No. 3. 21–28

McAfee, A. (2007). How to Hit the Enterprise 2.0 Bullseye. Blog Post, http://blog.hbs.edu/faculty/macafee/, November 3.

McAfee, A. (2008). Talk at PARC Forum. In the "Going Beyond 2.0" Speaker Series, http://www.parc.com/events/forum/, February 21.

Mello, S. (2002). *Customer-centric product definition: the key to great product development.* AMACOM, USA.

O'Reilly, T. (2005). What is web 2.0: Design Patterns and Business Models for the next Generation of Software. *Social Science Research Network Working Paper Series.*

Surowiecki, J. (2004). *The Wisdom of Crowds: Why the Many Are Smarter Than the Few and How Collective Wisdom Shapes Business*, Economies, Societies and Nations. Doubleday, New York.

Tang, J., Drews, C., Smith, M., Wu, F., Sue, A. and Lau. T. (2007). Exploring Patterns of Social Commonality Among File Directories at Work. *Proceedings of CHI'07*, San Jose, CA, USA, April 28–May 3.

Tapscott, D., Williams, A.D. (2006). *Wikinomics: How Mass Collaboration Changes Everything*. Penguin Group, New York.

Tomkins, C. (2001). Interdependencies, trust and information in relationships, alliances and networks. *Accounting, Organizations and Society, Vol. 26.* 161–191.

Vander Wal, T. (2007). Folksonomy. http://www.vanderwal.net/folksonomy.html

von Hippel, E. (1986). Lead Users: An Important Source of Novel Product Concepts. *Management Science. Vol. 32.* No. 7. 791–805.

Winograd, T. (2008). Design Education for Business and Engineering Management Students: A New Approach. *Interactions*. January/February.

Chapter 10
The Interplay of Web 2.0 and Collaboration Support Systems: Leveraging Synergies

Michael Prilla and Carsten Ritterskamp

10.1 Web 2.0: Substitute for or Update to Collaboration Support?

In recent years, we have experienced the rise of so-called Web 2.0 applications, in which a large number of users voluntarily engage in collaborative work. The characteristics of *Web 2.0* can be best described as an "architecture of participation" (O'Reilly 2005), which includes *simplicity of usage*, immediate *feedback* on UI and structural level, and *valuing each user's contributions* (Grudin 2006; Kittur et al. 2007). Web 2.0 orchestrates available technology in a way that encourages users to participate actively as its architecture of participation helps to balance effort and benefit even in work-related settings.[1] The success of these applications – e.g., Wikis, Word Processors on the Web, or Social Tagging systems – supports this point of view. *This immediately leads to the question whether Web 2.0 applications are the new generation of collaboration support systems.*

Looking at the state of CSS in practice, the idea of turning to Web 2.0 applications instead of "traditional" *collaboration support systems* (CSS) becomes even more tempting. Consequently, in current discussions in research and practice, this is often seen as a solution to existing problems. A look at the state of the art in CSS tells us why inspite of CSS being commonly used in practice, they often lack adoption by users (Grudin 1988; Mark and Poltrock 2003). There are three main reasons for this: *First*, as Grudin (1988) puts it, in CSS there is a "disparity between those who do the work and those who get the benefit." *Second*, participation of users in collaboration is hindered by missing support for frictionless transitions between personal and group work. *Third*, integration of CSS into daily work and tool

---

[1]See (Millen et al. 2007) for an example on how social bookmarking services can be applied to improve search for information sources and social navigation in a corporate environment.

M. Prilla (✉) and C. Ritterskamp
Information and Technology Management, Ruhr University of Bochum, Germany
e-mail: michael.prilla@rub.de

D. Randall and P. Salembier (eds.), *From CSCW to Web 2.0: European Developments in Collaborative Design*, Computer Supported Cooperative Work,
DOI 10.1007/978-1-84882-965-7_10, © Springer-Verlag London Limited 2010

interoperability have to be improved. Web 2.0 applications seem to solve these problems, making them a tempting alternative to CSS.

Facing the question whether Web 2.0 can replace CSS, the discussion provided above tells only half of the story. This is because there is also a downside to Web 2.0 applications: features known from CSS are missing in some application types and known problems resurrect, resulting in poor support for, e.g., awareness and communication,[2] which are indispensable requirements for enterprise-grade applications. Tackling the question stated above needs an answer to the question whether current Web 2.0 applications are capable of covering all aspects of CSS. In this chapter, we analyze both domains and conclude that this is not the case. We then argue that Web 2.0 applications and CSS can *complement* each other, resulting in synergies providing enhanced collaboration support. The resulting prototypes provide opportunities to evaluate the impact of Web 2.0 mechanisms on collaboration in existing CSS. However, as we have not conducted such an evaluation yet, the chapter provides no data on that.

There are various fields of application for the approach proposed in this article. Most of them can be subsumed by the concept of *knowledge work*, which today's economy is vastly dependent on (cf. Davenport 2005). Collaborative knowledge work done by highly educated professionals (Davenport 2005) appears to impose the biggest challenges on CSS design. This type of knowledge work involves both individual work and phases of intensive collaboration and it oftentimes cannot be described in terms of work processes or daily routine. For successful *knowledge workers*, tools supporting them in their work have to be adaptable to the work situation at a given time and they have to match personal preferences of work organization and usage. As a consequence, support for knowledge workers has to be accomplished in a lightweight fashion both on an individual and a group level, resulting in a transition from personal to group information management.

However, despite influential and beneficiary outcomes of, e.g., CSCW and Groupware research in this area, available *Collaboration Support Systems* (CSS) *still* lack important aspects needed for these tasks (McAfee 2006). While – due to its shortcomings described above – Web 2.0 mechanisms and systems cannot fully solve these issues, in this chapter we describe problem scenarios and corresponding prototypes demonstrating how combinations of CSS and Web 2.0 functionality can cope with difficulties arising from the needs of knowledge work support.

We have taken an exploratory approach for research, which is based on prototyping and iteratively improving each prototype. To get an impression, we performed informal tests of our prototypes asking students how they perceived each prototype. Additionally, we integrated our prototypes into the productive system of our CSS and observed how they were adopted by students using the system. We are aware of the fact that our approach cannot result in generalizable findings. However, bringing together domains such as Web 2.0 and CSS makes up a complex setting, including questions such as how to meaningfully design the resulting prototypes.

---

[2]It should be noted that some types of Web 2.0 applications such as Social Networking provide sufficient awareness support, whereas such support has to be improved in, e.g., Social Tagging and Applications on the Web.

Therefore, we decided to set our focus to the exploration of the problem space and find out more about our task of meaningful integration.

The contribution of this article is manifold. *First*, we provide a new approach toward distinguishing between the domains of Groupware, CSCW, and Web 2.0. This distinction has to be seen as a *conceptual* and *nonselective* way of analyzing the intentions each domain was associated with originally. While there are other perspectives one could take on these domains, this way enables us to map needs of collaborations support with the capabilities resulting from the design rationales of each domain. *Second*, we analyze Web 2.0 concepts and mechanisms, concerning their ability to foster collaboration. In this chapter, we derive the potential of each mechanism analyzed to support specific tasks of collaborative knowledge work. *Third*, by describing collaboration problem-oriented prototypes of an existing CSS in combination with Web 2.0 mechanisms, we show a way how this potential can be set free. Additionally, we discuss the potential benefits resulting from this combination on a theoretical basis and – in cases in which we performed small test scenarios – according to our experiences in using the prototypes. *Fourth*, we reflect on the lessons we draw from realizing these prototypes by describing follow-up tasks needed to systematically apply our approach in practice. Furthermore, the reflection leads to a concept of collaboration support as a network of services and consideration concerning the feasibility and implementation of this concept.

In what follows, we will provide the background our approach is built on. This includes a distinction covering differences and dependencies between the domains of CSCW, Groupware, and Web 2.0 applications. Additionally, we discuss the major aim of this article – making Web 2.0 mechanisms usable and useful in enterprise settings and making the stages clear for this. In Section 10.2, we analyze mechanisms known from Web 2.0 applications regarding their potential to foster collaborative work. In the following section we then take a pattern approach describing strategies suitable to meaningfully combine CSS and Web 2.0 applications for enhanced collaboration. We illustrate our considerations and their potential impact by three prototypical extensions to an existing CSS. Drawing from our experiences in designing and implementing them, in Section 10.5 we discuss how the future of Web 2.0 enhanced collaboration support may look like and how resulting changes can be supported systematically. The article concludes with our ideas and thoughts for further work on our approach.

10.2   On the Relationship Between Web 2.0 and Collaboration Support

10.2.1   CSCW, Groupware and Web 2.0 – Similarities, Differences, and Synergies

More often than not, in the discussion of Web 2.0 and its relations to existing approaches on collaboration support and corresponding systems, terms such as

Groupware, CSCW, and Web 2.0 are used ambiguously. In some discussions, Web 2.0 is seen as an aspect or part of one domain subsuming CSCW and Groupware. In other discussions, Web 2.0 is separated from the other two domains. In our opinion, the truth has to be seen in the middle: Answering the question whether Web 2.0 applications may replace traditional CSS needs an understanding of what these areas are all about and the differences and overlaps between terms and domains like Groupware, CSCW, and Web 2.0. However, it should be noted that there cannot be a *selective* distinction on these domains, and providing it is not what researchers in these fields should aim at. Instead, we should focus on the (original) *intentions* of these domains to find *conceptual* synergies between them. To accomplish this task, deriving differences and similarities from the usage and purposes of applications and processes of each domain is crucial.

Before we can derive similarities and differences between the domains mentioned above, we need to have an understanding of what is meant by terms like collaboration support systems and Web 2.0. While there are many ways to define or circumscribe CSS as a domain, by this term we mean systems that have been brought out or influenced by decades of CSCW and Groupware research. Namely, such systems can be found in sub-domains like knowledge management (KM) systems, computer-supported collaborative learning (CSCL), email, and office suites such as Lotus Notes or Microsoft Outlook as well as in various stand-alone tools such as instant messengers. In contrast to these well-known and more or less deeply researched classes of applications, we use the term Web 2.0 to describe a new kind of systems, which all share certain characteristics. Among these characteristics are strict orientation toward bottom-up processes and user democracy, hardly any prestructuring of the collaborative process as well as immediate benefit by participation. More than that, such applications have been built to provide rich user experiences and a playful approach to using them. The bottom line of this understanding of the two terms is that CSS and Web 2.0 should not be mixed up, as they come from different directions and intentions. However, there are also overlaps between them. In what follows, we will focus on such differences and overlaps.

Figure 10.1 provides a conceptual distinction between the domains of CSCW, Groupware, and Web 2.0 applications. The differentiation is based on three major characteristics present to a different extent in each domain: *goal and work orientation, communication and coordination* among peers in groups, and *playfulness and user experience*. Considering CSCW, this domain is concerned with the support for specific, *work-related* tasks in groups (cf. Baecker 1993). Therefore, the driving factor for this domain is work or goal orientation. Taking document management or intranet portals as typical examples of this domain, communication is another but minor goal. Playfulness and user experience play a subordinate role. For Groupware, in general communication and coordination among peers has to be seen as the major characteristic. Groupware supports more *generic* tasks that are not necessarily associated with particular business goals or tasks (Baecker 1993). Applications in this domain may serve different goals or no goal at all, as can be seen by typical examples such as instant messaging or chat. There is also an emphasis on user experience, but aspects like playfulness and individual adoption are not as important as

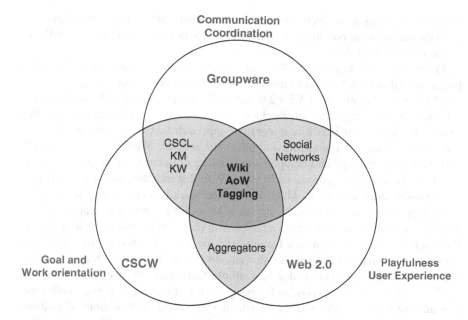

Fig. 10.1 Differentiation of CSCW, Groupware, and Web 2.0 applications

in Web 2.0 applications, which mainly focus on individual but also group benefits. Examples like Wikis or Tagging communities show that in such applications there is no need for a particular goal. In such applications, communication support varies and thus cannot be considered a major or decisive factor for this domain.

Besides differences between these domains, there are also overlaps. By *CSS* we refer to the *overlap between CSCW and Groupware*. Synergy potential with Web 2.0 can therefore be found in the overlap between *all* domains through, e.g., *Wikis, Applications on the Web (AoW)*, and *Tagging* applications. These applications all share a focus toward certain goals, a strong emphasis on communication and coordination, and rich user experiences and playfulness in their usage. Therefore, learning from principles of these applications such as high user motivation provides strong potential for improving CSS. The other way round, CSS mechanisms provide good opportunities to improve Web 2.0 applications. Our work focuses on exploring such mutual benefits.

10.2.2   Providing the Basis to Make Web 2.0 Sustainable

Those who propose Web 2.0 as a new generation of collaboration support sometimes tend to take the notion that just providing a tool taken from Web 2.0 will immediately solve problems with existing CSS. Again, we take another view of this by arguing that it is not sufficient to use a tempting mechanism from Web 2.0. Rather than that, we argue that measures have to be taken in order to make changes from the integration of Web 2.0 mechanisms sustainable. In what follows, we describe our view on building a technical basis for organizational sustainability of the benefits Web 2.0 bears.

From the characteristics of Web 2.0 applications it is easy to realize their potential to diminish problems known from the usage of CSS in practice. Equally, overlaps in the intentions of Web 2.0 and CSS can be seen, which provide room for meaningful integration of mechanisms taken from both domains. In this article, we argue that it is this integrative approach that makes the potential of both Web 2.0 and CSS available and paves the way for Web 2.0 mechanisms to systematically leverage and complement existing collaboration support systems.

There are different approaches in using Web 2.0 mechanisms in enterprise or other professional settings in which knowledge work is to be supported. Most of these approaches use applications such as wikis or blogs and try to map collaborative scenarios on or support these scenarios with these applications. Besides the fact that such applications often lack features and mechanisms known from collaboration support systems, we argue that this should not be the way of integrating Web 2.0 into such settings. This is due to a simple fact: Web 2.0 mechanisms such as applications on the web, wikis, and tagging stem from settings of mass collaboration and we should be skeptical about whether they work well without adaptations in other settings such as on enterprise level. Existing research confirms this notion by reporting on, e.g., additional mechanisms necessary to use wikis in organizations (Happel and Treitz 2008). Other approaches underpin this by purposefully and cleverly adapting mechanisms such as tagging and generating benefits out of it in enterprise settings (e.g., Farrell et al. 2007; Millen et al. 2007). Overall, we argue that in order to make Web 2.0 mechanisms usable for organizational settings in a sustainable manner, a meaningful and carefully analyzed integration should be managed in order to avoid the usual hype.

To underpin and explain this argument, we use a framework made popular by Malcolm Gladwell (2000) in his well-known book "The Tipping Point." In this book, Gladwell argues that for an idea to reach a critical mass of supporters or popularity, contextual knowledge as well as special roles are needed. Besides these needs, he describes the stages to the success of ideas by three steps: an idea being *tempting*, *sticky*, and *contagious*. By *tempting*, he refers to a status in which an idea is seen as possibly advantageous. There are many ideas and most of them will in the end not be followed up or only used in small settings. For an idea to reach beyond that, Gladwell argues that it has to at least be *sticky*. By sticky he means a situation in which people memorize the idea and thus may think about it to a deeper extent. Even this is not sufficient for an idea to have its breakthrough: For this, it has to be recognized as beneficiary *and* to spread among people until it reaches a critical point, which Gladwell calls the *tipping point*. The characteristic an idea has to have for this to happen is being *contagious*. If we replace the notion of an idea being tempting, sticky, and contagious by mechanisms or applications having these characteristics, we can describe our aims presented in this article along this framework.

Looking at the discussion of Web 2.0 in both practice and science, there is no doubt that Web 2.0 is *tempting* as a concept for collaboration support: who has not heard of a company planning to use or actually using wikis or blogs for, e.g., having their employees note down valuable information or enabling customers to give their feedback on products or services? Such applications have an appeal of voluntary participation, benefit for each participant, and playful interaction with the respective applications. Thus, they seem to do the magic that CSS has been missing in the minds of managers: once such applications are available, they will fill as of themselves because people are motivated just by the existence of these applications. Yet, this magic of "if we provide it, they will come" has not been observed in many cases. This is not a big surprise, as most of knowledge and assumptions available on such applications is taken from settings on the web, in which only voluntary participants engage in, e.g., Wikipedia. Thus, being tempting is not sufficient for Web 2.0 on enterprise level and therefore, just transferring applications to these settings will not do the deal in most cases.

For a successful implementation of Web 2.0 mechanisms in enterprise settings, we need to have a better understanding of the way they work, the way they motivate participants, and the way they can be used for specific scenarios. For such an understanding, we have to go beyond phenomenological levels and try to understand what makes, e.g., wikis or tagging so interesting for people on the web. Getting such an understanding, applying it to existing problems in collaboration support, and systemizing its usage are steps resulting in making Web 2.0 mechanisms *sticky* for collaboration support. This will then enable designers and developers to meaningfully integrate Web 2.0 mechanisms into applications such as CSS and make use of their potential. While we are aware that there is still some work to do in order to reach sufficiently broad and deep knowledge on Web 2.0 mechanisms, our analysis in Section 10.1 tries to contribute to this goal. Additionally, our efforts in using patterns of Web 2.0 integration (cf. Sections 10.4.2 and 10.5.1) aim at increasing the stickiness of these mechanisms.

In this article, we argue for the integration of Web 2.0 mechanisms into existing CSS and corresponding processes. By this, benefits of Web 2.0 can be applied and shortcomings carry no weight. Moreover, integrating such mechanisms into meaningful contexts shows users that Web 2.0 mechanisms can alleviate collaborative tasks by enriching the functionality of CSS. This is a situation in which Web 2.0 mechanisms can become *contagious*. Once people understand that using embedded mechanisms such as tagging in document management or wikis in publishing results of collaborative work results in their *own and others' benefit*, there is a fair chance that these mechanisms will be seen as beneficiary and thus be used extensively on a broader basis. The prototypes we present in Section 10.4 can be seen as a step toward this aim.

Taken together, the metaphors of stickiness and contagiousness can be seen as stages to be cleared toward making Web 2.0 useable and useful in enterprise settings. They also show that just transferring popular mechanisms to such settings is not enough. In what follows, we describe our approach of making Web 2.0 sticky and contagious for collaborative settings. While we are aware of different approaches which have been successful in special settings (cf. Farrell et al. 2007; Millen et al. 2007), we believe that our way can be a step forward toward using the potential of such applications. However, as we discuss in Section 10.5, dynamic and self-organized integration of such mechanisms has yet to be developed.

10.3   Web 2.0 Mechanisms to Support Collaboration – the Usual Suspects

10.3.1   Applications on the Web

Despite the fact that web-based applications and networked distributed software systems have been extensively discussed in the field of CSCW, with the advent of UI frameworks and technologies (e.g., AJAX) offering a desktop-like user experience in a web browser, the concept of Applications on the Web (AoW) have come to widespread attention in recent years. In using the browser as a substitute for desktop-based runtime environments, the concept of AoW has been underpinned by the idea of the Web as a platform (cf. O'Reilly 2005). With a still increasing number of online office suites like Google Docs & Spreadsheets[3] as the most prominent example, AoW enable users to fulfill tasks that formerly required rich clients or desktop applications within a web browser. One of the major advantages of AoW is that they free a knowledge worker's applications from the necessity of being installed and configured on a specific device. As a web browser is the only prerequisite for gaining access to relevant documents and applications in conjunction, AoW contribute to the ubiquitous availability of knowledge work's means of production. In this way, AoW allow a mobile workforce to work anytime and anywhere, providing technological scaffolding for a nomadic organization of work.

In an ICT infrastructure that supports document-centric knowledge work, AoW may help to bridge the gap between group-oriented, web-based document repositories supporting collaboration and desktop-based applications supporting the individual production and editing of documents. By allowing their users to do individual and collaboration work in one place, AoW may lower transitional costs that result from application switches and by this means increase efficiency.

Summing up, AoW provide to major potential benefits for CSS: first, they enable ubiquitous availability of content access and editing. Second, they intertwine individual and group work on content.

10.3.2   Wikis

Wikis are amongst the most prominent tools associated with the term Web 2.0. Analogous to its Hawaiian meaning "quick," a wiki provides easy content sharing and editing to a multitude of users. Wikis have been known to a larger audience

---

[3] Google docs & spreadsheets provide an online word processor (http://docs.google.com).

since the emergence of the "WikiWikiWeb,"[4] developed and made popular by Ward Cunningham in the 1990s (Leuf and Cunningham 2001). Yet, their acceptance in science and business and the resulting dissemination of wikis in these days stems from the remarkable success of the well-known Wikipedia,[5] which was started in 2001. Consequently, there are many studies and other contributions concerning wikis and their application available (e.g., Forte and Bruckman 2005; Tapscott and Williams 2006; Nov 2007). Thus, concerning Web 2.0 mechanisms, wikis can be seen as settled and well-researched applications.

Despite the coverage of wikis in scientific work and their acceptance in business and everyday life, there is an important thing to mention, which sometimes leads to misunderstandings: the potential and applicability of wikis should not be equalized with observations made on Wikipedia. While Wikipedia is based on wiki technology and provides the most prominent and successful example of wiki-based mass collaboration, we should not limit the applicability and scope of wikis to encyclopedia-like settings. Unfortunately, this is oftentimes done in current discussions on wikis. Nevertheless, studies available on Wikipedia and other contributions related to it can serve as good examples to learn about the potential and power of wikis in general. However, in using such studies to analyze the power of wikis needs careful consideration whether certain aspects of these studies are attributed to the special case of Wikipedia or hold true for wikis in general.

Wikis can serve as a role model for Web 2.0 applications providing and organizing user-generated content. They are organized in a democratic manner, meaning that – notwithstanding the possibility to restrict access to a closed group – everybody has equal rights to add, change, and link content in a wiki. While at first sight one could think that this leads to chaotic organization, at least Wikipedia in reality shows that the community associated to a wiki is capable of organizing a wiki's content properly. This is a phenomenon that can be seen throughout the whole Web 2.0 and can thus also be found in, e.g., tagging sites (cf. Section 10.3.3). In Wikipedia, this effect is caused by people from the community feeling responsible for proper content and its organization. However, recent studies on wikis in organizations show that such responsibility is needed urgently, as without it wikis and their structure might deteriorate (cf. Viégas et al. 2004; Happel and Treitz 2008).

The ease of accessing a wiki in a browser and its openness can be seen as two of the main success factors of wikis, which at the time wikis appeared paved the way of a writable web (Desilets et al. 2005). Nowadays, wikis still have the charm of bottom-up knowledge production environments giving everybody a voice and providing the benefit to those who do the work (cf. Grudin 1988; Grudin 2006). This is reflected by studies investigating motivational factors of Wikipedia users. Due to the exposed and anticommercial position of Wikipedia, such studies rank ideologically or ethically motivated factors such as freedom of knowledge and

---

[4] The "WikiWikiWeb" is still alive and can be found at Ward Cunningham's company web site (http://c2.com/cgi/wiki?WikiWikiWeb).

[5] The Wikipedia Foundation provides online encyclopedias in a multitude of languages and is nowadys one of the most popular sites on the web (http://wikipedia.org).

altruism among the top motivational factors (Nov 2007), surprisingly the most important factor can be found in *fun to write for Wikipedia* (Nov 2007). This not only reflects our notion of playfulness as one of the leading characteristics of Web 2.0, but also shows the potential of wikis in general: besides reasons only applying to some special wikis such as Wikipedia, wikis provide a joyful way of sharing content. Moreover, Forte and Bruckman (2005) found that another motivation to take part in Wikipedia can be found in gaining credit from others. This corresponds to the criterion of user experience mentioned as another leading characteristic of Web 2.0 applications above. While the study of Forte and Bruckman (2005) does not elaborate on the generalizability of this factor in other settings, we can conclude that wikis in general are capable of establishing and supporting social structures based on trust and credit.

From a pragmatic viewpoint, another aspect of a wiki's power corresponds to the well-known notion of providing a *low threshold* while having a *high ceiling*. Considering the ease of use of a wiki, such applications provide a huge set of possibilities ranging from easy, high-quality publishing including nontextual content (Viégas 2007) to making content accessible via, e.g., categories. Additionally, users of a wiki can prepare an article in privacy, check it carefully and then publish it by linking their freshly created page to other pages in the wiki. However, using a wiki still means using hypertext systems. Thus, certain syntax rules have to be known to make use of the full potential a wiki bears. Recently, this problem has been seen by wiki developers, resulting in more and more online word processors (cf. Section 10.1) being part of wiki input and therefore further lowering the threshold of wiki usage.

Considering the potential of wikis in supporting collaboration and complementing traditional CSS, factors such as easy access and publishing, providing the benefit to those who do the work and playfulness have to be taken into account. Thus, learning from wikis means learning from the interplay of openness and publishing of content on one side, while giving users means to thoroughly and easily prepare material on the other side. Additionally, another key learning factor – as can be seen by the example of Wikipedia – can be taken from the fact that the simple yet playful interface of wikis can foster the creation of content.

10.3.3 Tagging

Since their first appearances on the web in late 2003, tagging sites such as Delicious[6] and Flickr[7] have become enormously popular with users of the Internet. On such sites, users can assign freely chosen keywords to content. While at first sight this seems to end up in a chaotic distribution of various terms associated

---

[6] Delicious is a tagging sites managing bookmarks of users (http://delicious.com).
[7] The Flickr tagging service manages photographs of users (http://flickr.com).

with content units, recent studies have shown that *from tagging sites rich and well-structured vocabularies emerge* (cf. Golder and Huberman 2006; Cattuto et al. 2007). The distribution of tags in tagging applications forms a power law curve, which is considered as a typical sign of self-organized and converging human behavior (Cattuto et al. 2007).

Besides typical examples for tagging applications such as Flickr or Delicious, there are several contributions describing the applicability of tagging mechanisms in organizations for, e.g., expert finding (cf. Farrell et al. 2007) or information sharing (cf. Millen et al. 2007; Damianos et al. 2006). Applications of social tagging have also found to be useful in environments such as museums, in which visitors contribute to catalogs by assigning tags to artifacts (cf. Trant 2006). The adoption of tagging in so many contexts makes it attractive as a candidate for collaboration support.

It should be mentioned, however, that tagging is not a completely new idea. The need for contextualization of content has been observed earlier on. Before tagging emerged, metadata in, e.g., knowledge management and learning contexts (Heath et al. 2005) and semantic technologies like ontologies (Gruber 1993; Gomez-Perez and Fernandez-Lopez 2004) have been applied to solve this problem. While these are valuable approaches, which have been shown to be useful in many settings, they do not wholly solve the problem of contextualization. Studies show that, e.g., metadata templates in CSS are not used the way they were intended to be used, often resulting in trivial descriptions that could have been computed by a system as well (Heath et al. 2005). Ontologies, on the other hand, are powerful and computable means of descriptions, but they impose high learning efforts and do not represent users' language in general (refs). Tagging as a *bottom-up* means of description with no restrictions in keywords to be used may provide a better way of describing content. It *keeps the cognitive effort needed for contextualization low* (cf. Grudin 2006) and thereby reflects the playful and user-oriented approach of Web 2.0 mechanisms.

To understand how tagging may help in collaboration, at first we have to understand the different ways in which tagging mechanisms work. While at first sight there are no differences between the mechanisms used at, e.g., Flickr and Delicious, there are several ways in which so-called *folksonomies* resulting from tagging can be implemented. A first distinction has to be made between *narrow* and *broad* folksonomies. In narrow folksonomies such as Flickr,[8] only the creator of an item can assign tags to content while in broad mechanisms like del.icio.us everybody may tag everything. Regarding collaboration, this is a major difference, as broad folksonomies allow for much more interaction than narrow ones do. Thus, only broad folksonomies can be said to use a *social* tagging mechanism. Furthermore, tagging mechanisms may either use a *bag-model* or a *set-model* for managing tags (cf. Marlow et al. 2006). Using a bag-model, tags assigned to a resource are

---

[8] Flickr started out as a typical narrow tagging mechanism. Nowadays, a user's friends are also allowed to assign tags to his or her content. However, this still differs from the situation of broad tagging.

weighted according to the number of times they have been assigned to this resource. In contrast, a set-model only registers that a tag has been assigned to the resource and does not count its assignments. For collaboration support, both models may be beneficial: while the bag-model allows for finding popular content, the set-model gives newly created content a better chance to catch up on older content that has already been tagged many times. Besides other distinctions (Marlow et al. 2006), these differences have to be known when collaborative activities are to be supported by tagging mechanisms.

One of the major advantages of tagging is its *universal applicability to different content types*. There is no restriction whatsoever on the content types these sites manage: While Flickr is an archive of pictures, Delicious manages bookmarks and successors such as CiteULike or Bibsonomy[9] contain scientific content. Based on this success, tagging has also spread to other contexts such as enterprises and everyday life. In collaborative settings, the type of information needed or currently being worked on should not play a decisive role. However, contemporary retrieval methods still favor textual content over other types such as pictures (cf. Prilla 2008). Tagging can provide a means to overcome this by capturing the associations a user has toward certain content and thus putting content resources on the same semantic level when it comes to retrieval. Moreover, tagging can scale. With the low cognitive effort associated with tagging (cf. Grudin 2006), tags may be assigned to text fragments or parts of images without inducing too much effort on the user. These factors make tagging an ideal mechanism to contextually provide arbitrary content to users (cf. Jorgensen 2007). An application of these benefits can be found in a system developed in our group, which integrates complex content types such as process maps into activities of knowledge management (Prilla and Herrmann 2007; Prilla 2008).

Reasoning about the potential tagging has for collaboration support needs an understanding of the way tagging works for users and why it makes sense for them. Studies show that there are various reasons for users to voluntarily participate in tagging sites. Following Ames and Naaman (2007), these reasons include individual and collaborative characteristics. In their study, they describe tagging as a means for personal retrieval and contextualization as well as a way to make content findable for others. Other studies (cf. Marlow et al. 2006) show similar reasons for tagging, underpinning the notion that *while keeping up the individual perspective of the user, tagging also contributes to a group's perspective and awareness*. In collaborative settings, this can be used to make others aware of content that could be valuable for them. If some of these motivational factors can be transferred into enterprise settings and respective collaborative applications, collaboration support can clearly benefit from social tagging mechanisms.

Summing up, tagging shows several potential benefits for collaborative activities and corresponding systems: It can be used to *contextualize* content *individually* as well as on a *collective* level and it is *easy to use* with respect to

---

[9] CiteULike and Bibsonomy offer tagging for scientific resources such as articles and papers (http://www.citeulike.org, http://bibsonomy.org).

the cognitive effort needed to provide tags to content. Furthermore, it provides a means of *grounding by collaboratively producing a vocabulary* to describe content. Additionally, it makes *no assumptions on content types* to be tagged and can therefore be applied to relevant non-textual content as well. In Section 10.4.2.3, we will show how some of these potential benefits can be implemented in a CSS.

10.3.4   The Remainder of Web 2.0

Besides the Web 2.0 applications and services discussed in the previous sections, there are further services and applications that could also be helpful to support collaboration. Among these, Blogs, Social Networking Services, and Feeds are mechanisms offering a great potential for collaboration support: they will be discussed in brief in the remainder of this section.

Blogs are at the very heart of Web 2.0 and represent an archetype of user-generated content, one of the big ideas behind the Web 2.0 (cf. O'Reilly 2005). In its simplest form, a blog (web-log) is a webpage containing posts (i.e., short paragraphs of information on a particular topic) by a primary author and related comments by other users in chronological order. Today's blogging platforms offer good support to get a blog up and running within minutes, the processes of creating and commenting a post are effortless. One underlying and value-adding principle of blogs is connectedness: posts from different blogs can be linked to each other in a variety of ways, resulting in a deepened conversational nature of blogging and contributing to its sense of immediacy (Anderson 2007), meaning that blogs are held capable of conveying up-to-the-minute information.

Social Networking Services provide opportunities to share information and get in touch with like-minded people in both professional and personal networks. From the perspective of collaboration support, social networking services may help to make use of network effects in organizations. They may be applied to establish connections between people who work on similar tasks, providing the opportunity for information exchange on a common problem domain.

Feeds are heavily used on the Web 2.0 to provide information about updates and recent changes to resources like websites, blogs, and wikis. Usually, Feeds are summarizing, text-based representations of these resources. Although the underlying protocols depend on client-side pull requests, most Feed readers are capable of providing a user experience similar to push mail, i.e., the information is held up to date without requiring the user to take any action. In this way, feeds contribute to the Web 2.0's sense of immediacy. From the perspective of collaboration support, feeds can contribute to a knowledge worker's awareness of collaborations he or she is involved in, e.g., if they are used to convey information about changes to a shared workspace.

10.4   Integrating Web 2.0 and Collaboration Support: a Pattern Approach

10.4.1   Patterns in Groupware and CSCW

In the past decades, so-called patterns have become popular in many disciplines. Patterns can be defined as generalized solutions to frequent and recurring problems or the core of a solution, "to a problem that occurs over and over again""(Alexander et al. 1977). Stemming from the famous work of Alexander et al. (1977) in architecture, the utility of patterns has been made visible to a broader audience by so-called design patterns used to build software systems (Gamma et al. 1995).[10] By now, the concept of patterns has reached and inspired a multitude of disciplines such as, e.g., pedagogy (e.g., Fincher and Utting 2002), in which patterns are used to give examples of good teaching. In general, patterns are derived from observations of existing solutions in practice and generalizing the corresponding approaches to a solution of the problem they have in common.

Patterns have also become popular in research and practice concerning Groupware, CSCW, and HCI in general.[11] The scope of such patterns reaches from descriptive patterns depicting good practice and patterns oriented toward providing support for the development of, e.g., CSS applications. Examples of patterns in HCI can be found in Herrmann et al. (2003) providing patterns in the context of knowledge management and corresponding system as well as in Borchers (2001), who uses patterns for user interface design. A comprehensive approach to building a pattern language can be found in the approach of Schümmer and Lukosch (2007), who describe a pattern language for the domains of Groupware and CSCW. This language comprises organizational support as well as its technical implementation and can be seen as an example of the support patterns can provide in HCI.

Notwithstanding the domain a pattern is used in, the applicability of patterns is strongly influenced by the structure used to describe patterns. This structure always includes the division of problem and solution description. Most approaches additionally give examples of the pattern in use and relate a pattern to patterns it can be combined with. From our viewpoint, it is this structure that makes a pattern not only readable but also perceptible. Additionally, the strengths of pattern descriptions can be found in the explicit problem statement, which sets the solution following it into the right context.

In general, the success and ubiquity of patterns and their structure show their benefit for multiple purposes. Moreover, the dissemination of solutions can be

---

[10] While Gamma et al. (1995) made patterns popular, in the context of this chapter it should be noticed that the motiviation for the above-mentioned "WikiWikiWeb" was to provide a design pattern respository and discussion space.

[11] A huge choice of patterns related tot he field of HCI can be seen at, e.g., http://www.hcipatterns.org/patterns.html.

fostered by using a pattern approach and, e.g., setting own solution into context with others. This encouraged us to document our work in synergizing and complementing CSS and Web 2.0 as described in Section 10.4.2 with each other in the form of patterns.

10.4.2 Three Patterns of Web 2.0 Enhanced Collaboration Support

So far, we have argued that challenges related to CSS and Web 2.0 applications can be overcome by finding synergies between these domains. Therefore, our work on this subject was mainly concerned with finding such synergies and implementing them to demonstrate and later evaluate their impact. Here, we show three prototypical implementations that add Web 2.0 functionalities to KOLUMBUS 2 (*K2*, Prilla and Ritterskamp 2006), a CSS that has already been evaluated *on its own* in prior studies. Selecting KOLUMBUS 2 as a basis for the integration of Web 2.0 mechanisms in CSS offers the possibility to evaluate the effects of these functionalities in CSS.

As we have argued above, by using a pattern-like approach to describe our prototypes, we aim at pointing out the problems to be tackled and set our solution into context. For our description, we use the typical *problem* statement and *solution* description and extend this structure by describing the *implementation* of the respective prototype in KOLUMBUS 2, the *impact* potentially resulting from it and *similar solutions* pointing out that our solutions are viable pattern candidates. It should be noted, however, that our approach differs from the approaches mentioned in Section 10.4.1 in that it derives the patterns from our prototypes and therefore *proposes* them rather than analyzing existing solutions. Additionally, we give examples of similar solutions in other approaches.

10.4.2.1 Integrating AoW for Content Production: K2 Co-Writer

Problem Though collaboration support systems still heavily rely on secondary tools to, e.g., produce the content that is managed by them,[12] they lack proper application integration. This imposes an additional usage burden, as for creating and editing content a switch of applications is necessary. Instead of this extra effort, collaborative work should be fostered on the web, meaning that for, e.g., content creation there should be convenient means to perform these tasks in collaboration support systems. This not only lowers the usage barrier but also contributes to user acceptance of the respective system.

---

[12] It should be noticed, however, that there are existing approaches allowing for, e.g., content editing such as GROVE (Ellis et al. 2006), but these do not include the full set offered by secondary tools such as word processors.

Solution Recently, Applications on the Web (AoW) such as Google Docs & Spreadsheets have become very popular. These applications enable users to fulfill several tasks known from desktop applications in a web browser – resulting in ubiquitous availability of content creation and editing. The integration of AoW into CSS may provide a solution to the lack of application integration and the resulting application switches described above.

Implementation The K2 Co-Writer (Prilla and Ritterskamp 2007) was designed to support students in collaborative learning as well as professionals in science and business in collaborative writing. It is based on the integration of a web-based word processor into K2. To ensure proper support for content creation in CSS, the word processor was implemented to complement the existing system and adapted to its characteristics (see Fig. 10.2).

Whereas online word processors usually do not divide content into separate paragraphs that can be edited and owned by different users, the Co-Writer uses the fine-granular item structure of K2 and therefore enables multi-user support in asynchronous editing. We also integrated the contextualized communication and awareness features available in K2 to enhance the usability of the word processor. Furthermore, the word processor is implemented to be one of the different content views K2 provides. This way, users can decide whether to, e.g., browse content or edit it.

Impact The Co-Writer fulfills the requirements made up by the lack of content creation support in CSS in terms of collaborative writing (Prilla and Ritterskamp 2006). It is integrated into the system and provides a convenient way to edit and

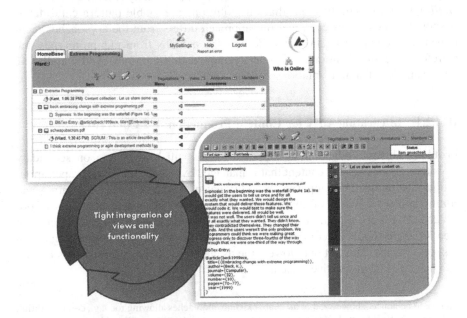

Fig. 10.2 The K2 Co-Writer extension

structure content, resulting in enhanced user experience. The other way round, this integration also diminishes AoW shortcomings like lacking awareness or communication support by using corresponding mechanisms *already present* in K2. The Co-Writer further illustrates how tool interoperability might foster knowledge work by reducing frictional losses resulting from frequent application switches. The effort for integrating such applications is moderate. It also demonstrates the stickiness and contagiousness of Web 2.0 in collaboration support: the Co-Writer approaches an existing problem and gives it a solution by providing an online word processor for frictionless content production. This makes the mechanism of the AoW *sticky*. Moreover, using the Co-Writer provides the personal benefit of easy content production and formatting while also providing others with higher quality in content, making the mechanism *contagious* as well.

In a small test setting with students, we told the participants to work with Google Docs & Spreadsheets and the KOLUMBUS 2 Co-Writer and asked them to tell us differences and problems of both solutions. In general, they told us that it was difficult to work collaboratively in Google Docs & Spreadsheets due to missing awareness features. In contrast, communication support and awareness features of the Co-Writer were regarded as helpful while using its online word processor.

Similar Solutions In many CSS and Web 2.0 applications, AoW have become popular. Taking wikis as an example, web-based word processors are becoming more and more popular enabling a user to create content without the need to know wiki syntax. This encourages us in regarding the integration of AoW into CSS as a pattern contributing to collaborations support.

10.4.2.2 Publishing Content: Wiki-like Sharing

Problem The creation of content in CSS is mainly limited to groups registered to these applications. While this makes sense in situations where content should be shared among a closed group, it prevents users outside these groups to contribute. Today, there is growing demands to involve parties external to a core group of collaborators in the creation and sharing of (selected) content. This holds true for diverse settings like distributed work in global software development (cf. Redmiles et al. 2007) and processes of open innovation (Chesbrough 2003). In any of these domains, the creation of content can benefit from contributions of (expert) users external to a group working in a certain application. With knowledge work increasingly depending on such participation in multi-project settings, corresponding functionality has to be provided by CSS.

Solution Wiki-like content creation with its ease of use and powerful means of content structuring provides a means to extend the scope of content production and sharing. The combination of publishing functionalities known from Wikis and sophisticated access control strategies known from the domain of CSS offers the potential of integrating formerly closed groups into a larger network of collaborators in a controlled manner. Being a playful approach of preparing and publishing content, wiki-like functionality also enables users from inside and outside of a group to come together an easily share and discuss content.

Implementation Learning from Wikis, we provided K2 with functionality to enable anonymous read-and-write access to certain parts of content. In the "go public" extension of the system, the creation of content can benefit from contributions of external users. Vice versa, results created internally may be well suited for public use. We therefore added functionality that allows users to negotiate public content and even enable anonymous access to it *within the application*. Whether content is to be published or not is always decided by the group producing the content: K2 supports such decisions by a negotiation mechanism that lets the assignment of access rights become subject to a group decision (Prilla and Ritterskamp 2006). The "go public" extension is combined with the Co-Writer for simplified content production.

Impact Integrating extended Wiki-like publishing functionalities into collaboration support systems as described above enables users to easily enlarge the scope of visibility and contribution for certain content sections while other resources remain accessible only to a closed group. Tackling an existing shortcoming of closed-group CSS, this makes the wiki functionality *sticky*. Multiproject knowledge work may benefit from functionalities that allow for project- and group-independent sharing and editing of content: by this means knowledge assets are no more bound to a single project but become available for others, too. Given that it is by some means relevant to them, there is a fair chance that public content will be enhanced by the contributions of external users. This provides the opportunity that the mechanism becomes *contagious* and will be adopted by others as well. Also, Wikis benefit from integrating sophisticated access control mechanisms, which is a prerequisite to their application in business settings.

The mechanism described here is currently being tested in a project aiming at publishing its results instantly to the public. While there are no evaluation results yet, our observation shows a good adoption of the feature and recurring usage by individuals, indicating the benefit provided by the mechanism.

Similar Solutions The notion of public content has already been adopted by some CSS, showing that public content has an impact on collaboration support. For example, public content is available in BSCW (Prinz et al. 2008). Currently, we are looking for other examples to harden our notion of wiki-like sharing as a viable collaboration support pattern.

10.4.2.3 Providing Metadata Support: Tagging

Problem Finding content and making individual perspectives on it visible is still a problem in collaboration support systems (Mathes 2004), especially if non-textual content is concerned (Prilla and Herrmann 2007). Metadata is widely accepted to be the remedy for this problem. However, existing approaches using predefined metadata have shown poor user acceptance due to an imbalance of work and benefit (Grudin 1988), and usually result in trivial descriptions that could also have been extracted automatically (Heath et al. 2005). Other approaches use formal semantics such as ontologies. While these mechanisms describe content properly, they impose an additional cognitive effort on users and may therefore not provide a solution to the problem (Golder and Huberman 2006; Grudin 2006).

Solution As described in Section 10.3.3, tagging provides an easy-to-use approach to produce metadata of fairly good quality. Additionally, this is done in a collaborative effort rather than in a top-down manner. Tagging also provides personal and collective benefit and can therefore be seen as a good candidate to increase the motivation of users to contribute to a CSS's metadata. Furthermore, tagging does not make any assumptions on the type of data to be tagged and therefore includes every single information unit into collaborative contextualization and work. Therefore, tagging mechanisms are likely to solve the metadata problem in CSS.

Implementation The K2 *Tagger* plugin aims at improvements for accessing, organizing, and sharing different content types on a group and personal level by integrating tagging into K2. It was designed to complement the existing content structure, meaning that well-known structures like folder hierarchies can be used in parallel to tagging (Fig. 10.3).

Like the Co-Writer, the Tagger plugin provides an additional view on content as shown in. Besides this view, the plugin includes a tag cloud (Rivadeneira et al. 2007) showing existing tags linked to content in the system. Furthermore, to foster the usage of tags, tagging functionality is integrated in all system dialogs used to create or edit content. Tagging here is not restricted to a single application: in K2, users are able to handle content from multiple applications *within a single structure*, allowing them to construct application independent content networks.

Impact The integration of a Tagging mechanism may solve existing problems related to the lack of metadata in CSS. Overall, it enriches the means to structure and contextualize content. Content may now be browsed via folders *and* tags, resulting in a richer user experience. The ability to tag content from other applications also contributes to cross-application content integration. Tagging mechanisms provide a lightweight and unobtrusive means to support the creation of beneficial

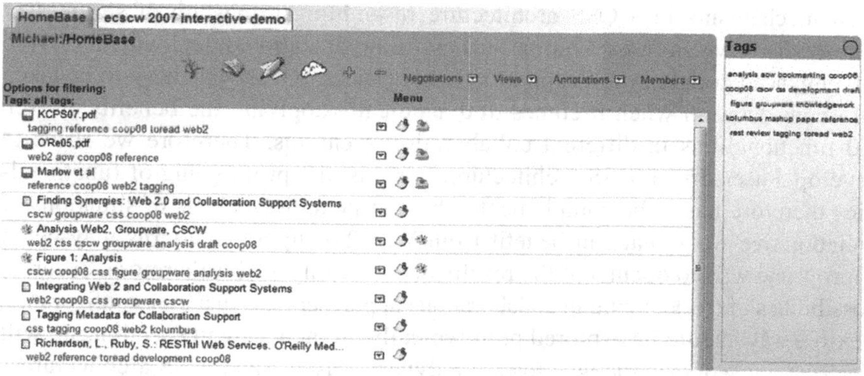

Fig. 10.3 The Tagger plugin

metadata both on a personal and group level: it therefore is a promising approach to intertwine a knowledge worker's personal information management with an organization's group information management processes. While its ability to solve the metadata problem fulfills the criterion of *stickiness*, the individual and group benefit of tagging makes it a *contagious* mechanism in a CSS: The other way round, tagging mechanisms also benefit from functionality already present in collaboration support systems: not only can tags be contextualized by folder structures but also by mechanisms such as awareness support and contextual communication.

To explore the adoption of the mechanism, we released it to our productive K2 environment for a fixed time period and observed its adoption. We integrated the tagging functionality in, e.g., dialogs supporting the creation of content in order to make people aware of the possibility to tag content. Surprisingly, we saw good adoption among the small group of students we observed, who instantly began to tag content. Without going into details, looking at their tags revealed that they used terminology with both personal (topics they worked on, etc.) and group (general topics for everybody, etc.) benefit.

Similar Solutions Tagging mechanisms have been shown to provide improvements on an enterprise level (Farrell et al. 2007; Millen et al. 2007). This encourages us to continue our work in integrating tagging into CSS and shows its potential as a pattern candidate.

10.4.3   Why Prototypes Are Not Enough: Lessons Learned

One major goal underlying the development of the prototypes described in the previous sections was to gain knowledge about the domain of Web 2.0 enhanced collaboration support. Whereas the prototypes helped us to better understand how Web 2.0 mechanisms could be applied to classic collaboration support systems in an advantageous way, only little can be learned about the interplay of such mechanisms in a CSS architecture resembling a mashup of services or factors that have an impact on the successful organizational deployment of Web 2.0 enhanced collaboration support systems. These two aspects have to be taken into consideration when it comes to dynamically applying the benefits of Web 2.0 functionalities in different collaboration scenarios. Therefore we strive to develop a user-driven CSS architecture. For this, the prototyping of functionalities therefore has to be complemented by a systematic analysis of situations of collaborative work that can benefit from Web 2.0 support. Patterns may be an appropriate way to document the results of such analysis. Furthermore, different possibilities of (re-)combining collaboration support services in a user-configurable, flexible way should be explored prototypically. In the following section, we will describe our work on the way toward a dynamic user-driven CSS architecture.

10.5 From Prototypes to Systematic Integration

10.5.1 Building a Pattern Language for Web 2.0 Enhanced Collaboration Support

As stated above, organizational support for leveraging synergies between web 2.0 applications and collaboration support systems can benefit from a systematic approach to providing problem-based patterns (see Section 10.4.1). The description of the prototypes given in Section 10.4.2 can serve as a preliminary example of such patterns. Though there is no empirical evidence that these solutions apply to more than one application setting (and can therefore finally be called *patterns*), other existing approaches given in the descriptions encourage us in thinking of them as viable pattern candidates. Nevertheless, the prototypes described in Section 10.4.2 only provide the beginning of building a pattern language concerned with the combinations of CSS and Web 2.0. As described in Section 10.3.4, there are more Web 2.0 applications which have the potential for complementing CSS. Additionally, there might also be other learning to take away from the applications used in our prototypes.

Future research should be aimed at both scrutinizing the pattern candidates presented in this article and extending the pattern collection describing beneficiary synergy potentials of Web 2.0 applications and collaboration support systems. Such patterns might also include result drawn from the efforts described in Sections 10.5.2 and 10.5.3. With some more patterns, we will then be able develop a small collection of patterns describing synergies between Web 2.0 and CSS. This collection can then be added to existing collections or pattern languages and complement them by the characteristics of Web 2.0 solutions in group work.

10.5.2 Designing Collaboration Support as a Mashup

The complex demands of collaboration support and the different contexts it is used in impose a huge amount of different requirements on collaboration support systems. Therefore, it is unlikely that the full potential of Web 2.0 enhanced collaboration support can be offered by extending a single application. Consequently, we regard the examples of, e.g., integrating tagging mechanisms or web-based word processors into collaboration support systems provided in Section 10.3 as feasibility studies or show-and-tell prototypes to explore the problem space. Therefore, the integration presented in Section 10.4 should be seen as a first step toward the intertwining of such mechanisms.

While our efforts provide a good point to start from, we suggest thinking of next generation systems as a network of applications or services rather than of stand-alone environments. In these networks, each service can be specialized in supporting a specific task and can be reused in several other networks. For example, the tagging mechanism discussed in Section 10.3.2 would be implemented as a service. Based on demands imposed by collaboration scenarios, this service can then be combined with any other service such as Kolumbus 2 content management. Using such an approach, different settings can be supported by providing a network of services suitable for the respective setting. To accomplish this, architectural concepts and their implementation that allow for individual orchestration of services and the construction of new mashups from existing services have to be developed. Such efforts can draw from the field of service-oriented architecture providing support for service orchestration and architectural styles like, e.g., REST (cf. Richardson and Ruby 2007), which is widely accepted in the domain of Web 2.0 mashups. In addition to these technical requirements, organizational support providing guidelines for building beneficial service networks and their deployment is needed.

10.5.3   Sorting Things: Building Blocks of Web 2.0 Enhanced CSS

How can the resources Web 2.0 enhanced CSS are built upon be orchestrated and recombined in a meaningful way? To answer this question, it is necessary to decide which functionalities affect the whole system (*aspects*), which technologies and strategies should be applied as *connectors* of different building blocks and information assets to each other and which functionalities can complement a CSS and therefore possibly be addressed by integrating third-party services as *partners*.

Functionalities that affect a system globally resemble cross-cutting concerns: usually, these functionalities enhance existing functionalities, e.g., to provide an open space for collaboration and are not limited to the support of subprocesses. In Web 2.0 enhanced CSS, functionality related to user-generated metadata like tagging can be considered to be a cross-cutting concern. As such, tagging should be integrated into all building blocks of a Web 2.0 enhanced CSS environment. While the prototype described in Section 10.4.2.3 may serve as an example for an integration of tagging on an UI level and can inspire similar projects, there is still a long way to go to answer the question how tagging functionality can be weaved into the exiting business logic of a CSS.

Building a Web 2.0 enhanced networked CSS from a collection of specialized services requires connectivity on different levels. Besides connectivity and interoperability on the level of software services or components being addressed by architectural styles like service-oriented architectures and REST, Web 2.0 enhanced CSS also require connectivity and interoperability with respect to user interaction and information provision. Feeds (see Section 10.3.4) and aggregators provide a good solution to integrate information from different sources; web portals and widget engines may serve as a basis to connect different building blocks on an UI level.

Finally, Web 2.0 enhanced CSS may benefit from the integration of third-party services that offer specialized functionalities. For example, if blogging or social networking functionalities are required to support collaboration, reverting to third-party solutions may turn out to be more efficient than reimplementing the functionalities in question. Connecting services from different domains and vendors is at the very heart of web service architectures. Besides architectural considerations and challenges (e.g., the design of simple but trustworthy single sign on mechanisms or the provision of unified straightforward but also potent interfaces as a prerequisite for the meaningful integration of services), the integration of third-party services in a CSS network raises questions about trust, intellectual property rights, and licensing.

10.5.4   CSS 2.0 by Example

Our current work is concerned with the development of a dynamic and user-centered CSS infrastructure. Figure 10.4 shows a prototype we have built upon the netvibes[13] platform to explore some of the issues raised in the previous sections.

The prototype integrates services from different sources (e.g., recent posts from a blog, information about appointments from a web calendar, content from a K2

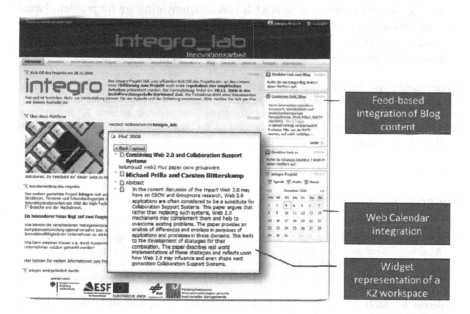

Fig. 10.4 Prototype of a networked CSS

---

[13] Netvibes is a portal that is capable of hosting a user-defined collection of widgets (http://netvibes.com).

workspace) on a UI level. Whereas the widgets used to integrate the blog and the web calendar have been developed by third parties, the representation of a K2 workspace within the platform is provided by a prototypic widget we have developed ourselves. The prototype provides valuable insights into benefits and shortcomings of building a widget-based CSS: whereas the integration on an UI level is well-supported, the integration of services on a functional level is hindered by a lack of support for interservice communication. Consequently, a remaining challenge to the development of a Web 2.0 enhanced CSS is the development of a coordinated approach to UI level integration (as offered by widget engines) and business level integration (ensured by SOA and REST). In our future work, we will address this problem.

10.6 Conclusion

In this paper we have argued that rather than replacing existing collaboration support systems by Web 2.0 mechanisms or regarding Web 2.0 as a part of collaboration support systems, both domains are distinct yet provide meaningful synergy potential. We have shown three prototypes demonstrating the potential of combinations between Web 2.0 mechanisms and an existing CSS. From these prototypes we derived a research agenda aiming at a CSS architecture allowing for problem-based and user-driven combinations of Web 2.0 and CSS services. Further work on the approach taken in this paper can help to overcome existing shortcomings in CSS and contribute to a new generation of collaboration support.

Acknowledgments This work has benefited from and was inspired by the contributions of others. We would like to thank all members of IMTM at the University of Bochum and the student groups who contributed to the Co-Writer and Tagging prototypes. Special thanks go to the K2 development team, namely Peter Schyma and Gergana Nalbantova, for their efforts in integrating all the ideas mentioned in this paper into the system.

References

Alexander, C., Ishikawa, S., Silverstein, M., Jacobson, M., Fiksdahl-King, I., Angel, S. (1977). *A pattern language: towns, buildings, construction.* Oxford University Press.

Ames, M., Naaman, M. (2007). Why we tag: motivations for annotation in mobile and online media. *Proceedings of the SIGCHI conference on Human factors in computing systems.* pp 971–980.

Anderson, P. (2007). What is Web 2.0? Ideas, technologies and implications for education. *JISC Technology and Standards Watch.*

Baecker, R. (1993). *Readings in Groupware and Computer-Supported Cooperative Work: Assisting Human-Human Collaboration.* Morgan Kaufmann.

Borchers, J. (2001). A pattern approach to interaction design. *AI & Society 15.* 359–376.

Cattuto, C., Loreto, V. and Pietronero, L. (2007). Collaborative Tagging and Semiotic Dynamics. *PNAS 104.* pp 1461–1464

Chesbrough, H. (2003). *Open Innovation: The New Imperative for Creating and Profiting from Technology*. Harvard Business School Press.

Damianos, L., Griffith, J., Cuomo, D., Hirst, D. and Smallwood, J. (2006). Onomi: Social Bookmarking on a Corporate Intranet. *Collaborative Web Tagging Workshop at WWW2006*, Edinburgh, Scotland.

Davenport, T. (2005). *Thinking for a living*. Harvard Business School Press.

Desilets, A., Paquet, S. and Vinson, N.G. (2005). Are wikis usable? In: *WikiSym '05: Proceedings of the 2005 international symposium on Wikis*. New York: ACM Press

Ellis, C., Simon, J. and Rein, G. (2006). Groupware: some issues and experiences. *Communications of the ACM 34*. 39–58.

Erickson, T. (2006). From PIM to GIM: personal information management in group contexts. *Communications of the ACM 49(1)*. 74–75.

Farrell, S., Lau, T., Wilcox, E., Nusser, S. and Muller, M. (2007). Socially augmenting employee profiles with people-tagging. *UIST '07: Proceedings of the 20th annual ACM symposium on User interface software and technology*. New York: ACM Press.

Fincher, S. and Utting, I. (2002). Pedagogical patterns: Their place in the genre. *Proceedings of the 7th Annual Conference on Innovation and Technology in Computer Science Education (ITiSCE'02)*. Aarhus, Denmark.

Forte, A. and Bruckman, A. (2005). Why Do People Write for Wikipedia? Incentives to Contribute to Open-Content Publishing. GROUP 5 workshop. http://www. cc. gatech. edu/~ aforte/

Gamma, E., Helm, R., Johnson, R. and Vlissides, J. (1995). *Design patterns: elements of reusable object-oriented software*. Boston, MA.: Addison-Wesley Longman Publishing Co., Inc.

Gladwell, M. (2000). *The Tipping Point: How Little Things Can Make a Big Difference*. Little, Brown and Company.

Golder, S. and Huberman, B. (2006). The structure of collaborative tagging systems. *Journal of Information Science*. 198–208

Gomez-Perez, A. and Fernandez-Lopez, M.: (2004). *Ontological Engineering: With Examples from the Areas of Knowledge Management, E-Commerce and the Semantic Web*. Springer.

Gruber, T. (1993). A translation approach to portable ontology specifications. *Knowledge Acquisition 5*. 199–220.

Grudin, J. (2006). Enterprise Knowledge Management and Emerging Technologies. *Proceedings of the 39th Annual Hawaii International Conference on System Sciences, 2006*. HICSS'06

Grudin, J. (1988). Why CSCW Applications fail: Problems in the Design and Evaluation of organizational Interfaces. *Conference on Computer Supported Cooperative Work*. New York: ACM Press. pp 85–93.

Happel, H., Treitz, M. (2008). Proliferation in enterprise wikis. *Proceedings of the 8th International Conference on the Design of Cooperative Systems (COOP 08)*. Carry-le-Rouet, France

Heath, B.P., McArthur, D.J., McClelland, M.K. and Vetter, R.J. (2005). Metadata lessons from the iLumina digital library. *Commun. ACM 48*. 68–74.

Herrmann, T., Hoffmann, M., Jahnke, I., Kienle, A., Kunau, G., Loser, K., and Menold, N. (2003). Concepts for usable patterns of groupware applications. *Proceedings of the 2003 international ACM SIGGROUP conference on Supporting group work*. New York: ACM Press.

Jorgensen, C. (2007). Image Access, the Semantic Gap, and Social Tagging as a Paradigm Shift. *Proceedings 18th Workshop of the American Society for Information Science and Technology Special Interest Group in Classification Research*, Milwaukee, Wisconsin

Kittur, A., Chi, E., Pendleton, B., Suh, B. and Mytkowicz, T. (2007). Power of the Few vs. Wisdom of the Crowd: Wikipedia and the Rise of the Bourgeoisie. *World Wide Web 1*

Leuf, B. and Cunningham, W. (2001). The Wiki way. Addison-Wesley

Mark, G. and Poltrock, S. (2003). Shaping technology across social worlds: groupware adoption in a distributed organization. *GROUP '03: Proceedings of the 2003 international ACM SIGGROUP conference on Supporting group work*. New York: ACM press.

Marlow, C., Naaman, M., Boyd, D. and Davis, M. (2006). HT06, tagging paper, taxonomy, Flickr, academic article, to read. *Proceedings of the seventeenth conference on Hypertext and hypermedia*. pp 31–40.

Mathes, A. (2004). Folksonomies-Cooperative Classification and Communication Through Shared Metadata. *Computer Mediated Communication, LIS590CMC* (Doctoral Seminar), Graduate School of Library and Information Science, University of Illinois Urbana-Champaign, December.

McAfee, A. (2006). Enterprise 2.0: The Dawn of Emergent Collaboration. *MIT Sloan Management Review 47.* 21–28.

Millen, D., Yang, M., Whittaker, S. and Feinberg, J. (2007). Social bookmarking and exploratory search. In: Bannon, L., Wagner, I., Gutwin, C., Harper, R. Schmidt, K. (eds.) *ECSCW'07: Proceedings of the Tenth European Conference on Computer Supported Cooperative Work.* Springer.

Nov, O. (2007). What motivates Wikipedians?. *Commun. ACM 50.* 60–64

O'Reilly, T. (2005). What is Web 2.0. Design Patterns and Business Models for the Next Generation of Software. *Social Science Research Network Working Paper Series*

Prilla, M. (2008). Semantic Integration of Process Models into Knowledge Management: A Social Tagging Approach. *Proceedings of BIS 08.*

Prilla, M., Herrmann, T. (2007) Semantically Integrating Heterogeneous Content: Applying Social Tagging as a Knowledge Management Tool for Process Model Development and Usage. *Proceedings of IKNOW ,07.*

Prilla, M., Ritterskamp, C. (2007). Kolumbus 2 Co-Writer: The Next Step in Collaborative Writing. *ECSCW 2007* (Demo.)

Prilla, M., Ritterskamp, C. (2006). Collaboration Support by Co-Ownership of Documents. In: Hassanaly, P., Herrmann, T., Kunau, G. Zacklad, M. (eds.) *Cooperative Systems Design. Seamless Integration of Artifacts and Conversations – Enhanced Concepts of Infrastructure for Communication: Proceedings of COOP 2006.* IOS Press.

Prinz, W., Hinrichs, E. and Kireyev, I. (2008). Anticipative Awareness in a Groupware System. *Proceedings of the 8th International Conference on the Design of Cooperative Systems (COOP '08)* Carry-Le-Rouet. France.

Redmiles, D., van der Hoek, A., Al-Ani, B., Hildenbrand, T., Quirk, S., Sarma, A., Silveira, R., Filho, S., De Souza, C. and Trainer, E. (2007). Continuous coordination a new paradigm to support globally distributed software development projects. *Wirtschaftsinformatik 49.* 28–38.

Richardson, L., Ruby, S. (2007). RESTful Web Services. O'Reilly Media, Inc.

Rivadeneira, A.W., Gruen, D.M., Muller, M.J. and Millen, D.R. (2007). Getting our head in the clouds: toward evaluation studies of tagclouds. In Rosson, M. B., Gilmore, D. J. (eds.) *Proceedings of CHI.* New York: ACM Press.

Schümmer, T. and Lukosch, S. (2007). *Patterns for Computer-Mediated Interaction.* John Wiley & Sons.

Tapscott, D., and Williams, A. (2006). *Wikinomics: how mass collaboration changes everything.* Portfolio.

Trant, J. (2006). Social classification and folksonomy in art museums: Early data from the steve. museum tagger prototype. *Proceedings of the 17th SIG Classification Research Workshop*

Viégas, F. (2007). The Visual Side of Wikipedia. *Proceedings of Hawaiian International Conference on System Sciences (HICCS'07)*

Viégas, F., Wattenberg, M. and Kushel, D. (2004). Studying cooperation and conflict between authors with history flow visualizations. *Proceedings of the 2004 conference on Human factors in computing systems.* pp 575–582

Index